Butterworths Student Statutes
Contract and Tort

Butterworths Student Statutes

Contract and Tort

Terence Prime, Solicitor
Lecturer
University of Liverpool

Butterworths
London, Dublin, Edinburgh
1993

United Kingdom	Butterworth & Co (Publishers) Ltd, 88 Kingsway, LONDON WC2B 6AB and 4 Hill Street, EDINBURGH EH2 3JZ
Australia	Butterworths Pty Ltd, SYDNEY, MELBOURNE, BRISBANE, ADELAIDE, PERTH, CANBERRA and HOBART
Belgium	Butterworth & Co (Publishers) Ltd, BRUSSELS
Canada	Butterworth Canada Ltd, TORONTO and VANCOUVER
Ireland	Butterworth (Ireland) Ltd, DUBLIN
Malaysia	Malayan Law Journal Sdn Bhd, KUALA LUMPUR
New Zealand	Butterworths of New Zealand Ltd, WELLINGTON and AUCKLAND
Puerto Rico	Equity de Puerto Rico, Inc, HATO REY
Singapore	Malayan Law Journal Pte Ltd, SINGAPORE
USA	Butterworth Legal Publishers, AUSTIN, Texas; BOSTON, Massachusetts; CLEARWATER, Florida (D & S Publishers); ORFORD, New Hampshire (Equity Publishing); ST PAUL, Minnesota; and SEATTLE, Washington

All rights reserved. No part of this publication may be reproduced in any material form (including photocopying or storing it in any medium by electronic means and whether or not transiently or incidentally to some other use of this publication) without the written permission of the copyright owner except in accordance with the provisions of the Copyright, Designs and Patents Act 1988 or under the terms of a licence issued by the Copyright Licensing Agency Ltd, 90 Tottenham Court Road, London, England, W1P 9HE. Application for the copyright owner's written permission to reproduce any part of this publication should be addressed to the publisher.

Warning: The doing of an unauthorised act in relation to a copyright work may result in both a civil claim for damages and criminal prosecution.

© Butterworth & Co (Publishers) Ltd 1993

A CIP catalogue record for this book is available from the British Library.

ISBN 0 406 02300 X

Printed and bound by Mackays of Chatham plc, Kent.

Preface

It has been a great advantage that the editors of two of the titles in the Butterworths Student Statutes series, namely *Contract and Tort*, and *Criminal Law*, are colleagues in the same institution, have a common approach to legal education, and have been involved with Butterworths from the very beginning of the discussions which led to this new series. It has meant that these two volumes have been prepared with a common vision to meet jointly agreed objectives. In view of this, it seems appropriate that the two volumes should be prefaced by a single joint statement.

With combined experience of 26 years of University teaching, we feel justified in stating that, in our view, there are serious weaknesses in the training of lawyers. Perhaps the most fundamental of such weaknesses is the failure to equip graduates to deal with statutory source materials. The average law student leaves law school with some degree of proficiency in dealing with case law, but with very little experience of dealing with statute law. There is nothing new in this: the same was true when the elder of us was a student thirty years ago. However, the vast growth of statute law in recent years means that it is now crucial that students develop the skills to deal with such legislation. The question for law teachers is how those skills can best be developed.

We both believe that statute books can play an important role in the change of direction which is necessary in legal education: with increasing demand for limited library resources, statute books allow the student immediate access to primary materials which are often not otherwise readily available, particularly in their amended form.

If law students are to use primary materials more frequently, and statute books are to play a part in the process, the books must meet certain objectives. These objectives are as follows:

1. The lay-out of the book should be clear and attractive so that students are encouraged to study the material and not merely to consult it occasionally.

2. At a time of ever-increasing financial pressure on students in higher education, the book must be available at a price which students can afford.

3. The range of material must be limited and, clearly, the book could not be both well presented and affordable unless this were so. There is, however, a strong educational reason for imposing a limit. Legal education is fundamentally about developing legal skills and this cannot be achieved by mere regurgitation of lecture notes covering a vast range of material. The quality of study is directly related to the extent to which a student uses his or her powers of analysis and it is therefore essential that students study statutory materials for themselves and in considerable depth. To encourage students to do this, we must provide them with a manageable selection of the most important legislation

rather than overwhelm them with a mass of material from which they will gain only a superficial understanding.

As part of the process of persuading students to study statutory material in order to construct legal argument, rather than simply learning provisions by rote, we welcome the use of statute books in examinations. It would be inappropriate to allow their use in examinations if the statutes were fully annotated with explanatory notes and, therefore, we have deliberately left the provisions in these volumes unannotated, except for amendment and commencement notes.

In making our selection of legislation we have consulted widely with colleagues and sought written reaction from as many institutions as possible. However, any selection will inevitably omit material that some readers would have found useful and we welcome comments and suggestions for future editions.

Terence Prime, Gary P Scanlan
Faculty of Law
The University
P.O. Box 147
Liverpool
L69 3BX

Contents

	page
Preface	v
Statute of Frauds 1677 (s 4)	1
Fires Prevention (Metropolis) Act 1774 (s 86)	1
Statute of Frauds Amendment Act 1828 (s 6)	2
Libel Act 1843 (ss 1, 2, 10)	2
Libel Act 1845 (s 2)	3
Gaming Act 1845 (s 18)	3
Law of Libel Amendment Act 1888 (ss 3, 10, 11)	4
Slander of Women Act 1891 (ss 1, 2)	4
Gaming Act 1892 (ss 1, 2)	5
Third Parties (Rights Against Insurers) Act 1930 (ss 1–3, 5)	5
Law Reform (Miscellaneous Provisions) Act 1934 (ss 1, 4)	8
Law Reform (Married Women and Tortfeasors) Act 1935 (ss 3, 4, 8)	9
Law Reform (Frustrated Contracts) Act 1943 (ss 1–3)	11
Law Reform (Contributory Negligence) Act 1945 (ss 1, 3, 4, 7)	13
Crown Proceedings Act 1947 (ss 2, 52, 54)	14
Law Reform (Personal Injuries) Act 1948 (ss 1, 6)	16
Defamation Act 1952 (ss 2–13, 16, 18, Sch)	17
Occupiers' Liability Act 1957 (ss 1–3, 5, 8)	24
Factories Act 1961 (ss 12–14, 28, 29, 176, 185)	27
Law Reform (Husband and Wife) Act 1962 (ss 1, 3)	30
Misrepresentation Act 1967 (ss 1–3, 5, 6)	31
Criminal Law Act 1967 (ss 3, 11, 14, 15)	33
Theatres Act 1968 (ss 4, 7, 20)	34
Civil Evidence Act 1968 (ss 11, 13, 20)	36
Employer's Liability (Defective Equipment) Act 1969 (ss 1, 2)	39
Employers' Liability (Compulsory Insurance) Act 1969 (ss 1, 2, 7)	40

	page
Employers' Liability (Compulsory Insurance) General Regulations 1971, SI 1971/1117	41
Animals Act 1971 (ss 1–13)	42
Defective Premises Act 1972 (ss 1–7)	47
Supply of Goods (Implied Terms) Act 1973 (ss 8–12, 14, 15, 18)	52
Congenital Disabilities (Civil Liability) Act 1976 (ss 1–4, 6)	56
Fatal Accidents Act 1976 (ss 1, 1A, 2–5, 7)	59
Resale Prices Act 1976 (ss 1, 30)	62
Torts (Interference with Goods) Act 1977 (ss 1–14, 16, 17, Schs 1, 2)	63
Unfair Contract Terms Act 1977 (ss 1–7, 9–14, 26, 27, 29, 31, 32, Schs 1, 2)	74
Civil Liability (Contribution) Act 1978 (ss 1–8, 10)	84
Sale of Goods Act 1979 (ss 2, 7–15, 34, 35, 49–53, 61, 64)	88
Limitation Act 1980 (ss 1–14B, 28–33, 36, 38, 41)	96
Highways Act 1980 (ss 58, 345)	115
Contempt of Court Act 1981 (ss 3, 4, 21)	116
Civil Aviation Act 1982 (ss 76, 110)	118
Supply of Goods and Services Act 1982 (ss 1–20)	119
Administration of Justice Act 1982 (ss 1, 2, 5, 77, 78)	128
Occupiers' Liability Act 1984 (ss 1, 3, 4)	130
Data Protection Act 1984 (ss 22, 23, 43)	132
Building Act 1984 (ss 1, 38, 135)	134
Police and Criminal Evidence Act 1984 (ss 17, 19, 22, 24, 25, 120, 122)	135
Companies Act 1985 (ss 14, 35, 35A, 35B, 36, 36A, 36C)	141
Landlord and Tenant Act 1985 (ss 8, 10, 40)	144
Latent Damage Act 1986 (ss 3, 5)	146
Financial Services Act 1986 (ss 162, 163, 166, 167, 212)	147
Minors' Contracts Act 1987 (ss 2, 3, 5)	151
Consumer Protection Act 1987 (ss 1–16, 18–46, 50, Sch 2)	152
Criminal Justice Act 1988 (ss 108–111, 115, 171–173)	194
Road Traffic Act 1988 (ss 38, 143–153, 197)	201
Law of Property (Miscellaneous Provisions) Act 1989 (ss 2, 5, 6)	213
Broadcasting Act 1990 (s 166, 204)	214
Access to Neighbouring Land Act 1992 (ss 1, 3, 9)	216
Provision and Use of Work Equipment Regulations 1992, SI 1992/2932	219

Index

STATUTE OF FRAUDS (1677)

(29 Car 2 c 3)

An Act for prevention of Frauds and Perjuryes

4 No action against executors, etc, upon a special promise, or upon any ageement, or contract for sale of lands, etc, unless agreement, etc, be in writing, and signed

... noe action shall be brought ... whereby to charge the defendant upon any speciall promise to answere for the debt default or miscarriages of another person ... unlesse the agreement upon which such action shall be brought or some memorandum or note thereof shall be in writeing and signed by the partie to be charged therewith or some other person thereunto by him lawfully authorized.

[1]

NOTE
Words omitted at the beginning of this section repealed by the Statute Law Revision Act 1883 and the Statute Law Revision Act 1948; words omitted in the second place repealed by the Law Reform (Enforcement of Contracts) Act 1954, s 1; words omitted in the third place repealed by the Law of Property Act 1925, s 207, Sch 7, and s 1 of the 1954 Act.

FIRES PREVENTION (METROPOLIS) ACT 1774

(C 78)

An Act ... for the more effectually preventing Mischiefs by Fire within the Cities of London and Westminster and the Liberties thereof, and other the Parishes, Precincts, and Places within the Weekly Bills of Mortality, the Parishes of Saint Mary-le-bon, Paddington, Saint Pancras and Saint Luke at Chelsea, in the County of Middlesex ...

NOTE
Long title: words omitted repealed by the Statute Law Revision Act 1887.

86 No action to lie against a person where the fire accidentally begins

And ... no action, suit or process whatever shall be had, maintained or prosecuted against any person in whose house, chamber, stable, barn or other building, or on whose estate any fire shall ... accidentally begin, nor shall any recompence be made by such person for any damage suffered thereby, any law, usage or custom to the contrary notwithstanding: ... provided that no contract or agreement made between landlord and tenant shall be hereby defeated or made void.

[2]

NOTE
First words omitted repealed by the Statute Law Revision Act 1888; second words omitted repealed by the Statute Law Revision Act 1948; final words omitted repealed by the Statute Law Revision Act 1958.

STATUTE OF FRAUDS AMENDMENT ACT 1828

(9 Geo 4 c 14)

An Act for rendering a written Memorandum necessary to the Validity of certain Promises and Engagements

[9 May 1828]

6 Action not maintainable on representations of character, etc, unless they be in writing sigend by the party chargeable

No action shall be brought whereby to charge any person upon or by reason of any representation or assurance made or given concerning or relating to the character, conduct, credit, ability, trade, or dealings of any other person, to the intent or purpose that such other person may obtain credit, money, or goods upon, unless such representation or assurance be made in writing, signed by the party to be charged therewith.

[3]

LIBEL ACT 1843

(C 96)

An Act to amend the Law respecting defamatory Words and Libel

[24 August 1843]

1 Offer of an apology admissible in evidence in mitigation of damages in action for defamation

... In any action for defamation it shall be lawful for the defendant (after notice in writing of his intention so to do, duly given to the plaintiff at the time of filing or delivering the plea in such action,) to give in evidence, in mitigation of damages, that he made or offered an apology to the plaintiff for such defamation before the commencement of the action, or as soon afterwards as he had an opportunity of doing so, in case the action shall have been commenced before there was an opportunity of making or offering such apology.

[4]

NOTE

Words omitted repealed by the Statute Law Revision Act 1891.

---

2 In an action against a newspaper for libel, the defendant may plead that it was inserted without malice and without negligence, and that he has published or offered to publish an apology

... In an action for libel contained in any public newspaper or other periodical publication it shall be competent to the defendant to plead that such libel was inserted in such newspaper or other periodical publication without actual malice, and without gross negligence, and that before the commencement of the action, or at the earliest opportunity afterwards, he inserted in such newspaper or other periodical publication a full apology for the said libel, or, if the newspaper or periodical publication in which the said libel appeared should be ordinarily published at intervals exceeding one week, had offered to publish the said apology in any newspaper or periodical publication to be selected by the plaintiff in such action; ... and ... to such plea to such action it shall be competent to the plaintiff to reply generally, denying the whole of such plea.

[5]

NOTE
Words omitted repealed by the Statute Law Revision Act 1891, and the Statute Law Revision Act 1892.

10 Commencement and extent of Act

... Nothing in this Act contained shall extend to Scotland.

[6]

NOTE
Words omitted repealed by the Statute Law Revision Act 1874 (No 2).

LIBEL ACT 1845

(C 75)

An Act to amend an Act passed in the Session of Parliament held in the Sixth and Seventh Years of the Reign of Her present Majesty, intituled "An Act to amend the Law respecting defamatory Words and Libel"

[31 July 1845]

2 Defendant not to file such plea without paying money into court by way of amends

... It shall not be competent to any defendant in such action, whether in England or in Ireland, to file any such plea, without at the same time making a payment of money into court by way of amends ... , but every such plea so filed without payment of money into court shall be deemed a nullity, and may be treated as such by the plaintiff in the action.

[7]

NOTE
Words omitted repealed by the Statute Law Revision Act 1891.

GAMING ACT 1845

(C 109)

An Act to amend the Law concerning Games and Wagers

[8 August 1845]

18 Contracts by way of gaming to be void, and wagers or sums deposited with stakeholders not to be recoverable at law—Saving for subscriptions for prizes

... All contracts or agreements, whether by parole or in writing, by way of gaming or wagering, shall be null and void; and ... no suit shall be brought or maintained in any court of law and equity for recovering any sum of money or valuable thing alleged to be won upon any wager, or which shall have been deposited in the hands of any person to abide the event on which any wager shall have been made: Provided always, that this enactment shall not be deemed to apply to any subscription or contribution, or agreement to subscribe or contribute, for or towards any plate, prize, or sum of money to be awarded to the winner or winners of any lawful game, sport, pastime, or exercise.

[8]

NOTE
Words omitted repealed by the Statute Law Revision Act 1891.

LAW OF LIBEL AMENDMENT ACT 1888

(C 64)

An Act to amend the Law of Libel

[24 December 1888]

3 Newspaper reports of proceedings in court privileged

A fair and accurate report in any newspaper of proceedings publicly heard before any court exercising judicial authority shall, if published contemporaneously with such proceedings, be privileged: Provided that nothing in this section shall authorise the publication of any blasphemous or indecent matter.

[9]–[10]

10 Extent of Act

This Act shall not apply to Scotland.

[11]

11 Short title

This Act may be cited as the Law of Libel Amendment Act 1888.

[12]

SLANDER OF WOMEN ACT 1891

(C 51)

An Act to amend the Law relating to the Slander of Women

[5 August 1891]

1 Amendment of law

Words spoken and published ... which impute unchastity or adultery to any woman or girl shall not require special damage to render them actionable.

Provided always, that in any action for words spoken and made actionable by this Act, a plaintiff shall not recover more costs than damages, unless the judge shall certify that there was reasonable ground for bringing the action.

[13]

NOTE
Words omitted repealed by the Statute Law Revision Act 1908.

2 Short title and extent

This Act may be cited as the Slander of Women Act 1891 and shall not apply to Scotland.

[14]

GAMING ACT 1892

(C 9)

An Act to amend the Act of the eighth and ninth Victoria, chapter one hundred and nine, intituled "An Act to amend the Law concerning Games and Wagers"

[20 May 1892]

1 Promises to repay sums paid under contracts void by 8 & 9 Vict c 109 to be null and void

Any promise, express or implied, to pay any person any sum of money paid by him under or in respect of any contract or agreement rendered null and void by the Gaming Act 1845 or to pay any sum of money by way of commission, fee, reward, or otherwise in respect of any such contract, or of any services in relation thereto or in connexion therewith, shall be null and void, and no action shall be brought or maintained to recover any such sum of money.

[15]

2 Short title

This Act may be cited as the Gaming Act 1892.

[16]

THIRD PARTIES (RIGHTS AGAINST INSURERS) ACT 1930

(C 25)

An Act to confer on third parties rights against insurers of third-party risks in the event of the insured becoming insolvent, and in certain other events

[10 July 1930]

1 Rights of third parties against insurers on bankruptcy, etc, of the insured

(1) Where under any contract of insurance a person (hereinafter referred to as the insured) is insured against liabilities to third parties which he may incur, then—
    (a) in the event of the insured becoming bankrupt or making a composition or arrangement with his creditors; or
    (b) in the case of the insured being a company, in the event of a winding-up order [or an administration order] being made, or a resolution for a voluntary winding-up being passed, with respect to the company, or of a receiver or manager of the company's business or undertaking being duly appointed,

or of possession being taken, by or on behalf of the holders of any debentures secured by a floating charge, of any property comprised in or subject to the charge [or of [a voluntary arrangement proposed for the purposes of Part I of the Insolvency Act 1986 being approved under that Part]];

if, either before or after that event, any such liability as aforesaid is incurred by the insured, his rights against the insurer under the contract in respect of the liability shall, notwithstanding anything in any Act or rule of law to the contrary, be transferred to and vest in the third party to whom the liability was so incurred.

(2) Where [the estate of any person falls to be administered in accordance with an order under section [421 of the Insolvency Act 1986]], then, if any debt provable in bankruptcy ... is owing by the deceased in respect of a liability against which he was insured under a contract of insurance as being a liability to a third party, the deceased debtor's rights against the insurer under the contract in respect of that liability shall, notwithstanding anything in [any such order], be transferred to and vest in the person to whom the debt is owing.

(3) In so far as any contract of insurance made after the commencement of this Act in respect of any liability of the insured to third parties purports, whether directly or indirectly, to avoid the contract or to alter the rights of the parties thereunder upon the happening to the insured of any of the events specified in paragraph (a) or paragraph (b) of subsection (1) of this section or upon the [estate of any person falling to be administered in accordance with an order under section [421 of the Insolvency Act 1986]], the contract shall be of no effect.

(4) Upon a transfer under subsection (1) or subsection (2) of this section, the insurer shall, subject to the provisions of section three of this Act, be under the same liability to the third party as he would have been under to the insured, but—
   (a) if the liability of the insurer to the insured exceeds the liability of the insured to the third party, nothing in this Act shall affect the rights of the insured against the insurer in respect of the excess; and
   (b) if the liability of the insurer to the insured is less than the liability of the insured to the third party, nothing in this Act shall affect the rights of the third party against the insured in respect of the balance.

(5) For the purposes of this Act, the expression "liabilities to third parties", in relation to a person insured under any contract of insurance, shall not include any liability of that person in the capacity of insurer under some other contract of insurance.

(6) This Act shall not apply—
   (a) where a company is wound up voluntarily merely for the purposes of reconstruction or of amalgamation with another company; or
   (b) to any case to which subsections (1) and (2) of section seven of the Workmen's Compensation Act 1925 applies.

[17]

NOTES
Sub-s (1): words in first pair of square brackets and words in second (outer) pair of square brackets added with savings by the Insolvency Act 1985, s 235, Sch 8, para 7 and the Insolvency Act 1986, s 437, Sch 11; other amendment in square brackets made by s 439(2) of, and Sch 14 to, the 1986 Act.

Sub-s (2): first and final words in square brackets substituted by the Insolvency Act 1985, s 235, Sch 8, para 7 and the Insolvency Act 1986, s 437, Sch 11; second amendment made by s 439(2) of, and Sch 14 to, the 1986 Act.

Sub-s (3): first words in square brackets substituted by the Insolvency Act 1985, s 235, Sch 8, para 7 and the Insolvency Act 1986, s 437, Sch 11; further amended by s 439(2) of, and Sch 14 to, the 1986 Act.

2 Duty to give necessary information to third parties

(1) In the event of any person becoming bankrupt or making a composition or arrangement with his creditors, or in the event of [the estate of any person falling to be administered in accordance with an order under section [421 of the Insolvency Act 1986]], or in the event of a winding-up order [or an administration order] being made, or a resolution for a voluntary winding-up being passed, with respect to any company or of a receiver or manager of the company's business or undertaking being duly appointed or of possession being taken by or on behalf of the holders of any debentures secured by a floating charge of any property comprised in or subject to the charge it shall be the duty of the bankrupt, debtor, personal representative of the deceased debtor or company, and, as the case may be, of the trustee in bankruptcy, trustee, liquidator, [administrator,] receiver, or manager, or person in possession of the property to give at the request of any person claiming that the bankrupt, debtor, deceased debtor, or company is under a liability to him such information as may reasonably be required by him for the purpose of ascertaining whether any rights have been transferred to and vested in him by this Act and for the purpose of enforcing such rights, if any, and any contract of insurance, in so far as it purports, whether directly or indirectly, to avoid the contract or to alter the rights of the parties thereunder upon the giving of any such information in the events aforesaid or otherwise to prohibit or prevent the giving thereof in the said events shall be of no effect.

[(1A) The reference in subsection (1) of this section to a trustee includes a reference to the supervisor of a [voluntary arrangement proposed for the purposes of, and approved under, Part I or Part VIII of the Insolvency Act 1986].]

(2) If the information given to any person in pursuance of subsection (1) of this section discloses reasonable ground for supposing that there have or may have been transferred to him under this Act rights against any particular insurer, that insurer shall be subject to the same duty as is imposed by the said subsection on the persons therein mentioned.

(3) The duty to give information imposed by this section shall include a duty to allow all contracts of insurance, receipts for premiums, and other relevant documents in the possession or power of the person on whom the duty is so imposed to be inspected and copies thereof to be taken.

[18]

NOTES
Sub-s (1): first, third and final words in square brackets substituted or added by the Insolvency Act 1985, s 235, Sch 8, para 7 and the Insolvency Act 1986, s 437, Sch 11; other amendment made by s 439(2) of, and Sch 14 to, the 1986 Act.
Sub-s (1A): added by the Insolvency Act 1985, s 235, Sch 8, para 7 and the Insolvency Act 1986, s 437, Sch 11; amended by s 439(2) of, and Sch 14 to, the 1986 Act.

---

3 Settlement between insurers and insured persons

Where the insured has become bankrupt or where in the case of the insured being a company, a winding-up order [or an administration order] has been made or a resolution for a voluntary winding-up has been passed, with respect to the company, no agreement made between the insurer and the insured after liability has been incurred to a third party and after the commencement of the bankruptcy or winding-up [or the day of the making of the administration order], as the case may be, nor any waiver, assignment, or other disposition made by, or payment made to the insured after the commencement [or day] aforesaid shall be effective to defeat or affect the rights transferred to the third party under this Act, but those rights shall be the same as if no such agreement, waiver, assignment, disposition or payment had been made.

[19]

NOTE
Words in square brackets added with savings by the Insolvency Act 1985, s 235, Sch 8, para 7 and the Insolvency Act 1986, s 437, Sch 11.

---

5 Short title

This Act may be cited as the Third Parties (Rights Against Insurers) Act 1930.

[20]

LAW REFORM (MISCELLANEOUS PROVISIONS) ACT 1934

(C 41)

An Act to amend the law as to the effect of death in relation to causes of action and as to the awarding of interest in civil proceedings.

[25 July 1934]

1 Effect of death on certain causes of action

(1) Subject to the provisions of this section, on the death of any person after the commencement of this Act all causes of action subsisting against or vested in him shall survive against, or, as the case may be, for the benefit of, his estate. Provided that this subsection shall not apply to causes of action for defamation ...

[(1A) The right of a person to claim under section 1A of the Fatal Accidents Act 1976 (bereavement) shall not survive for the benefit of his estate on his death.]

(2) Where a cause of action survives as aforesaid for the benefit of the estate of a deceased person, the damages recoverable for the benefit of the estate of that person:—
  [(a) shall not include—
    (i) any exemplary damages;
    (ii) any damages for loss of income in respect of any period after that person's death;]
  (b) ...
  (c) where the death of that person has been caused by the act or omission which give rise to the cause of action, shall be calculated without reference to any loss or gain to his estate consequent on his death, except that a sum in respect of funeral expenses may be included.

(3) ...

(4) Where damage has been suffered by reason of any act or omission in respect of which a cause of action would have subsisted against any person if that person had not died before or at the same time as the damage was suffered, there shall be deemed, for the purposes of this Act, to have been subsisting against him before his death such

cause of action in respect of that act or omission as would have subsisted if he had died after the damage was suffered.

(5) The rights conferred by this Act for the benefit of the estates of deceased persons shall be in addition to and not in derogation of any rights conferred on the dependants of deceased persons by the Fatal Accidents Acts 1846 to 1908 ... and so much of this Act as relates to causes of action against the estates of deceased persons shall apply in relation to causes of action under the said Acts as it applies in relation to other causes of action not expressly excepted from the operation of subsection (1) of this section.

(6) In the event of the insolvency of an estate against which proceedings are maintainable by virtue of this section, any liability in respect of the cause of action in respect of which the proceedings are maintainable shall be deemed to be a debt provable in the administration of the estate, notwithstanding that it is a demand in the nature of unliquidated damages arising otherwise than by a contract, promise or breach of trust.

(7) ...

NOTES
Sub-ss (1), (2): words omitted repealed by the Law Reform (Miscellaneous Provisions) Act 1970, s 7, Schedule and the Administration of Justice Act 1982, ss 4(2), 75, Sch 9, Part I; amendment in square brackets made with a saving by the Administration of Justice Act 1982, ss 4(2), 75, Sch 9, Part I.
Sub-s (1A): added with a saving by the Administration of Justice Act 1982, s 4(1).
Sub-s (3): repealed by the Proceedings Against Estates Act 1970, s 1.
Sub-s (5): words omitted repealed by the Carriage by Air Act 1961, s 14(3), Sch 2.
Sub-s (7): repealed by the Statute Law Revision Act 1950.

4 Short title and extent

(1) This Act may be cited as the Law Reform (Miscellaneous Provisions) Act 1934.

(2) This Act shall not extend to Scotland or Northern Ireland.

LAW REFORM (MARRIED WOMEN AND TORTFEASORS) ACT 1935

(C 30)

An Act to to amend the law relating to the capacity, property, and liabilities of married women, and the liabilities of husbands; and to amend the law relating to proceedings against, and contribution between, tortfeasors

[22 August 1935]

Part I
Capacity, Property, and Liabilities of Married Women; and Liabilities of Husbands

3 Abolition of husband's liability for wife's torts and ante-nuptial contracts, debts, and obligations

Subject to the provisions of this Part of this Act, the husband of a married woman shall not, by reason only of his being her husband, be liable—

(a) in respect of any tort committed by her whether before or after the marriage, or in respect of any contract entered into, or debt or obligation incurred, by her before the marriage; or
(b) to be sued, or made a party to any legal proceeding brought, in respect of any such tort, contract, debt, or obligation.

4 Savings

(1) Nothing in this Part of this Act shall—
(a) during coverture which began before the first day of January eighteen hundred and eighty-three, affect any property to which the title (whether vested or contingent, and whether in possession, reversion, or remainder) of a married woman accrued before that date, except property held for her separate use in equity;
(b) affect any legal proceeding in respect of any tort if proceedings had been instituted in respect thereof before the passing of this Act;
(c) enable any judgement or order against a married woman in respect of a contract entered into, or debt or obligation incurred, before the passing of this Act, to be enforced in bankruptcy or to be enforced otherwise than against her property.

(2) For the avoidance of doubt it is hereby declared that nothing in this Part of this Act—
(a) renders the husband of a married woman liable in respect of any contract entered into, or debt or obligation incurred, by her after the marriage in respect of which he would not have been liable if this Act had not been passed;
(b) exempts the husband of a married woman from liability in respect of any contract entered into, or debt or obligation (not being a debt or obligation arising out of the commission of a tort) incurred, by her after the marriage in respect of which he would have been liable if this Act had not been passed;
(c) prevents a husband and wife from acquiring, holding, and disposing of, any property jointly or as tenants in common, or from rendering themselves, or being rendered, jointly liable in respect of any tort, contract, debt or obligation, and of suing and being sued either in tort or in contract or otherwise, in like manner as if they were not married;
(d) prevents the exercise of any joint power given to a husband and wife.

Part III
Supplementary

8 Short title, extent and construction of references

(1) This Act may be cited as the Law Reform (Married Women and Tortfeasors) Act 1935.

(2) This Act shall not extend to Scotland or to Northern Ireland.

(3) Any reference in this Act to any other enactment or to any provision of any other enactment shall, unless the context otherwise requires, be construed as a reference to that enactment, or that provision, as the case may be, as amended by any subsequent enactment including this Act.

LAW REFORM (FRUSTRATED CONTRACTS) ACT 1943

(C 40)

An Act to amend the law relating to the frustration of contracts

[5 August 1943]

1 Adjustment of rights and liabilities of parties to frustrated contracts

(1) Where a contract governed by English law has become impossible of performance or been otherwise frustrated, and the parties thereto have for that reason been discharged from the further performance of the contract, the following provisions of this section shall, subject to the provisions of section two of this Act, have effect in relation thereto.

(2) All sums paid or payable to any party in pursuance of the contract before the time when the parties were so discharged (in this Act referred to as "the time of discharge") shall, in the case of sums so paid, be recoverable from him as money received by him for the use of the party by whom the sums were paid, and, in the case of sums so payable, cease to be so payable:

Provided that, if the party to whom the sums were so paid or payable incurred expenses before the time of discharge in, or for the purpose of, the performance of the contract, the court may, if it considers it just to do so having regard to all the circumstances of the case, allow him to retain or, as the case may be, recover the whole or any part of the sums so paid or payable, not being an amount in excess of the expenses so incurred.

(3) Where any party to the contract has, by reason of anything done by any other party thereto in, or for the purpose of, the performance of the contract, obtained a valuable benefit (other than a payment of money to which the last foregoing subsection applies) before the time of discharge, there shall be recoverable from him by the said other party such sum (if any), not exceeding the value of the said benefit to the party obtaining it, as the court considers just, having regard to all the circumstances of the case and, in particular,—
  (a) the amount of any expenses incurred before the time of discharge by the benefited party in, or for the purpose of, the performance of the contract, including any sums paid or payable by him to any other party in pursuance of the contract and retained or recoverable by that party under the last foregoing subsection, and
  (b) the effect, in relation to the said benefit, of the circumstances giving rise to the frustration of the contract.

(4) In estimating, for the purposes of the foregoing provisions of this section, the amount of any expenses incurred by any party to the contract, the court may, without prejudice to the generality of the said provisions, include such sum as appears to be reasonable in respect of overhead expenses and in respect of any work or services performed personally by the said party.

(5) In considering whether any sum ought to be recovered or retained under the foregoing provisions of this section by any party to the contract, the court shall not take into account any sums which have, by reason of the circumstances giving rise to the frustration of the contract, become payable to that party under any contract of

insurance unless there was an obligation to insure imposed by an express term of the frustrated contract or by or under any enactment.

(6) Where any person has assumed obligations under the contract in consideration of the conferring of a benefit by any other party to the contract upon any other person, whether a party to the contract or not, the court may, if in all the circumstances of the case it considers it just to do so, treat for the purposes of subsection (3) of this section any benefit so conferred as a benefit obtained by the person who has assumed the obligations as aforesaid.

2 Provision as to application of this Act

(1) This Act shall apply to contracts, whether made before or after the commencement of this Act, as respects which the time of discharge is on or after the first day of July, nineteen hundred and forty-three, but not to contracts as respects which the time of discharge is before the said date.

(2) This Act shall apply to contracts to which the Crown is a party in like manner as to contracts between subjects.

(3) Where any contract to which this Act applies contains any provision which, upon the true construction of the contract, is intended to have effect in the event of circumstances arising which operate, or would but for the said provision operate, to frustrate the contract, or is intended to have effect whether such circumstances arise or not, the court shall give effect to the said provision and shall only give effect to the foregoing section of this Act to such extent, if any, as appears to the court to be consistent with the said provision.

(4) Where it appears to the court that a part of any contract to which this Act applies can properly be severed from the remainder of the contract, being a part wholly performed before the time of discharge, or so performed except for the payment in respect of that part of the contract of sums which are or can be ascertained under the contract, the court shall treat that part of the contract as if it were a separate contract and had not been frustrated and shall treat the foregoing section of this Act as only applicable to the remainder of that contract.

(5) This Act shall not apply—
  (a) to any charterparty, except a time charterparty or a charterparty by way of demise, or to any contract (other than a charterparty) for the carriage of goods by sea; or
  (b) to any contract of insurance, save as is provided by subsection (5) of the foregoing section; or
  (c) to any contract to which [section 7 of the Sale of Goods Act 1979] (which avoids contracts for the sale of specific goods which perish before the risk has passed to the buyer) applies, or to any other contract for the sale, or for the sale and delivery, of specific goods, where the contract is frustrated by reason of the fact that the goods have perished.

NOTE
Sub-s (5): amended by the Sale of Goods Act 1979, s 63, Sch 2, para 2.

3 Short title and interpretation

(1) This Act may be cited as the Law Reform (Frustrated Contracts) Act 1943.

(2) In this Act the expression "court" means, in relation to any matter, the court or arbitrator by or before whom the matter falls to be determined.

LAW REFORM (CONTRIBUTORY NEGLIGENCE) ACT 1945

(C 28)

An Act to amend the law relating to contributory negligence and for purposes connected therewith
[15 June 1945]

1 Apportionment of liability in case of contributory negligence

(1) Where any person suffers damage as the result partly of his own fault and partly of the fault of any other person or persons, a claim in respect of that damage shall not be defeated by reason of the fault of the person suffering the damage, but the damages recoverable in respect thereof shall be reduced to such extent as the court thinks just and equitable having regard to the claimant's share in the responsibility for the damage:

Provided that—
  (a) this subsection shall not operate to defeat any defence arising under a contract;
  (b) where any contract or enactment providing for the limitation of liability is applicable to the claim, the amount of damages recoverable by the claimant by virtue of this subsection shall not exceed the maximum limit so applicable.

(2) Where damages are recoverable by any person by virtue of the foregoing subsection subject to such reduction as is therein mentioned, the court shall find and record the total damages which would have been recoverable if the claimant had not been at fault.

(3), (4) ...

(5) Where, in any case to which subsection (1) of this section applies, one of the persons at fault avoids liability to any other such person or his personal representative by pleading the Limitation Act 1939, or any other enactment limiting the time within which proceedings may be taken, he shall not be entitled to recover any damages ... from that other person or representative by virtue of the said subsection.

(6) Where any case to which subsection (1) of this section applies is tried with a jury, the jury shall determine the total damages which would have been recoverable if the claimant had not been at fault and the extent to which those damages are to be reduced.

(7) ...

NOTES
  Sub-ss (3), (5): words omitted repealed by the Civil Liability (Contribution) Act 1978, s 9(2), Sch 2.
  Sub-s (4): repealed by the Fatal Accidents Act 1976, s 6(2), Sch 2.

Sub-s (7): repealed by the Carriage by Air Act 1961, s 14(3), Sch 2.

3 Saving for Maritime Conventions Act 1911, and past cases

(1) This Act shall not apply to any claim to which section one of the Maritime Conventions Act 1911, applies and that Act shall have effect as if this Act had not been passed.

(2) This Act shall not apply to any case where the Acts or omissions giving rise to the claim occurred before the passing of this Act.

[30]

4 Interpretation

The following expressions have the meanings hereby respectively assigned to them, that is to say—

"court" means, in relation to any claim, the court or arbitrator by or before whom the claim falls to be determined;

"damage" includes loss of life and personal injury;

...

"fault" means negligence, breach of statutory duty or other act or omission which gives rise to a liability in tort or would, apart from this Act, give rise to the defence of contributory negligence.

[31]

NOTE

Words omitted repealed by the Fatal Accidents Act 1976, s 6(2), Sch 2, and the National Insurance (Industrial Injuries) Act 1946, s 89 (1), Sch 9.

7 Short title and extent

This Act may be cited as the Law Reform (Contributory Negligence) Act 1945.

[32]

CROWN PROCEEDINGS ACT 1947

(C 44)

An Act to amend the law relating to the civil liabilities and rights of the Crown and to civil proceedings by and against the Crown, to amend the law relating to the civil liabilities of persons other than the Crown in certain cases involving the affairs or property of the Crown, and for purposes connected with the matters aforesaid

[31 July 1947]

Part I
Substantive Law

2 Liability of the Crown in tort

(1) Subject to the provisions of this Act, the Crown shall be subject to all those li-

abilities in tort to which, if it were a private person of full age and capacity, it would be subject:—
   (a) in respect of torts committed by its servants or agents;
   (b) in respect of any breach of those duties which a person owes to his servants or agents at common law by reason of being their employer; and
   (c) in respect of any breach of the duties attaching at common law to the ownership, occupation, possession or control of property:

Provided that no proceedings shall lie against the Crown by virtue of paragraph (a) of this subsection in respect of any act or omission of a servant or agent of the Crown unless the act or omission would apart from the provisions of this Act have given rise to a cause of action in tort against that servant or agent or his estate.

(2) Where the Crown is bound by a statutory duty which is binding also upon persons other than the Crown and its officers, then, subject to the provisions of this Act, the Crown shall, in respect of a failure to comply with that duty, be subject to all those liabilities in tort (if any) to which it would be so subject if it were a private person of full age and capacity.

(3) Where any functions are conferred or imposed upon an officer of the Crown as such either by any rule of the common law or by statute, and that officer commits a tort while performing or purporting to perform those functions, the liabilities of the Crown in respect of the tort shall be such as they would have been if those functions had been conferred or imposed solely by virtue of instructions lawfully given by the Crown.

(4) Any enactment which negatives or limits the amount of the liability of any Government department or officer of the Crown in respect of any tort committed by that department or officer shall, in the case of proceedings against the Crown under this section in respect of a tort committed by that department or officer, apply in relation to the Crown as it would have applied in relation to that department or officer if the proceedings against the Crown had been proceedings against that department or officer.

(5) No proceedings shall lie against the Crown by virtue of this section in respect of anything done or omitted to be done by any person while discharging or purporting to discharge any responsibilities of a judicial nature vested in him, or any responsibilities which he has in connection with the execution of judicial process.

(6) No proceedings shall lie against the Crown by virtue of this section in respect of any act, neglect or default of any officer of the Crown, unless that officer has been directly or indirectly appointed by the Crown and was at the material time paid in respect of his duties as an officer of the Crown wholly out of the Consolidated Fund of the United Kingdom, moneys provided by Parliament ... or any other Fund certified by the Treasury for the purposes of this subsection or was at the material time holding an office in respect of which the Treasury certify that the holder thereof would normally be so paid.

NOTE
Sub-s (6): words omitted repealed by the Statute Law (Repeals) Act 1981.

Part VI
Extent, Commencement, Short Title, etc

52 Extent of Act

Subject to the provisions hereinafter contained with respect to Northern Ireland, this Act shall not affect the law enforced in courts elsewhere than in England and Scotland, or the procedure in any such courts.

54 Short title and commencement

(1) This Act may be cited as the Crown Proceedings Act 1947.

(2) ...

NOTE
Sub-s (2): repealed by the Statute Law Revision Act 1950.

LAW REFORM (PERSONAL INJURIES) ACT 1948

(C 41)

An Act to abolish the defence of common employment, to amend the law relating to the measure of damages for personal injury or death, and for purposes connected therewith.

[30 June 1948]

1 Common employment

(1) It shall not be a defence to an employer who is sued in respect of personal injuries caused by the negligence of a person employed by him, that that person was at the time the injuries were caused in common employment with the person injured.

(2) Accordingly the Employers' Liability Act 1880 shall cease to have effect, and is hereby repealed.

(3) Any provision contained in a contract of service or apprenticeship, or in an agreement collateral thereto, (including a contract or agreement entered into before the commencement of this Act) shall be void in so far as it would have the effect of excluding or limiting any liability of the employer in respect of personal injuries caused to the person employed or apprenticed by the negligence of persons in common employment with him.

6 Short title and commencement

(1) This Act may be cited as the Law Reform (Personal Injuries) Act 1948.

(2) Section one and subsection (1) of section two of this Act shall apply only where the cause of action accrues on or after the day appointed for the National Insurance (Industrial Injuries) Act 1946 to take effect, but subsections (4) and (5) of the said

section two shall apply whether the cause of action accrued or the action was commenced before or after the commencement of this Act.

[37]

DEFAMATION ACT 1952

(C 66)

An Act to amend the law relating to libel and slander and other malicious falsehoods

[30 October 1952]

2 Slander affecting official, professional or business reputation

In an action for slander in respect of words calculated to disparage the plaintiff in any office, profession, calling, trade or business held or carried on by him at the time of the publication, it shall not be necessary to allege or prove special damage, whether or not the words are spoken of the plaintiff in the way of his office, profession, calling, trade or business.

[38]

NOTE
Commencement: 30 November 1952.

3 Slander of title, etc

(1) In an action for slander of title, slander of goods or other malicious falsehood, it shall not be necessary to allege or prove special damage—

- (a) if the words upon which the action is founded are calculated to cause pecuniary damage to the plaintiff and are published in writing or other permanent form; or
- (b) if the said words are calculated to cause pecuniary damage to the plaintiff in respect of any office, profession, calling, trade or business held or carried on by him at the time of the publication.

(2) Section one of this Act shall apply for the purposes of this section as it applies for the purposes of the law of libel and slander.

[39]

NOTES
Commencement: 30 November 1952.

4 Unintentional defamation

(1) A person who has published words alleged to be defamatory of another person may, if he claims that the words were published by him innocently in relation to that other person, make an offer of amends under this section; and in any such case—

- (a) if the offer is accepted by the party aggrieved and is duly performed, no proceedings for libel or slander shall be taken or continued by that party against the person making the offer in respect of the publication in question (but without prejudice to any cause of action against any other person jointly responsible for that publication);

(b) if the offer is not accepted by the party aggrieved, then, except as otherwise provided by this section, it shall be a defence, in any proceedings by him for libel or slander against the person making the offer in respect of the publication in question, to prove that the words complained of were published by the defendant innocently in relation to the plaintiff and that the offer was made as soon as practicable after the defendant received notice that they were or might be defamatory of the plaintiff, and has not been withdrawn.

(2) An offer of amends under this section must be expressed to be made for the purposes of this section, and must be accompanied by an affidavit specifying the facts relied upon by the person making it to show that the words in question were published by him innocently in relation to the party aggrieved; and for the purposes of a defence under paragraph (b) of subsection (1) of this section no evidence, other than evidence of facts specified in the affidavit, shall be admissible on behalf of that person to prove that the words were so published.

(3) An offer of amends under this section shall be understood to mean an offer—
   (a) in any case, to publish or join in the publication of a suitable correction of the words complained of, and a sufficient apology to the party aggrieved in respect of those words;
   (b) where copies of a document or record containing the said words have been distributed by or with the knowledge of the person making the offer, to take such steps as are reasonably practicable on his part for notifying persons to whom copies have been so distributed that the words are alleged to be defamatory of the party aggrieved.

(4) Where an offer of amends under this section is accepted by the party aggrieved—
   (a) any question as to the steps to be taken in fulfilment of the offer as so accepted shall in default of agreement between the parties be referred to and determined by the High Court, whose decision thereon shall be final;
   (b) the power of the court to make orders as to costs in proceedings by the party aggrieved against the person making the offer in respect of the publication in question, or in proceedings in respect of the offer under paragraph (a) of this subsection, shall include power to order the payment by the person making the offer to the party aggrieved of costs on an indemnity basis and any expenses reasonably incurred or to be incurred by that party in consequence of the publication in question;

and if no such proceedings as aforesaid are taken, the High Court may, upon application made by the party aggrieved, make any such order for the payment of such costs and expenses as aforesaid as could be made in such proceedings.

(5) For the purposes of this section words shall be treated as published by one person (in this subsection referred to as the publisher) innocently in relation to another person if and only if the following conditions are satisfied, that is to say—
   (a) that the publisher did not intend to publish them of and concerning that other person, and did not know of circumstances by virtue of which they might be understood to refer to him; or
   (b) that the words were not defamatory on the face of them, and the publisher did not know of circumstances by virtue of which they might be understood to be defamatory of that other person,

and in either case that the publisher exercised all reasonable care in relation to the publication; and any reference in this subsection to the publisher shall be construed as including a reference to any servant or agent of his who was concerned with the contents of the publication.

(6) Paragraph (b) of subsection (1) of this section shall not apply in relation to the publication by any person of words of which he is not the author unless he proves that the words were written by the author without malice.

[40]

NOTE
Commencement: 30 November 1952.

5 Justification

In an action for libel or slander in respect of words containing two or more distinct charges against the plaintiff, a defence of justification shall not fail by reason only that the truth of every charge is not proved if the words not proved to be true do not materially injure the plaintiff's reputation having regard to the truth of the remaining charges.

[41]

NOTE
Commencement: 30 November 1952.

6 Fair comment

In an action for libel or slander in respect of words consisting partly of allegations of fact and partly of expression of opinion, a defence of fair comment shall not fail by reason only that the truth of every allegation of fact is not proved if the expression of opinion is fair comment having regard to such of the facts alleged or referred to in the words complained of as are proved.

[42]

NOTE
Commencement: 30 November 1952.

7 Qualified privilege of newspapers

(1) Subject to the provisions of this section, the publication in a newspaper of any such report or other matter as is mentioned in the Schedule to this Act shall be privileged unless the publication is proved to be made with malice.

(2) In an action for libel in respect of the publication of any such report or matter as is mentioned in Part II of the Schedule to this Act, the provisions of this section shall not be a defence if it is proved that the defendant has been requested by the plaintiff to publish in the newspaper in which the original publication was made a reasonable letter or statement by way of explanation or contradiction, and has refused or neglected to do so, or has done so in a manner not adequate or not reasonable having regard to all the circumstances.

(3) Nothing in this section shall be construed as protecting the publication of any matter the publication of which is prohibited by law, or of any matter which is not of public concern and the publication of which is not for the public benefit.

(4) Nothing in this section shall be construed as limiting or abridging any privilege subsisting (otherwise than by virtue of section four of the Law of Libel Amendment Act 1888) immediately before the commencement of this Act.

(5) In this section the expression "newspaper" means any paper containing public news or observations thereon, or consisting wholly or mainly of advertisements, which is printed for sale and is published in the United Kingdom either periodically or in parts or numbers at intervals not exceeding thirty-six days.

NOTE
Commencement: 30 November 1952.

8 Extent of Law of Libel Amendment Act 1888, s 3

Section three of the Law of Libel Amendment Act 1888 (which relates to contemporary reports of proceedings before courts exercising judicial authority) shall apply and apply only to courts exercising judicial authority within the United Kingdom.

NOTE
Commencement: 30 November 1952.

9 Extension of certain defences to broadcasting

(1) Section three of the Parliamentary Papers Act 1840 (which confers protection in respect of proceedings for printing extracts from or abstracts of parliamentary papers) shall have effect as if the reference to printing included a reference to broadcasting by means of wireless telegraphy.

(2) Section seven of this Act and section three of the Law of Libel Amendment Act 1888, as amended by this Act shall apply in relation to reports or matters broadcast by means of wireless telegraphy as part of any programme or service provided by means of a broadcasting station within the United Kingdom, and in relation to any broadcasting by means of wireless telegraphy of any such report or matter, as they apply in relation to reports and matters published in a newspaper and to publication in a newspaper; and subsection (2) of the said section seven shall have effect in relation to any such broadcasting, as if for the words "in the newspaper in which" there were substituted the words "in the manner which."

(3) In this section "broadcasting station" means any station in respect of which a licence granted by the Postmaster General under the enactments relating to wireless telegraphy is in force, being a licence which (by whatever form of words) authorises the use of the station for the purpose of providing broadcasting services for general reception.

NOTE
Commencement: 30 November 1952.

10 Limitation on privilege at elections

A defamatory statement published by or on behalf of a candidate in any election to a local government authority or to Parliament shall not be deemed to be published on a privileged occasion on the ground that it is material to a question in issue in the election, whether or not the person by whom it is published is qualified to vote at the election.

NOTE
Commencement: 30 November 1952.

11 Agreements for indemnity

An agreement for indemnifying any person against civil liability for libel in respect of the publication of any matter shall not be unlawful unless at the time of the publication that person knows that the matter is defamatory, and does not reasonably believe there is a good defence to any action brought upon it.

[47]

NOTE
Commencement: 30 November 1952.

12 Evidence of other damages recovered by plaintiff

In any action for libel or slander the defendant may give evidence in mitigation of damages that the plaintiff has recovered damages, or has brought actions for damages, for libel or slander in respect of the publication of words to the same effect as the words on which the action is founded, or has received or agreed to receive compensation in respect of any such publication.

[48]

NOTE
Commencement: 30 November 1952.

13 Consolidation of actions for slander, etc

Section five of the Law of Libel Amendment Act 1888 (which provides for the consolidation, on the application of the defendants, of two or more actions for libel by the same plaintiff) shall apply to actions for slander and to actions for slander of title, slander of goods or other malicious falsehood as it applies to actions for libel; and references in that section to the same, or substantially the same, libel shall be construed accordingly.

[49]

NOTE
Commencement: 30 November 1952.

16 Interpretation

(1) Any reference in this Act to words shall be construed as including a reference to pictures, visual images, gestures and other methods of signifying meaning.

(2) The provisions of Part III of the Schedule to this Act shall have effect for the purposes of the interpretation of that Schedule.

(3) In this Act "broadcasting by means of wireless telegraphy" means publication for general reception by means of wireless telegraphy within the meaning of the Wireless Telegraphy Act 1949 and "broadcast by means of wireless telegraphy" shall be construed accordingly.

(4) ...

[50]

NOTES
Commencement: 30 November 1952.
Sub-s (4): repealed by the Cable and Broadcasting Act 1984, s 57(2), Sch 6.

18 Short title, commencement, extent and repeals

(1) This Act may be cited as the Defamation Act 1952 and shall come into operation one month after the passing of this Act.

(2) This Act ... shall not extend to Northern Ireland.

(3) ...

NOTES
Commencement: 30 November 1952.
Sub-s (2): words omitted repealed by the Northern Ireland Constitution Act 1973, s 41(1), Sch 6, Part I.
Sub-s (3): repealed by the Statute Law (Repeals) Act 1974.

SCHEDULE

Sections 7, 16

NEWSPAPER STATEMENTS HAVING QUALIFIED PRIVILEGE

PART I

STATEMENTS PRIVILEGED WITHOUT EXPLANATION OR CONTRADICTION

1 A fair and accurate report of any proceedings in public of the legislature of any part of Her Majesty's dominions outside Great Britain.

2 A fair and accurate report of any proceedings in public of an international organisation of which the United Kingdom or Her Majesty's Government in the United Kingdom is a member, or of any international conference to which that government sends a representative.

3 A fair and accurate report of any proceedings in public of an international court.

4 A fair and accurate report of any proceedings before a court exercising jurisdiction throughout any part of Her Majesty's dominions outside the United Kingdom, or of any proceedings before a court-martial held outside the United Kingdom under the Naval Discipline Act, [the Army Act 1955 or the Air Force Act 1955.]

5 A fair and accurate report of any proceedings in public of a body or person appointed to hold a public inquiry by the government or legislature of any part of Her Majesty's dominions outside the United Kingdom.

6 A fair and accurate copy of or extract from any register kept in pursuance of any Act of Parliament which is open to inspection by the public, or of any other document which is required by the law of any part of the United Kingdom to be open to inspection by the public.

7 A notice or advertisement published by or on the authority of any court within the United Kingdom or any judge or officer of such a court.

NOTES
Commencement: 30 November 1952.
Para 4: words in square brackets substituted by the Army and Air Force Acts (Transitional Provisions) Act 1955, s 3, Sch 2, para 16.

PART II
STATEMENTS PRIVILEGED SUBJECT TO EXPLANATION OR CONTRADICTION

8 A fair and accurate report of the findings or decision of any of the following associations, or of any committee or governing body thereof, that is to say—
   (a) an association formed in the United Kingdom for the purpose of promoting or encouraging the exercise of or interest in any art, science, religion or learning, and empowered by its constitution to exercise control over or adjudicate upon matters of interest or concern to the association, or the actions or conduct of any persons subject to such control or adjudication;
   (b) an association formed in the United Kingdom for the purpose of promoting or safeguarding the interests of any trade, business, industry or profession, or of the persons carrying on or engaged in any trade, business, industry or profession, and empowered by its constitution to exercise control over or adjudicate upon matters connected with the trade, business, industry or profession, or the actions or conduct of those persons;
   (c) an association formed in the United Kingdom for the purpose of promoting or safeguarding the interests of any game, sport or pastime to the playing or exercise of which members of the public are invited or admitted, and empowered by its constitution to exercise control over or adjudicate upon persons connected with or taking part in the game, sport or pastime,

being a finding or decision relating to a person who is a member of or is subject by virtue of any contract to the control of the association.

9 A fair and accurate report of the proceedings at any public meeting held in the United Kingdom, that is to say, a meeting bona fide and lawfully held for a lawful purpose and for the furtherance or discussion of any matter of public concern, whether the admission to the meeting is general or restricted.

10 A fair and accurate report of the proceedings at any meeting or sitting in any part of the United Kingdom of—
   (a) any local authority or committee of a local authority or local authorities;
   (b) any justice or justices of the peace acting otherwise than as a court exercising judicial authority;
   (c) any commission, tribunal, committee or person appointed for the purposes of any inquiry by Act of Parliament, by Her Majesty or by a Minister of the Crown;
   (d) any person appointed by a local authority to hold a local inquiry in pursuance of any Act of Parliament;
   (e) any other tribunal, board, committee or body constituted by or under, and exercising functions under an Act of Parliament,

not being a meeting or sitting admission to which is denied to representatives of newspapers and other members of the public.

11 A fair and accurate report of the proceedings at a general meeting of any company or association constituted, registered or certified by or under any Act of Parliament or incorporated by Royal Charter, not being a private company within the meaning of the Companies Act 1948.

12 A copy or fair and accurate report or summary of any notice or other matter issued for the information of the public by or on behalf of any government department, officer of state, local authority or chief officer of police.

[53]

PART III
INTERPRETATION

13 [(1)] In this Schedule the following expressions have the meanings hereby respectively assigned to them, that is to say:—

"Act of Parliament" includes an Act of the Parliament of Northern Ireland, and the reference to the Companies Act 1948 includes a reference to any corresponding enactment of the Parliament of Northern Ireland;

"government department" includes a department of the Government of Northern Ireland;

"international court" means the International Court of Justice and any other judicial or arbitral tribunal deciding matters in dispute between States;

"legislature", in relation to any territory comprised in Her Majesty's dominions which is subject to a central and a local legislature, means either of those legislatures;

["local authority means—
  (a) any principal council within the meaning of the Local Government Act 1972, any body falling within any paragraph of section 100J(1) of that Act and any local authority, within the meaning of the Local Government (Scotland) Act 1973;
  (b) any authority or body to which the Public Bodies (Admission to Meetings) Act 1960 applies; and
  (c) any authority or body to which sections 23 to 27 of the Local Government Act (Northern Ireland) 1972 apply;

and any reference to a committee of a local authority shall be construed in accordance with sub-paragraph (2) below;]

"part of Her Majesty's dominions" means the whole of any territory within those dominions which is subject to a separate legislature.

[(2) Any reference in this Schedule to a committee of a local authority includes a reference—
  (a) to any committee or sub-committee in relation to which sections 100A to 100D of the Local Government Act 1972 apply by virtue of section 100E of that Act (whether or not also by virtue of section 100J of that Act); and
  (b) ...

14 In relation to the following countries and territories, that is to say, India, the Republic of Ireland, any protectorate, protected state or trust territory within the meaning of the British Nationality Act 1948, any territory administered under the authority of a country mentioned in [Schedule 3 to the British Nationality Act 1981], the Sudan and the New Hebrides, the provisions of this Schedule shall have effect as they have effect in relation to Her Majesty's dominions, and references therein to Her Majesty's dominions shall be construed accordingly.

NOTES

Commencement: 30 November 1952.

Para 13 was renumbered 13(1), and the definition of "local authority" was substituted, and a new sub-para (2) was added, by the Local Government (Access to Information) Act 1985, s 3(1), Sch 2, para 2.

Sub-para (b) applies to Scotland only.

Para 14: words in square brackets substituted by the British Nationality Act 1981, s 52(6), Sch 7.

OCCUPIERS' LIABILITY ACT 1957

(C 31)

An Act to amend the law of England and Wales as to the liability of occupiers and others for injury or damage resulting to persons or goods lawfully on any land or other property from dangers due to the state of the property or to things done or omitted to be done there, to make provision as to the operation in relation to the Crown of laws made by the Parliament of Northern Ireland for similar purposes or otherwise amending the law of tort, and for purposes connected therewith

[6 June 1957]

Liability in tort

1 Preliminary

(1) The rules enacted by the two next following sections shall have effect, in place of the rules of the common law, to regulate the duty which an occupier of premises owes to his visitors in respect of dangers due to the state of the premises or to things done or omitted to be done on them.

(2) The rules so enacted shall regulate the nature of the duty imposed by law in consequence of a person's occupation or control of premises and of any invitation or permission he gives (or is to be treated as giving) to another to enter or use the premises, but they shall not alter the rules of the common law as to the persons on whom a duty is so imposed or to whom it is owed; and accordingly for the purpose of the rules so enacted the persons who are to be treated as an occupier and as his visitors are the same (subject to subsection (4) of this section) as the persons who would at common law be treated as an occupier and as his invitees or licensees.

(3) The rules so enacted in relation to an occupier of premises and his visitors shall also apply, in like manner and to the like extent as the principles applicable at common law to an occupier of premises and his invitees or licensees would apply, to regulate—
  (a) the obligations of a person occupying or having control over any fixed or moveable structure, including any vessel, vehicle or aircraft; and
  (b) the obligations of a person occupying or having control over any premises or structure in respect of damage to property, including the property of persons who are not themselves his visitors.

(4) A person entering any premises in exercise of rights conferred by virtue of an access agreement or order under the National Parks and Access to the Countryside Act 1949, is not, for the purposes of this Act, a visitor of the occupier of those premises.

2 Extent of occupier's ordinary duty

(1) An occupier of premises owes the same duty, the "common duty of care", to all his visitors, except in so far as he is free to and does extend, restrict, modify or exclude his duty to any visitor or visitors by agreement or otherwise.

(2) The common duty of care is a duty to take such care as in all the circumstances of the case is reasonable to see that the visitor will be reasonably safe in using the premises for the purposes for which he is invited or permitted by the occupier to be there.

(3) The circumstances relevant for the present purpose include the degree of care, and of want of care, which would ordinarily be looked for in such a visitor, so that (for example) in proper cases—
  (a) an occupier must be prepared for children to be less careful than adults; and
  (b) an occupier may expect that a person, in the exercise of his calling, will appreciate and guard against any special risks ordinarily incident to it, so far as the occupier leaves him free to do so.

(4) In determining whether the occupier of premises has discharged the common duty of care to a visitor, regard is to be had to all the circumstances, so that (for example)—

(a) where damage is caused to a visitor by a danger of which he had been warned by the occupier, the warning is not to be treated without more as absolving the occupier from liability, unless in all the circumstances it was enough to enable the visitor to be reasonably safe; and

(b) where damage is caused to a visitor by a danger due to the faulty execution of any work of construction, maintenance or repair by an independent contractor employed by the occupier, the occupier is not to be treated without more as answerable for the danger if in all the circumstances he had acted reasonably in entrusting the work to an independent contractor and had taken such steps (if any) as he reasonably ought in order to satisfy himself that the contractor was competent and that the work had been properly done.

(5) The common duty of care does not impose on an occupier any obligation to a visitor in respect of risks willingly accepted as his by the visitor (the question whether a risk was so accepted to be decided on the same principles as in other cases in which one person owes a duty of care to another).

(6) For the purposes of this section, persons who enter premises for any purpose in the exercise of a right conferred by law are to be treated as permitted by the occupier to be there for that purpose, whether they in fact have his permission or not.

[56]

3 Effect of contract on occupier's liability to third party

(1) Where an occupier of premises is bound by contract to permit persons who are strangers to the contract to enter or use the premises, the duty of care which he owes to them as his visitors cannot be restricted or excluded by that contract, but (subject to any provision of the contract to the contrary) shall include the duty to perform his obligations under the contract, whether undertaken for their protection or not, in so far as those obligations go beyond the obligations otherwise involved in that duty.

(2) A contract shall not by virtue of this section have the effect, unless it expressly so provides, of making an occupier who has taken all reasonable care answerable to strangers to the contract for dangers due to the faulty execution of any work of construction, maintenance or repair or other like operation by persons other than himself, his servants and persons acting under his direction and control.

(3) In this section "stranger to the contract" means a person not for the time being entitled to the benefit of the contract as a party to it or as the successor by assignment or otherwise of a party to it or as the successor by assignment or otherwise of a party to it, and accordingly includes a party to the contract who has ceased to be so entitled.

(4) Where by the terms or conditions governing any tenancy (including a statutory tenancy which does not in law amount to a tenancy) either the landlord or the tenant is bound, though not by contract, to permit persons to enter or use premises of which he is the occupier, this section shall apply as if the tenancy were a contract between the landlord and the tenant.

(5) This section, in so far as it prevents the common duty of care from being restricted or excluded, applies to contracts entered into and tenancies created before the commencement of this Act, as well as to those entered into or created after its commencement; but, in so far as it enlarges the duty owed by an occupier beyond the common duty of care, it shall have effect only in relation to obligations which are

undertaken after that commencement or which are renewed by agreement (whether express or implied) after that commencement.

[57]

Liability in contract

5 Implied term in contracts

(1) Where persons enter or use, or bring or send goods to, any premises in exercise of a right conferred by contract with a person occupying or having control of the premises, the duty he owes them in respect of dangers due to the state of the premises or to things done or omitted to be done on them, in so far as the duty depends on a term to be implied in the contract by reason of its conferring that right, shall be the common duty of care.

(2) The foregoing subsection shall apply to fixed and moveable structures as it applies to premises.

(3) This section does not affect the obligations imposed on a person by or by virtue of any contract for the hire of, or for the carriage for reward of persons or goods in, any vehicle, vessel, aircraft or other means of transport, or by or by virtue of any contract of bailment.

(4) This section does not apply to contracts entered into before the commencement of this Act.

[58]

General

8 Short title etc

(1) This Act may be cited as the Occupiers' Liability Act 1957.

(2) This Act shall not extend to Scotland, nor to Northern Ireland except in so far as it extends the powers of the Parliament of Northern Ireland.

(3) This Act shall come into force on the first day of January, nineteen hundred and fifty-eight.

[59]

FACTORIES ACT 1961

(C 34)

An Act to consolidate the Factories Acts 1937 to 1959, and certain other enactments relating to the safety, health and welfare of employed persons

[22 June 1961]

PART II
SAFETY (GENERAL PROVISIONS)

12 *Prime movers*

(1) Every flywheel directly connected to any prime mover and every moving part of any prime

mover, except such prime movers as are mentioned in subsection (3) of this section, shall be securely fenced, whether the flywheel or prime mover is situated in an engine-house or not.

(2) The head and tail race of every water wheel and of every water turbine shall be securely fenced.

(3) Every part of electric generators, motors and rotary converters, and every flywheel directly connected thereto, shall be securely fenced unless it is in such a position or of such construction as to be as safe to every person employed or working on the premises as it would be if securely fenced.

[60]

NOTE
Prospective repeal: this section, and ss 13, 14 of this Act, are repealed, in so far as applying to work equipment provided for use before 1 January 1993, by the Provision of Use of Work Equipment Regulations 1992, SI 1992/2932, regs 1(3), 27, Sch 2, Pt I, as from 1 January 1997.

13 Transmission machinery

(1) Every part of the transmission machinery shall be securely fenced unless it is in such a position or of such construction as to be as safe to every person employed or working on the premises as it would be if securely fenced.

(2) Efficient devices or appliances shall be provided and maintained in every room or place where work is carried on by which the power can promptly be cut off from the transmission machinery in that room or place.

(3) No driving belt when not in use shall be allowed to rest or ride upon a revolving shaft which forms part of the transmission machinery.

(4) Suitable striking gear or other efficient mechanical appliances shall be provided and maintained and used to move driving belts to and from fast and loose pulleys which form part of the transmission machinery, and any such gear or appliances shall be so constructed, placed and maintained as to prevent the driving belt from creeping back on to the fast pulley.

(5) ...

[61]

NOTES
Sub-s (5): repealed by SI 1974/1941.
Prospective repeal: see the note to s 12 ante.

14 Other machinery

(1) Every dangerous part of any machinery, other than prime movers and transmission machinery, shall be securely fenced unless it is in such a position or of such construction as to be as safe to every person employed or working on the premises as it would be if securely fenced.

(2) In so far as the safety of a dangerous part of any machinery cannot by reason of the nature of the operation be secured by means of a fixed guard, the requirements of subsection (1) of this section shall be deemed to have been complied with if a device is provided which automatically prevents the operator from coming into contact with that part.

(3), (4) ...

(5) Any part of a stock-bar which projects beyond the headstock of a lathe shall be securely fenced unless it is in such a position as to be as safe to every person employed or working on the premises as it would be if securely fenced.

(6) ...

[62]

NOTES
Sub-ss (3), (4), (6): repealed by SI 1974/1941.
Prospective repeal: see the note to s 12 ante.

28 Floors, passages and stairs

(1) All floors, steps, stairs, passages and gangways shall be of sound construction and properly maintained and shall, so far as is reasonably practicable, be kept free from any obstruction and from any substance likely to cause persons to slip.

(2) For every staircase in a building or affording a means of exit from a building, a substantial hand-rail shall be provided and maintained, which, if the staircase has an open side, shall be on that side, and in the case of a staircase having two open sides or of a staircase which, owing to the nature of its construction or the condition of the surface of the steps or other special circumstances, is specially liable to cause accidents, such a hand-rail shall be provided and maintained on both sides.

(3) Any open side of a staircase shall also be guarded by the provision and maintenance of a lower rail or other effective means.

(4) All openings in floors shall be securely fenced, except in so far as the nature of the work renders such fencing impracticable.

(5) All ladders shall be soundly constructed and properly maintained.

[63]

NOTE
Repealed for certain purposes and prospectively repealed for remaining purposes, as from 1 January 1996, by SI 1992/3004, reg 27(1), Sch 2, Part I.

29 Safe means of access and safe place of employment

(1) There shall, so far as is reasonably practicable, be provided and maintained safe means of access to every place at which any person has at any time to work and every such place shall, so far as is reasonably practicable, be made and kept safe for any person working there.

(2) ...

[64]

NOTE
Repealed for certain purposes and prospectively repealed for remaining purposes, as from 1 January 1996, by SI 1992/3004, reg 27(1), Sch 2, Part I.

PART XIV
INTERPRETATION AND GENERAL

Interpretation

176 General interpretation

(1) In this Act, unless the context otherwise requires, the following expressions have the meanings hereby assigned to them respectively, that is to say:-

...

"prime mover" means every engine, motor or other appliance which provides mechanical energy derived from steam, water, wind, electricity, the combustion of fuel or other source;

...

"transmission machinery" means every shaft, wheel, drum, pulley, system of fast and loose pulleys, coupling, clutch, driving-belt or other device by which the motion of a prime mover is transmitted to or received by any machine or appliance;

...

[65]

185 Short title, commencement and extent

(1) This Act may be cited as the Factories Act 1961.

(2) This Act shall come into force on the first day of April, nineteen hundred and sixty-two.

(3) This Act, except subsections (1) and (2) of section seventy-seven ... does not extend to Northern Ireland.

[66]

NOTE
Sub-s (3): words omitted repealed by the Statute Law (Repeals) Act 1974.

LAW REFORM (HUSBAND AND WIFE) ACT 1962

(C 48)

An Act to amend the law with respect to civil proceedings between husband and wife
[1 August 1962]

1 Actions in tort between husband and wife

(1) Subject to the provisions of this section, each of the parties to a marriage shall have the like right of action in tort against the other as if they were not married.

(2) Where an action in tort is brought by one of the parties to a marriage against the other during the subsistence of the marriage, the court may stay the action if it appears—
  (a) that no substantial benefit would accrue to either party from the continuation of the proceedings; or
  (b) that the question or questions in issue could more conveniently be disposed of on an application made under section seventeen of the Married Women's Property Act 1882 (determination of questions between husband and wife as to the title to or possession of property);

and without prejudice to paragraph (b) of this subsection the court may, in such an action, either exercise any power which could be exercised on an application under the said section seventeen, or give such directions as it thinks fit for the disposal under that section of any question arising in the proceedings.

(3) Provision shall be made by rules of court for requiring the court to consider at an early stage of the proceedings whether the power to stay an action under subsection (2) of this section should or should not be exercised; ...

(4) ...

[67]

NOTES
Commencement: 1 August 1962 (RA).
Sub-s (3): words omitted repealed by the County Courts Act 1984, s 148(3), Sch 4.
Sub-s (4): applies to Scotland only.

3 Short title, repeal, interpretation, saving and extent

(1) This Act may be cited as the Law Reform (Husband and Wife) Act 1962.

(2) ...

(3) The references in subsection (1) of section one and subsection (1) of section two of this Act to the parties to a marriage include references to the persons who were parties to a marriage which has been dissolved.

(4) This Act does not apply to any cause of action which arose, or would but for the subsistence of a marriage have arisen, before the commencement of this Act.

(5) This Act does not extend to Northern Ireland.

[68]

NOTES
Sub-s (2): repealed by the Statute Law (Repeals) Act 1974.

MISREPRESENTATION ACT 1967

(C 7)

An Act to amend the law relating to innocent misrepresentations and to amend sections 11 and 35 of the Sale of Goods Act 1893

[22 March 1967]

1 Removal of certain bars to rescission for innocent misrepresentation

Where a person has entered into a contract after a misrepresentation has been made to him, and—
    (a) the misrepresentation has become a term of the contract; or
    (b) the contract has been performed;

or both, then, if otherwise he would be entitled to rescind the contract without alleging fraud, he shall be so entitled, subject to the provisions of this Act, notwithstanding the matters mentioned in paragraphs (a) and (b) of this section.

[69]

NOTE
Commencement: 22 April 1967.

2 Damages for misrepresentation

(1) Where a person has entered into a contract after a misrepresentation has been made to him by another party thereto and as a result thereof he has suffered loss, then, if the person making the misrepresentation would be liable to damages in respect thereof had the misrepresentation been made fraudulently, that person shall be so liable notwithstanding that the misrepresentation was not made fraudulently, unless he proves that he had reasonable ground to believe and did believe up to the time the contract was made that the facts represented were true.

(2) Where a person has entered into a contract after a misrepresentation has been made to him otherwise than fraudulently, and he would be entitled, by reason of the misrepresentation, to rescind the contract, then, if it is claimed, in any proceedings arising out of the contract, that the contract ought to be or has been rescinded the court or arbitrator may declare the contract subsisting and award damages in lieu of rescission, if of opinion that it would be equitable to do so, having regard to the nature of the misrepresentation and the loss that would be caused by it if the contract were upheld, as well as to the loss that rescission would cause to the other party.

(3) Damages may be awarded against a person under subsection (2) of this section whether or not he is liable to damages under subsection (1) thereof, but where he is so liable any award under the said subsection (2) shall be taken into account in assessing his liability under the said subsection (1).

[70]

NOTE
Commencement: 22 April 1967.

[3 Avoidance of provision excluding liability for misrepresentation]

If a contract contains a term which would exclude or restrict—
   (a) any liability to which a party to a contract may be subject by reason of any misrepresentation made by him before the contract was made; or
   (b) any remedy available to another party to the contract by reason of such a misrepresentation,

that term shall be of no effect except in so far as it satisfies the requirement of reasonableness as stated in section 11(1) of the Unfair Contract Terms Act 1977; and it is for those claiming that the term satisfies that requirement to show that it does.]

[71]

NOTES
Commencement: 1 February 1978.
Substituted by the Unfair Contract Terms Act 1977, s 8(1).

5 Saving for past transactions

Nothing in this Act shall apply in relation to any misrepresentation or contract of sale which is made before the commencement of this Act.

NOTE
Commencement: 22 April 1967.

6 Short title, commencement and extent

(1) This Act may be cited as the Misrepresentation Act 1967.

(2) This Act shall come into operation at the expiration of the period of one month beginning with the date on which it is passed.

(3) ...

(4) This Act does not extend to Northern Ireland.

NOTE
Commencement: 22 April 1967.
Sub-s (3): applies to Scotland only.

CRIMINAL LAW ACT 1967

(C 58)

An Act to amend the law of England and Wales by abolishing the division of crimes into felonies and misdemeanours and to amend and simplify the law in respect of matters arising from or related to that division or the abolition of it; to do away (within or without England and Wales) with certain obsolete crimes together with the torts of maintenance and champerty; and for purposes connected therewith

[21 July 1967]

PART I
FELONY AND MISDEMEANOUR

3 Use of force in making arrest, etc

(1) A person may use such force as is reasonable in the circumstances in the prevention of crime, or in effecting or assisting in the lawful arrest of offenders or suspected offenders or of persons unlawfully at large.

(2) Subsection (1) above shall replace the rules of the common law on the question when force used for a purpose mentioned in the subsection is justified by that purpose.

NOTE
Commencement: 1 January 1968.

11 Extent of Part I, and provision for Northern Ireland

(1) Subject to subsections (2) to (4) below, this Part of this Act shall not extend to Scotland or to Northern Ireland.

(2) Subsection (1) above shall not restrict the operation of this Part of this Act—
   (a) in so far as it affects—
      (i) ...
      (ii) the Army Act 1955, the Air Force Act 1955 or the Naval Discipline Act 1957; or
      (iii) section 2 of the Forfeiture Act 1870 or any other enactment or rule of law relating to any parliamentary disqualification or other disability or penal consequence arising from an offence being felony; or
   (b) in so far as (by paragraph 10 of Schedule 2) it amends the Regimental Debts Act 1893.

(3), (4) ...

NOTES
Commencement: 1 January 1968.
Sub-s (2): words omitted repealed by the Extradition Act 1989, s 37(2), Sch 2.
Sub-s (3): applies to Scotland only; repealed by the Public Order Act 1986, s 40(3), Sch 3.
Sub-s (4): repealed by the Northern Ireland Constitution Act 1973, s 41(1), Sch 6.

Part III
Supplementary

14 Civil rights in respect of maintenance and champerty

(1) No person shall, under the law of England and Wales, be liable in tort for any conduct on account of its being maintenance or champerty as known to the common law, except in the case of a cause of action accruing before this section has effect.

(2) The abolition of criminal and civil liability under the law of England and Wales for maintenance and champerty shall not affect any rule of that law as to the cases in which a contract is to be treated as contrary to public policy or otherwise illegal.

NOTE
Commencement: 21 July 1967 (RA).

15 Short title

This Act may be cited as the Criminal Law Act 1967.

THEATRES ACT 1968

(c 54)

An Act to abolish censorship of the theatre and to amend the law in respect of theatres and theatrical performances

[26 July 1968]

4 Amendment of law of defamation

(1) For the purposes of the law of libel and slander (including the law of criminal libel so far as it relates to the publication of defamatory matter) the publication of words in the course of a performance of a play shall, subject to section 7 of this Act, be treated as publication in permanent form.

(2) The foregoing subsection shall apply for the purposes of section 3 (slander of title, etc) of the Defamation Act 1952 as it applies for the purposes of the law of libel and slander.

(3) In this section "words" includes pictures, visual images, gestures and other methods of signifying meaning.

(4) . . .

[78]

NOTES
Commencement: 26 September 1968.
Sub-s (4): applies to Scotland only.

7 Exceptions for performances given in certain circumstances

(1) Nothing in sections 2 to 4 of this Act shall apply in relation to a performance of a play given on a domestic occasion in a private dwelling.

(2) Nothing in sections 2 to 6 of this Act shall apply in relation to a performance of a play given solely or primarily for one or more of the following purposes, that is to say—
 (a) rehearsal; or
 (b) to enable—
  (i) a record or cinematograph film to be made from or by means of the performance; or
  (ii) the performance to be broadcast; or
  (iii) the performance to be [included in a cable programme service which is or does not require to be licensed];

but in any proceedings for an offence under section 2, ... or 6 of this Act alleged to have been committed in respect of a performance of a play or an offence at common law alleged to have been committed in England and Wales by the publication of defamatory matter in the course of a performance of a play, if it is proved that the performance was attended by persons other than persons directly connected with the giving of the performance or the doing in relation thereto of any of the things mentioned in paragraph (b) above, the performance shall be taken not to have been given solely or primarily for one or more of the said purposes unless the contrary is shown.

(3) In this section—
 "broadcast" means broadcast by wireless telegraphy (within the meaning of the Wireless Telegraphy Act 1949), whether by way of sound broadcasting or television;
 "cinematograph film" means any print, negative, tape or other article on which a performance of a play or any part of such a performance is recorded for the purposes of visual reproduction;
 "record" means any record or similar contrivance for reproducing sound, including the sound-track of a cinematograph film;
 . . .

NOTES
Commencement: 26 September 1968.
Sub-s (2): words in square brackets substituted by the Cable and Broadcasting Act 1984, s 57, Sch 5, para 21; figure omitted thereof repealed by the Public Order Act 1986, s 40(3), Sch 3.
Sub-s (3): words omitted repealed by the Cable and Broadcasting Act 1984, s 57, Sch 6.

20 Short title, commencement, extent and application to Isles of Scilly

(1) This Act may be cited as the Theatres Act 1968.

(2) The provisions of this Act mentioned in subsection (3) below shall come into force on the passing of this Act, and the other provisions of this Act shall come into force on the expiration of a period of two months beginning with the date on which this Act is passed; ...

(3) ...

(4) This Act does not extend to Northern Ireland.

(5) ...

NOTE
Words omitted at the end of sub-s (2) and sub-ss (3) and (5) are not relevant to this work.

[80]

CIVIL EVIDENCE ACT 1968

(C 64)

An Act to amend the law of evidence in relation to civil proceedings, and in respect of the privilege against self-incrimination to make corresponding amendments in relation to statutory powers of inspection or investigation

[25 October 1968]

Part II
Miscellaneous and General

Convictions, etc as evidence in civil proceedings

11 Convictions as evidence in civil proceedings

(1) In any civil proceedings the fact that a person has been convicted of an offence by or before any court in the United Kingdom or by a court-martial there or elsewhere shall (subject to subsection (3) below) be admissible in evidence for the purpose of proving, where to do so is relevant to any issue in those proceedings, that he committed that offence, whether he was so convicted upon a plea of guilty or otherwise and whether or not he is a party to the civil proceedings; but no conviction other than a subsisting one shall be admissible in evidence by virtue of this section.

(2) In any civil proceedings in which by virtue of this section a person is proved to have been convicted of an offence by or before any court in the United Kingdom or by a court-martial there or elsewhere—

(a) he shall be taken to have committed that offence unless the contrary is proved; and
(b) without prejudice to the reception of any other admissible evidence for the purpose of identifying the facts on which the conviction was based, the contents of any document which is admissible as evidence of the conviction, and the contents of the information, complaint, indictment or charge-sheet on which the person in question was convicted, shall be admissible in evidence for that purpose.

(3) Nothing in this section shall prejudice the operation of section 13 of this Act or any other enactment whereby a conviction or a finding of fact in any criminal proceedings is for the purposes of any other proceedings made conclusive evidence of any fact.

(4) Where in any civil proceedings the contents of any document are admissible in evidence by virtue of subsection (2) above, a copy of that document, or of the material part thereof, purporting to be certified or otherwise authenticated by or on behalf of the court or authority having custody of that document shall be admissible in evidence and shall be taken to be a true copy of that document or part unless the contrary is shown.

(5) Nothing in any of the following enactments, that is to say—
(a) [section 1C] of the Powers of Criminal Courts Act 1973] (under which a conviction leading to ... discharge is to be disregarded except as therein mentioned);
(b) section 9 of the Criminal Justice (Scotland) Act 1949 (which makes similar provision in respect of convictions on indictment in Scotland); and
(c) section 8 of the Probation Act (Northern Ireland) 1950 (which corresponds to the said section 12) or any corresponding enactment of the Parliament of Northern Ireland for the time being in force,

shall affect the operation of this section; and for the purposes of this section any order made by a court of summary jurisdiction in Scotland under section 1 or section 2 of the said Act of 1949 shall be treated as a conviction.

(6) In this section "court-martial" means a court-martial constituted under the Army Act 1955, the Air Force Act 1955 or the Naval Discipline Act 1957 or a disciplinary court constituted under section 50 of the said Act of 1957, and in relation to a court-martial "conviction", as regards a court-martial constituted under either of the said Acts of 1955, means a finding of guilty which is, or falls to be treated as, a finding of the court duly confirmed and, as regards a court-martial or disciplinary court constituted under the said Act of 1957, means a finding of guilty which is, or falls to be treated as, the finding of the court, and "convicted" shall be construed accordingly.

[81]

NOTES
Commencement: 2 December 1968.
Sub-s (5): first words in square brackets substituted by the Powers of Criminal Courts Act 1973, ss 56(1), 60(2), Sch 5, para 31, words in square brackets therein substituted and words omitted repealed, by the Criminal Justice Act 1991, ss 100, 101(2), Sch 11, para 5, Sch 13.

13 Conclusiveness of convictions for purposes of defamation actions

(1) In an action for libel or slander in which the question whether a person did or did not commit a criminal offence is relevant to an issue arising in the action, proof

that at the time when that issue falls to be determined, that person stands convicted of that offence shall be conclusive evidence that he committed that offence; and his conviction thereof shall be admissible in evidence accordingly.

(2) In any such action as aforesaid in which by virtue of this section a person is proved to have been convicted of an offence, the contents of any document which is admissible as evidence of the conviction, and the contents of the information, complaint, indictment or charge-sheet on which that person was convicted, shall, without prejudice to the reception of any other admissible evidence for the purpose of identifying the facts on which the conviction was based, be admissible in evidence for the purpose of identifying those facts.

(3) For the purposes of this section a person shall be taken to stand convicted of an offence if but only if there subsists against him a conviction of that offence by or before a court in the United Kingdom or by a court-martial there or elsewhere.

(4) Subsections (4) to (6) of section 11 of this Act shall apply for the purposes of this section as they apply for the purposes of that section, but as if in the said subsection (4) the reference to subsection (2) were a reference to subsection (2) of this section.

(5) The foregoing provisions of this section shall apply for the purposes of any action begun after the passing of this Act, whenever the cause of action arose, but shall not apply for the purposes of any action begun before the passing of this Act or any appeal or other proceedings arising out of any such action.

[82]

NOTES
Commencement: 25 October 1968.

General

20 Short title, repeals, extent and commencement

(1) This Act may be cited as the Civil Evidence Act 1968.

(2) ...

(3) This Act shall not extend to Scotland or, ... to Northern Ireland.

(4) The following provisions of this Act, namely sections 13 to 19, this section (except subsection (2)) and the Schedule, shall come into force on the day this Act is passed, and the other provisions of this Act shall come into force on such day as the Lord Chancellor may by order made by statutory instrument appoint; and different days may be so appointed for different purposes of this Act or for the same purposes in relation to different courts or proceedings or otherwise in relation to different circumstances.

[83]

NOTES
Sub-s (2): repeals the Evidence Act 1938, ss 1, 2, 6(1) in part, 6 (2)(b)
Commencement: 25 October 1968 (except sub-s (2)).

EMPLOYER'S LIABILITY (DEFECTIVE EQUIPMENT) ACT 1969

(C 37)

An Act to make further provision with respect to the liability of an employer for injury to his employee which is attributable to any defect in equipment provided by the employer for the purposes of the employer's business; and for purposes connected with the matter aforesaid.

[25 July 1969]

1 Extension of employer's liability for defective equipment

(1) Where after the commencement of this Act—
   (a) an employee suffers personal injury in the course of his employment in consequence of a defect in equipment provided by his employer for the purposes of the employer's business; and
   (b) the defect is attributable wholly or partly to the fault of a third party (whether identified or not),

the injury shall be deemed to be also attributable to negligence on the part of the employer (whether or not he is liable in respect of the injury apart from this subsection), but without prejudice to the law relating to contributory negligence and to any remedy by way of contribution or in contract or otherwise which is available to the employer in respect of the injury.

(2) In so far as any agreement purports to exclude or limit any liability of an employer arising under subsection (1) of this section, the agreement shall be void.

(3) In this section—
   "business" includes the activities carried on by any public body;
   "employee" means a person who is employed by another person under a contract of service or apprenticeship and is so employed for the purposes of a business carried on by that other person, and "employer" shall be construed accordingly;
   "equipment" includes any plant and machinery, vehicle, aircraft and clothing;
   "fault" means negligence, breach of statutory duty or other act or omission which gives rise to liability in tort in England and Wales or which is wrongful and gives rise to liability in damages in Scotland; and
   "personal injury" includes loss of life, any impairment of a person's physical or mental condition and any disease.

(4) This section binds the Crown, and persons in the service of the Crown shall accordingly be treated for the purposes of this section as employees of the Crown if they would not be so treated apart from this subsection.

NOTE
Commencement: 25 October 1969.

2 Short title, commencement and extent

(1) This Act may be cited as the Employer's Liability (Defective Equipment) Act 1969.

(2) This Act shall come into force on the expiration of the period of three months beginning with the date on which it is passed.

(3) ...

(4) This Act ... does not extend to Northern Ireland.

NOTES
Commencement: 25 October 1969.
Sub-ss (3), (4): words omitted repealed by the Northern Ireland Constitution Act 1973, s 41, Sch 6, Part I.

EMPLOYERS' LIABILITY (COMPULSORY INSURANCE) ACT 1969

(C 57)

An Act to require employers to insure against their liability for personal injury to their employees; and for purposes connected with the matter aforesaid.

[22 October 1969]

1 Insurance against liability for employees

(1) Except as otherwise provided by this Act, every employer carrying on any business in Great Britain shall insure, and maintain insurance, under one or more approved policies with an authorised insurer or insurers against liability for bodily injury or disease sustained by his employees, and arising out of and in the course of their employment in Great Britain in that business, but except in so far as regulations otherwise provide not including injury or disease suffered or contracted outside Great Britain.

(2) Regulations may provide that the amount for which an employer is required by this Act to insure and maintain insurance shall, either generally or in such cases or classes of case as may be prescribed by the regulations, be limited in such manner as may be so prescribed.

(3) For the purposes of this Act—
  (a) "approved policy" means a policy of insurance not subject to any conditions or exceptions prohibited for those purposes by regulations;
  (b) "authorised insurer" means a person or body of persons lawfully carrying on in [the United Kingdom insurance business of a class specified in Schedule 1 or 2 to the Insurance Companies Act [1982]] and issuing the policy or policies in the course thereof;
  (c) "business" includes a trade or profession, and includes any activity carried on by a body of persons, whether corporate or unincorporate;
  (d) except as otherwise provided by regulations, an employer not having a place of business in Great Britain shall be deemed not to carry on business there.

NOTES
Commencement: 1 January 1972.
Sub-s (3): amended by the Insurance Companies Act 1981, s 36, Sch 4, Part II, para 19, further amended by the Insurance Companies Act 1982, s 99(2), Sch 5, para 8.

2 Employees to be covered

(1) For the purposes of this Act the term "employee" means an individual who has entered into or works under a contract of service or apprenticeship with an employer whether by way of manual labour, clerical work or otherwise, whether such contract is expressed or implied, oral or in writing.

(2) This Act shall not require an employer to insure—
   (a) in respect of an employee of whom the employer is the husband, wife, father, mother, grandfather, grandmother, step-father, step-mother, son, daughter, grandson, granddaughter, stepson, stepdaughter, brother, sister, half-brother or half-sister; or
   (b) except as otherwise provided by regulations, in respect of employees not ordinarily resident in Great Britain.

[87]

NOTES
Commencement: 1 January 1972.
Sub-s (2): first words in square brackets added by the National Health Service and Community Care Act 1990, s 60, Sch 8, Part I, para 1; first words omitted repealed by the Local Government Act 1985, s 102, Sch 17; second words omitted repealed by the Local Government Act 1972, s 272(1), Sch 30; second words in square brackets added by the Norfolk and Suffolk Broads Act 1988, s 21, Sch 6, para 7; third amendment in square brackets made by the Local Government Act 1985, s 84, Sch 14, para 46, words omitted therein repealed by the Education Reform Act 1988, s 237, Sch 13, Part I.
Modified by the Waste Regulation and Disposal (Authorities) Order 1985, SI 1985 /1884, art 10, Sch 3.

7 Short title, extent and commencement

(1) This Act may be cited as the Employers' Liability (Compulsory Insurance) Act 1969.

(2) This Act shall not extend to Northern Ireland.

(3) This Act shall come into force for any purpose on such date as the Secretary of State may by order contained in a statutory instrument appoint, and the purposes for which this Act is to come into force at any time may be defined by reference to the nature of an employer's business, or to that of an employee's work, or in any other way.

[88]

NOTE
Commencement: 1 January 1972.

EMPLOYERS' LIABILITY (COMPULSORY INSURANCE) GENERAL REGULATIONS 1971

(SI 1971/1117)

1 Commencement, citation and interpretation

(1) These Regulations may be cited as the Employers' Liability (Compulsory Insurance) General Regulations 1971 and shall come into operation on 1st January 1972, with the exception of Regulations 6 and 7 which shall come into operation on 1st January 1973.

(2) The Interpretation Act 1889 shall apply to the interpretation of these Regulations as it applies to the interpretation of an Act of Parliament.

2 Prohibition of certain conditions in policies of insurance

(1) Any condition in a policy of insurance issued or renewed in accordance with the requirements of the Act after the coming into operation of this Regulation which provides (in whatever terms) that no liability (either generally or in respect of a particular claim) shall arise under the policy, or that any such liability so arising shall cease—
    (a) in the event of some specified thing being done or omitted to be done after the happening of the event giving rise to a claim under the policy;
    (b) unless the policy holder takes reasonable care to protect his employees against the risk of bodily injury or disease in the course of their employment;
    (c) unless the policy holder complies with the requirements of any enactment for the protection of employees against the risk of bodily injury or disease in the course of their employment; and
    (d) unless the policy holder keeps specified records or provides the insurer with or makes available to him information therefrom,

is hereby prohibited for the purposes of the Act.

(2) Nothing in this Regulation shall be taken as prejudicing any provision in a policy requiring the policy holder to pay to the insurer any sums which the latter may have become liable to pay under the policy and which have been applied to the satisfaction of claims in respect of employees or any costs and expenses incurred in relation to such claims.

3 Limit of amount of compulsory insurance

The amount for which an employer is required by the Act to insure and maintain insurance shall be two million pounds in respect of claims relating to any one or more of his employees arising out of any one occurrence.

ANIMALS ACT 1971

(C 22)

An Act to make provision with respect to civil liability for damage done by animals and with respect to the protection of livestock from dogs; and for purposes connected with those matters

[12 May 1971]

Strict liability for damage done by animals

1 New provisions as to strict liability for damage done by animals

(1) The provisions of sections 2 to 5 of this Act replace—
    (a) the rules of the common law imposing a strict liability in tort for damage done by an animal on the ground that the animal is regarded as ferae naturea or that its vicious or mischievous propensities are known or presumed to be known;

(b) subsections (1) and (2) of section 1 of the Dogs Act 1906 as amended by the Dogs (Amendment) Act 1928 (injury to cattle or poultry); and
(c) the rules of the common law imposing a liability for cattle trespass.

(2) Expressions used in those sections shall be interpreted in accordance with the provisions of section 6 (as well as those of section 11) of this Act.

2 Liability for damage done by dangerous animals

(1) Where any damage is caused by an animal which belongs to a dangerous species, any person who is a keeper of the animal is liable for the damage, except as otherwise provided by this Act.

(2) Where damage is caused by an animal which does not belong to a dangerous species, a keeper of the animal is liable for the damage, except as otherwise provided by this Act, if—
(a) the damage is of a kind which the animal, unless restrained, was likely to cause or which, if caused by the animal, was likely to be severe; and
(b) the likelihood of the damage or of its being severe was due to characteristics of the animal which are not normally found in animals of the same species or are not normally so found except at particular times or in particular circumstances: and
(c) those characteristics were known to that keeper or were at any time known to a person who at that time had charge of the animal as that keeper's servant or, where that keeper is the head of a household, were known to another keeper of the animal who is a member of that household and under the age of sixteen.

3 Liability for injury done by dogs to livestock

Where a dog causes damage by killing or injuring livestock, any person who is a keeper of the dog is liable for the damage, except as otherwise provided by this Act.

4 Liability for damage and expenses due to trespassing livestock

(1) Where livestock belonging to any person strays on to land in the ownership or occupation of another and—
(a) damage is done by the livestock to the land or to any property on it which is in the ownership or possession of the other person; or
(b) any expenses are reasonably incurred by that other person in keeping the livestock while it cannot be restored to the person to whom it belongs or while it is detained in pursuance of section 7 of this Act, or in ascertaining to whom it belongs;

the person to whom the livestock belongs is liable for the damage or expenses, except as otherwise provided by this Act.

(2) For the purposes of this section any livestock belongs to the person in whose possession it is.

5 Exceptions from liability under sections 2 to 4

(1) A person is not liable under sections 2 to 4 of this Act for any damage which is due wholly to the fault of the person suffering it.

(2) A person is not liable under section 2 of this Act for any damage suffered by a person who has voluntarily accepted the risk thereof.

(3) A person is not liable under section 2 of this Act for any damage caused by an animal kept on any premises or structure to a person trespassing there, if it is proved either—
- (a) that the animal was not kept there for the protection of persons or property; or
- (b) (if the animal was kept there for the protection of persons or property) that keeping it there for that purpose was not unreasonable.

(4) A person is not liable under section 3 of this Act if the livestock was killed or injured on land on to which it had strayed and either the dog belonged to the occupier or its presence on the land was authorised by the occupier.

(5) A person is not liable under section 4 of this Act where the livestock strayed from a highway and its presence there was a lawful use of the highway.

(6) In determining whether any liability for damage under section 4 of this Act is excluded by subsection (1) of this section the damage shall not be treated as due to the fault of the person suffering it by reason only that he could have prevented it by fencing; but a person is not liable under that section where it is proved that the straying of the livestock on to the land would not have occurred but for a breach by any other person, being a person having an interest in the land, of a duty to fence.

6 Interpretation of certain expressions used in sections 2 to 5

(1) The following provisions apply to the interpretation of sections 2 to 5 of this Act.

(2) A dangerous species is a species—
- (a) which is not commonly domesticated in the British Islands; and
- (b) whose fully grown animals normally have such characteristics that they are likely, unless restrained, to cause severe damage or that any damage they may cause is likely to be severe.

(3) Subject to subsection (4) of this section, a person is a keeper of an animal if—
- (a) he owns the animal or has it in his possession; or
- (b) he is the head of a household of which a member under the age of sixteen owns the animal or has it in his possession;

and if at any time an animal ceases to be owned by or to be in the possession of a person, any person who immediately before that time was a keeper thereof by virtue of the preceding provisions of this subsection continues to be a keeper of the animal until another person becomes a keeper thereof by virtue of those provisions.

(4) Where an animal is taken into and kept in possession for the purpose of preventing it from causing damage or of restoring it to its owner, a person is not a keeper of it by virtue only of that possession.

(5) Where a person employed as a servant by a keeper of an animal incurs a risk incidental to his employment he shall not be treated as accepting it voluntarily.

Detention and sale of trespassing livestock

7 Detention and sale of trespassing livestock

(1) The right to seize and detain any animal by way of distress damage feasant is hereby abolished.

(2) Where any livestock strays on to any land and is not then under the control of any person the occupier of the land may detain it, subject to subsection (3) of this section, unless ordered to return it by a court.

(3) Where any livestock is detained in pursuance of this section the right to detain it ceases—
- (a) at the end of a period of forty-eight hours, unless within that period notice of the detention has been given to the officer in charge of a police station and also, if the person detaining the livestock knows to whom it belongs, to that person; or
- (b) when such amount is tendered to the person detaining the livestock as is sufficient to satisfy any claim he may have under section 4 of this Act in respect of the livestock; or
- (c) if he has no such claim, when the livestock is claimed by a person entitled to its possession.

(4) Where livestock has been detained in pursuance of this section for a period of not less than fourteen days the person detaining it may sell it at a market or by public auction, unless proceedings are then pending for the return of the livestock or for any claim under section 4 of this Act in respect of it.

(5) Where any livestock is sold in the exercise of the right conferred by this section and the proceeds of the sale, less the costs thereof and any costs incurred in connection with it, exceed the amount of any claim under section 4 of this Act which the vendor had in respect of the livestock, the excess shall be recoverable from him by the person who would be entitled to the possession of the livestock but for the sale.

(6) A person detaining any livestock in pursuance of this section is liable for any damage caused to it by a failure to treat it with reasonable care and supply it with adequate food and water while it is so detained.

(7) References in this section to a claim under section 4 of this Act in respect of any livestock do not include any claim under that section for damage done by or expenses incurred in respect of the livestock before the straying in connection with which it is detained under this section.

Animals straying on to highway

8 Duty to take care to prevent damage from animals straying on to the highway

(1) So much of the rules of the common law relating to liability for negligence as excludes or restricts the duty which a person might owe to others to take such care as is reasonable to see that damage is not caused by animals straying on to a highway is hereby abolished.

(2) Where damage is caused by animals straying from unfenced land to a highway a person who placed them on the land shall not be regarded as having committed a breach of the duty to take care by reason only of placing them there if—
: (a) the land is common land, or is land situated in an area where fencing is not customary, or is a town or village green; and
: (b) he had a right to place the animals on that land.

Protection of livestock against dogs

9 Killing of or injury to dogs worrying livestock

(1) In any civil proceedings against a person (in this section referred to as the defendant) for killing or causing injury to a dog it shall be a defence to prove—
: (a) that the defendant acted for the protection of any livestock and was a person entitled to act for the protection of that livestock; and
: (b) that within forty-eight hours of the killing or injury notice thereof was given by the defendant to the officer in charge of a police station.

(2) For the purposes of this section a person is entitled to act for the protection of any livestock if, and only if—
: (a) the livestock or the land on which it is belongs to him or to any person under whose express or implied authority he is acting; and
: (b) the circumstances are not such that liability for killing or causing injury to the livestock would be excluded by section 5(4) of this Act.

(3) Subject to subsection (4) of this section, a person killing or causing injury to a dog shall be deemed for the purposes of this section to act for the protection of any livestock if, and only if, either—
: (a) the dog is worrying or is about to worry the livestock and there are no other reasonable means of ending or preventing the worrying; or
: (b) the dog has been worrying livestock, has not left the vicinity and is not under the control of any person and there are no practicable means of ascertaining to whom it belongs.

(4) For the purposes of this section the condition stated in either of the paragraphs of the preceding subsection shall be deemed to have been satisfied if the defendant believed that it was satisfied and had reasonable ground for that belief.

(5) For the purposes of this section—
: (a) an animal belongs to any person if he owns it or has it in his possession; and
: (b) land belongs to any person if he is the occupier thereof.

Supplemental

10 Application of certain enactments to liability under sections 2 to 4

For the purposes of the Fatal Accidents Acts 1846 to 1959, the Law Reform (Contributory Negligence) Act 1945 and the Limitation Acts 1939 to 1963 any damage for which a person is liable under sections 2 to 4 of this Act shall be treated as due to his fault.

11 General interpretation

In this Act—

"common land", and "town or village green" have the same meanings as in the Commons Registration Act 1965;

"damage" includes the death of, or injury to, any person (including any disease and any impairment of physical or mental condition);

"fault" has the same meaning as in the Law Reform (Contributory Negligence) Act 1945;

"fencing" includes the construction of any obstacle designed to prevent animals from straying;

"livestock" means cattle, horses, asses, mules, hinnies, sheep, pigs, goats and poultry, and also deer not in the wild state and, in sections 3 and 9, also, while in captivity, pheasants, partridges and grouse;

"poultry" means the domestic varieties of the following, that is to say, fowls, turkeys, geese, ducks, guinea-fowls, pigeons, peacocks and quails; and

"species" includes sub-species and variety.

[102]

12 Application to Crown

(1) This Act binds the Crown, but nothing in this section shall authorise proceedings to be brought against Her Majesty in her private capacity.

(2) Section 38(3) of the Crown Proceedings Act 1947 (interpretation of references to Her Majesty in her private capacity) shall apply as if this section were contained in that Act.

[103]

13 Short title, repeal, commencement and extent

(1) This Act may be cited as the Animals Act 1971.

(2) ...

(3) This Act shall come into operation on 1st October 1971.

(4) This Act does not extend to Scotland or to Northern Ireland.

[104]

NOTE
Sub-s (2): amends the Dogs Act 1906, s 1, and the Dogs (Amendment) Act 1928, s 1(1).

DEFECTIVE PREMISES ACT 1972

(C 35)

An Act to impose duties in connection with the provision of dwellings and otherwise to amend the law of England and Wales as to liability for injury or damage caused to persons through defects in the state of premises

[29 June 1972]

1 Duty to build dwellings properly

(1) A person taking on work for or in connection with the provision of a dwelling (whether the dwelling is provided by the erection or by the conversion or enlargement of a building) owes a duty—

(a) if the dwelling is provided to the order of any person, to that person; and

(b) without prejudice to paragraph (a) above, to every person who acquires an interest (whether legal or equitable) in the dwelling;

to see that the work which he takes on is done in a workmanlike or, as the case may be, professional manner, with proper materials and so that as regards that work the dwelling will be fit for habitation when completed.

(2) A person who takes on any such work for another on terms that he is to do it in accordance with instructions given by or on behalf of that other shall, to the extent to which he does it properly in accordance with those instructions, be treated for the purposes of this section as discharging the duty imposed on him by subsection (1) above except where he owes a duty to that other to warn him of any defects in the instructions and fails to discharge that duty.

(3) A person shall not be treated for the purposes of subsection (2) above as having given instructions for the doing of work merely because he has agreed so the work being done in a specified manner, with specified materials or to a specified design.

(4) A person who—
   (a) in the course of a business which consists of or includes providing or arranging for the provision of dwellings or installations in dwellings; or
   (b) in the exercise of a power of making such provision or arrangements conferred by or by virtue of any enactment;

arranges for another to take on work for or in connection with the provision of a dwelling shall be treated for the purposes of this section as included among the persons who have taken on the work.

(5) Any cause of action in respect of a breach of the duty imposed by this section shall be deemed, for the purposes of the Limitation Act 1939, the Law Reform (Limitation of Actions, &c.) Act 1954 and the Limitation Act 1963, to have accrued at the time when the dwelling was completed, but if after that time a person who has done work for or in connection with the provision of the dwelling does further work to rectify the work he has already done, any such cause of action in respect of that further work shall be deemed for those purposes to have accrued at the time when the further work was finished.

[105]

2 Cases excluded from the remedy under section 1

(1) Where—
   (a) in connection with the provision of a dwelling or its first sale or letting for habitation any rights in respect of defects in the state of the dwelling are conferred by an approved scheme to which this section applies on a person having or acquiring an interest in the dwelling; and
   (b) it is stated in a document of a type approved for the purposes of this section that the requirements as to design or construction imposed by or under the scheme have, or appear to have, been substantially complied with in relation to the dwelling;

no action shall be brought by any person having or acquiring an interest in the dwelling for breach of the duty imposed by section 1 above in relation to the dwelling.

(2) A scheme to which this section applies—
   (a) may consist of any number of documents and any number of agreements or other transactions between any number of persons; but

(b) must confer, by virtue of agreements entered into with persons having or acquiring an interest in the dwellings to which the scheme applies, rights on such persons in respect of defects in the state of the dwellings.

(3) In this section "approved" means approved by the Secretary of State, and the power of the Secretary of State to approve a scheme or document for the purposes of this section shall be exercisable by order, except that any requirements as to construction or design imposed under a scheme to which this section applies may be approved by him without making any order or, if he thinks fit, by order.

(4) The Secretary of State—
  (a) may approve a scheme or document for the purposes of this section with or without limiting the duration of his approval; and
  (b) may by order revoke or vary a previous order under this section or, without such an order, revoke or vary a previous approval under this section given otherwise than by order.

(5) The production of a document purporting to be a copy of an approval given by the Secretary of State otherwise than by order and certified by an officer of the Secretary of State to be a true copy of the approval shall be conclusive evidence of the approval, and without proof of the handwriting or official position of the person purporting to sign the certificate.

(6) The power to make an order under this section shall be exercisable by statutory instrument which shall be subject to annulment in pursuance of a resolution by either House of Parliament.

(7) Where an interest in a dwelling is compulsorily acquired—
  (a) no action shall be brought by the acquiring authority for breach of the duty imposed by section 1 above in respect of the dwelling; and
  (b) if any work for or in connection with the provision of the dwelling was done otherwise than in the course of a business by the person in occupation of the dwelling at the time of the compulsory acquisition, the acquiring authority and not that person shall be treated as the person who took on the work and accordingly as owing that duty.

[106]

3 Duty of care with respect to work done on premises not abated by disposal of premises

(1) Where work of construction, repair, maintenance or demolition or any other work is done on or in relation to premises, any duty of care owed, because of the doing of the work, to persons who might reasonably be expected to be affected by defects in the state of the premises created by the doing of the work shall not be abated by the subsequent disposal of the premises by the person who owed the duty.

(2) This section does not apply—
  (a) in the case of premises which are let, where the relevant tenancy of the premises commenced, or the relevant tenancy agreement of the premises was entered into, before the commencement of this Act;
  (b) in the case of premises disposed of in any other way, when the disposal of the premises was completed, or a contract for their disposal was entered into, before the commencement of this Act; or
  (c) in either case, where the relevant transaction disposing of the premises is

entered into in pursuance of an enforceable option by which the consideration for the disposal was fixed before the commencement of this Act.

[107]

4 Landlord's duty of care in virtue of obligation or right to repair premises demised

(1) Where premises are let under a tenancy which puts on the landlord an obligation to the tenant for the maintenance or repair of the premises, the landlord owes to all persons who might reasonably be expected to be affected by defects in the state of the premises a duty to take such care as is reasonable in all the circumstances to see that they are reasonably safe from personal injury or from damage to their property caused by a relevant defect.

(2) The said duty is owed if the landlord knows (whether as the result of being notified by the tenant or otherwise) or if he ought in all the circumstances to have known of the relevant defect.

(3) In this section "relevant defect" means a defect in the state of the premises existing at or after the material time and arising from, or continuing because of, an act or omission by the landlord which constitutes or would if he had had notice of the defect, have constituted a failure by him to carry out his obligation to the tenant for the maintenance or repair of the premises; and for the purposes of the foregoing provision "the material time" means—
    (a) where the tenancy commenced before this Act, the commencement of this Act; and
    (b) in all other cases, the earliest of the following times, that is to say—
        (i) the time when the tenancy commences;
        (ii) the time when the tenancy agreement is entered into;
        (iii) the time when possession is taken of the premises in contemplation of the letting.

(4) Where premises are let under a tenancy which expressly or impliedly gives the landlord the right to enter the premises to carry out any description of maintenance or repair of the premises, then, as from the time when he first is, or by notice or otherwise can put himself, in a position to exercise the right and so long as he is or can put himself in that position, he shall be treated for the purposes of subsections (1) to (3) above (but for no other purpose) as if he were under an obligation to the tenant for that description of maintenance or repair of the premises; but the landlord shall not owe the tenant any duty by virtue of this subsection in respect of any defect in the state of the premises arising from, or continuing because of, a failure to carry out an obligation expressly imposed on the tenant by the tenancy.

(5) For the purposes of this section obligations imposed or rights given by any enactment in virtue of a tenancy shall be treated as imposed or given by the tenancy.

(6) This section applies to a right of occupation given by contract or any enactment and not amounting to a tenancy as if the right were a tenancy, and "tenancy" and cognate expressions shall be construed accordingly.

[108]

5 Application to Crown

This Act shall bind the Crown, but as regards the Crown's liability in tort shall not bind the Crown further than the Crown is made liable in tort by the Crown Proceedings Act 1947.

[109]

6 Supplemental

(1) In this Act—
"disposal", in relation to premises, includes a letting, and an assignment or surrender of a tenancy, of the premises and the creation by contract of any other right to occupy the premises, and "dispose" shall be construed accordingly;
"personal injury" includes any disease and any impairment of a person's physical or mental condition;
"tenancy" means—
   (a) a tenancy created either immediately or derivatively out of the freehold, whether by a lease or underlease, by an agreement for a lease or underlease or by a tenancy agreement, but not including a mortgage term or any interest arising in favour of a mortgagor by his attorning tenant to his mortgagee; or
   (b) a tenancy at will or a tenancy on sufferance; or
   (c) a tenancy, whether or not constituting a tenancy at common law, created by or in pursuance of any enactment;
and cognate expressions shall be construed accordingly.

(2) Any duty imposed by or enforceable by virtue of any provision of this Act is in addition to any duty a person may owe apart from that provision.

(3) Any term of an agreement which purports to exclude or restrict, or has the effect of excluding or restricting, the operation of any of the provisions of this Act, or any liability arising by virtue of any such provision, shall be void.

(4) ...

NOTES
Sub-s (4): repeals the Occupiers' Liability Act 1957, s 4.

7 Short title, commencement and extent

(1) This Act may be cited as the Defective Premises Act 1972.

(2) This Act shall come into force on 1st January 1974.

(3) This Act does not extend to Scotland or Northern Ireland.

SUPPLY OF GOODS (IMPLIED TERMS) ACT 1973

(C 13)

An Act to amend the law with respect to the terms to be implied in contracts of sale of goods and hire-purchase agreements and on the exchange of goods for trading stamps, and with respect to the terms of conditional sale agreements: and for connected purposes

[18 April 1973]

Hire-purchase agreements

[8 Implied terms as to title

(1) In every hire-purchase agreement, other than one to which subsection (2) below applies, there is—
  (a) an implied condition on the part of the creditor that he will have a right to sell the goods at the time when the property is to pass; and
  (b) an implied warranty that—
    (i) the goods are free, and will remain free until the time when the property is to pass, from any charge or encumbrance not disclosed or known to the person to whom the goods are bailed or (in Scotland) hired before the agreement is made, and
    (ii) that person will enjoy quiet possession of the goods except so far as it may be disturbed by any person entitled to the benefit of any charge or encumbrance so disclosed or known.

(2) In a hire-purchase agreement, in the case of which there appears from the agreement or is to be inferred from the circumstances of the agreement an intention that the creditor should transfer only such title as he or a third person may have, there is—
  (a) an implied warranty that all charges or encumbrances known to the creditor and not known to the person to whom the goods are bailed or hired have been disclosed to that person before the agreement is made; and
  (b) an implied warranty that neither—
    (i) the creditor; nor
    (ii) in a case where the parties to the agreement intend that any title which may be transferred shall be only such title as a third person may have, that person; nor
    (iii) anyone claiming through or under the creditor or that third person otherwise than under a charge or encumbrance disclosed or known to the person to whom the goods are bailed or hired, before the agreement is made;

will disturb the quiet possession of the person to whom the goods are bailed or hired.]

[112]

NOTES
Commencement: 19 May 1985.
Substituted by the Consumer Credit Act 1974, s 192(3)(a), Sch 4, para 35.

[9 Bailing or hiring by description]

(1) Where under a hire-purchase agreement goods are bailed or (in Scotland) hired by description, there is an implied condition that the goods will correspond with the description, and if under the agreement the goods are bailed or hired by reference to

a sample as well as a description, it is not sufficient that the bulk of the goods corresponds with the sample if the goods do not also correspond with the description.

(2) Goods shall not be prevented from being bailed or hired by description by reason only that, being exposed for sale, bailment or hire, they are selected by the person to whom they are bailed or hired.]

[113]

NOTES
Commencement: 19 May 1985.
Substituted by the Consumer Credit Act 1974, s 192(3)(a), Sch 4, para 35.

[10 Implied undertakings as to quality or fitness

(1) Except as provided by this section and section 11 below and subject to the provisions of any other enactment, including any enactment of the Parliament of Northern Ireland, or the Northern Ireland Assembly there is no implied condition or warranty as to the quality or fitness for any particular purpose of goods bailed or (in Scotland) hired under a hire-purchase agreement.

(2) Where the creditor bails or hires goods under a hire-purchase agreement in the course of a business, there is an implied condition that the goods [supplied under the agreement] are of merchantable quality, except that there is no such condition—
  (a) as regards defects specifically drawn to the attention of the person to whom the goods are bailed or hired before the agreement is made; or
  (b) if that person examines the goods before the agreement is made, as regards defects which that examination ought to reveal.

(3) Where the creditor bails or hires goods under a hire-purchase agreement in the course of a business and the person to whom the goods are bailed or hired, expressly or by implication, makes known—
  (a) to the creditor in the course of negotiations conducted by the creditor in relation to the making of the hire-purchase agreement, or
  (b) to a credit-broker in the course of negotiations conducted by that broker in relation to goods sold by him to the creditor before forming the subject matter of the hire-purchase agreement,

any particular purpose for which the goods are being bailed or hired, there is an implied condition that the goods supplied under the agreement are reasonably fit for that purpose, whether or not that is a purpose for which such goods are commonly supplied, except where the circumstances show that the person to whom the goods are bailed or hired does not rely, or that it is unreasonable for him to rely, on the skill or judgment of the creditor or credit-broker.

(4) An implied condition or warranty as to quality or fitness for a particular purpose may be annexed to a hire-purchase agreement by usage.

(5) The preceding provisions of this section apply to a hire-purchase agreement made by a person who in the course of a business is acting as agent for the creditor as they apply to an agreement made by the creditor in the course of a business, except where the creditor is not bailing or hiring in the course of a business and either the person to whom the goods are bailed or hired knows that fact or reasonable steps are taken to bring it to the notice of that person before the agreement is made.

(6) In subsection (3) above and this subsection—
  (a) "credit-broker" means a person acting in the course of a business of credit brokerage.

(b) "credit brokerage" means the effecting of introductions of individuals desiring to obtain credit—
  (i) to persons carrying on any business so far as it relates to the provision of credit, or
  (ii) to other persons engaged in credit brokerage.]

[114]

NOTES
Commencement: 19 May 1985.
Substituted by the Consumer Credit Act 1974, s 192(3)(a), Sch 4, para 35.
Sub-s (2): amended by the Supply of Goods and Services Act 1982, s 17(1).

[11 Samples

Where under a hire-purchase agreement goods are bailed or (in Scotland) hired by reference to a sample, there is an implied condition—
  (a) that the bulk will correspond with the sample in quality; and
  (b) that the person to whom the goods are bailed or hired will have a reasonable opportunity of comparing the bulk with the sample; and
  (c) that the goods will be free from any defect, rendering them unmerchantable, which would not be apparent on reasonable examination of the sample.]

[115]

NOTES
Commencement: 19 May 1985.
Substituted by the Consumer Credit Act 1974, s 192(3)(a), Sch 4, para 35.

[12 Exclusion of implied terms and conditions

(1) An express condition or warranty does not negative a condition or warranty implied by this Act unless inconsistent with it.]

(2)–(9) ...

[116]

NOTES
Commencement: 19 May 1985.
Sub-s (1): substituted by the Consumer Credit Act 1974, s 192(3)(a), Sch 4, para 35.
Sub-ss (2)–(9): repealed by the Unfair Contract Terms Act 1977, s 31(4), Sch 4.

[14 Special provisions as to conditional sale agreements

(1) [Section 11(4) of the Sale of Goods Act 1979] (whereby in certain circumstances a breach of a condition in a contract of sale is treated only as a breach of warranty) shall not apply to [a conditional sale agreement where the buyer deals as consumer within Part I of the Unfair Contract Terms Act 1977 ... .]

(2) In England and Wales and Northern Ireland a breach of a condition (whether express or implied) to be fulfilled by the seller under any such agreement shall be treated as a breach of warranty, and not as grounds for rejecting the goods and treating the agreement as repudiated, if (but only if) it would have fallen to be so treated had the condition been contained or implied in a corresponding hire-purchase agreement as a condition to be fulfilled by the creditor.]

[117]

NOTES

Commencement: 19 May 1985.

Substituted by the Consumer Credit Act 1974, s 192(3)(a), Sch 4, para 36; first amendment made by the Sale of Goods Act 1979, s 63, Sch 2, para 16; second amendment made by the Unfair Contract Terms Act 1977, s 31(3), Sch 3; words omitted repealed by the Statute Law (Repeals) Act 1981, Sch 1, Pt XII.

[15 Supplementary

(1) In sections 8 to 14 above and this section—

"business" includes a profession and the activities of any government department (including a Northern Ireland department), [or local or public authority];

"buyer" and "seller" includes a person to whom rights and duties under a conditional sale agreement have passed by assignment or operation of law;

"condition" and "warranty", in relation to Scotland, mean stipulation, and any stipulation referred to in sections 8(1)(a), 9, 10 and 11 above shall be deemed to be material to the agreement.

"conditional sale agreement" means an agreement for the sale of goods under which the purchase price or part of it is payable by instalments, and the property in the goods is to remain in the seller (notwithstanding that the buyer is to be in possession of the goods) until such conditions as to the payment of instalments or otherwise as may be specified in the agreement are fulfilled;

...

"creditor" means the person by whom the goods are bailed or (in Scotland) hired under a hire-purchase agreement or the person to whom his rights and duties under the agreement have passed by assignment or operation of law; and

"hire-purchase agreement" means an agreement, other than a conditional sale agreement, under which—

(a) goods are bailed or (in Scotland) hired in return for periodical payments by the person to whom they are bailed or hired, and

(b) the property in the goods will pass to that person if the terms of the agreements are complied with and one or more of the following occurs—
   (i) the exercise of an option to purchase by that person,
   (ii) the doing of any other specified act by any party to the agreement,
   (iii) the happening of any other specified event.

(2) Goods of any kind are of merchantable quality within the meaning of section 10(2) above if they are as fit for the purpose or purposes for which goods of that kind are commonly bought as it is reasonable to expect having regard to any description applied to them, the price (if relevant) and all the other relevant circumstances; and in section 11 above "unmerchantable" shall be construed accordingly.

(3) In section 14(2) above "corresponding hire-purchase agreement" means, in relation to a conditional sale agreement, a hire-purchase agreement relating to the same goods as the conditional sale agreement and made between the same parties and at the same time and in the same circumstances and, as nearly as may be, in the same terms as the conditional sale agreement.

(4) Nothing in sections 8 to 13 above shall prejudice the operation of any other enactment including any enactment of the Parliament of Northern Ireland or the Northern Ireland Assembly or any rule of law whereby any condition or warranty, other than one relating to quality or fitness, is to be implied in any hire-purchase agreement.]

NOTES
Commencement: 19 May 1985.
Substituted by the Consumer Credit Act 1974, s 192(3)(a), Sch 4, para 36.
Sub-s (1): definition "business" amended, and words omitted repealed by the Unfair Contract Terms Act 1977, s 31(3), (4), Sch 4.

Miscellaneous

18 Short title, citation, interpretation, commencement, repeal and saving

(1) This Act may be cited as the Supply of Goods (Implied Terms) Act 1973.

(2) ...

(3) This Act shall come into operation at the expiration of a period of one month beginning with the date on which it is passed.

(4) ...

(5) This Act does not apply to contracts of sale or hire-purchase agreements made before its commencement.

NOTES
Commencement: 18 May 1973.
Sub-s (2): repealed by the Sale of Goods Act 1979, s 63(2), Sch 3.
Sub-s (4): repeals ss 17-20, 29(3)(c) of the Hire-Purchase Act 1965, the Hire-Purchase (Scotland) Act 1965 and the Hire- Purchase Act (Northern Ireland) 1966.

CONGENITAL DISABILITIES (CIVIL LIABILITY) ACT 1976

(C 28)

An Act to make provision as to civil liability in the case of children born disabled in consequence of some person's fault; and to extend the Nuclear Installations Act 1965, so that children so born in consequence of a breach of duty under that Act may claim compensation

[22 July 1976]

1 Civil liability to child born disabled

(1) If a child is born disabled as the result of such an occurrence before its birth as is mentioned in subsection (2) below, and a person (other than the child's own mother) is under this section answerable to the child in respect of the occurrence, the child's disabilities are to be regarded as damage resulting from the wrongful act of that person and actionable accordingly at the suit of the child.

(2) An occurrence to which this section applies is one which—
   (a) affected either parent of the child in his or her ability to have a normal, healthy child; or
   (b) affected the mother during her pregnancy, or affected her or the child in the course of its birth, so that the child is born with disabilities which would not otherwise have been present.

(3) Subject to the following subsections, a person (here referred to as "the defendant") is answerable to the child if he was liable in tort to the parent or would, if sued

in due time, have been so; and it is no answer that there could not have been such liability because the parent suffered no actionable injury, if there was a breach of legal duty which, accompanied by injury, would have given rise to the liability.

(4) In the case of an occurrence preceding the time of conception, the defendant is not answerable to the child if at that time either or both of the parents knew the risk of their child being born disabled (that is to say, the particular risk created by the occurrence); but should it be the child's father who is the defendant, this subsection does not apply if he knew of the risk and the mother did not.

(5) The defendant is not answerable to the child, for anything he did or omitted to do when responsible in a professional capacity for treating or advising the parent, if he took reasonable care having due regard to then received professional opinion applicable to the particular class of case; but this does not mean that he is answerable only because he departed from received opinion.

(6) Liability to the child under this section may be treated as having been excluded or limited by contract made with the parent affected, to the same extent and subject to the same restrictions as liability in the parent's own case; and a contract term which could have been set up by the defendant in an action by the parent, so as to exclude or limit his liability to him or her, operates in the defendant's favour to the same, but no greater, extent in an action under this section by the child.

(7) If in the child's action under this section it is shown that the parent affected shared the responsibility for the child being born disabled, the damages are to be reduced to such extent as the court thinks just and equitable having regard to the extent of the parent's responsibility.

[120]

NOTE
Commencement: 22 July 1976.

2 Liability of woman driving when pregnant

A woman driving a motor vehicle when she knows (or ought reasonably to know) herself to be pregnant is to be regarded as being under the same duty to take care for the safety of her unborn child as the law imposes on her with respect to the safety of other people; and if in consequence of her breach of that duty her child is born with disabilities which would not otherwise have been present, those disabilities are to be regarded as damage resulting from her wrongful act and actionable accordingly at the suit of the child.

[120A]

NOTE
Commencement: 22 July 1976.

3 Disabled birth due to radiation

(1) Section 1 of this Act does not affect the operation of the Nuclear Installations Act 1965 as to liability for, and compensation in respect of, injury or damage caused by occurrences involving nuclear matter or the emission of ionising radiations.

(2) For the avoidance of doubt anything which—
    (a) affects a man in his ability to have a normal, healthy child; or
    (b) affects a woman in that ability, or so affects her when she is pregnant that

her child is born with disabilities which would not otherwise have been present,

is an injury for the purposes of that Act.

(3) If a child is born disabled as the result of an injury to either of its parents caused in breach of a duty imposed by any of sections 7 to 11 of that Act (nuclear site licensees and others to secure that nuclear incidents do not cause injury to persons, etc), the child's disabilities are to be regarded under the subsequent provisions of that Act (compensation and other matters) as injuries caused on the same occasion, and by the same breach of duty, as was the injury to the parent.

(4) As respects compensation to the child, section 13(6) of that Act (contributory fault of person injured by radiation) is to be applied as if the reference there to fault were to the fault of the parent.

(5) Compensation is not payable in the child's case if the injury to the parent preceded the time of the child's conception and at that time either or both of the parents knew the risk of their child being born disabled (that is to say, the particular risk created by the injury).

[120B]

NOTE
Commencement: 22 July 1976.

4 Interpretation and other supplementary provisions

(1) References in this Act to a child being born disabled or with disabilities are to its being born with any deformity, disease or abnormality, including predisposition (whether or not susceptible of immediate prognosis) to physical or mental defect in the future.

(2) In this Act—
   (a) "born" means born alive (at the moment of a child's birth being when it first has a life separate from its mother), and "birth" has a corresponding meaning;
   (b) "motor vehicle" means a mechanically propelled vehicle intended or adapted for use on roads,

[and references to embryos shall be construed in accordance with section 1 of the Human Fertilisation and Embryology Act 1990].

(3) Liability to a child under section 1, [1A] or 2 of this Act is to be regarded—
   (a) as respects all its incidents and any matters arising or to arise out of it; and
   (b) subject to any contrary context or intention, for the purpose of construing references in enactments and documents to personal or bodily injuries and cognate matters,

as liability for personal injuries sustained by the child immediately after its birth.

(4) No damages shall be recoverable under [any] of those sections in respect of any loss of expectation of life, nor shall any such loss be taken into account in the compensation payable in respect of a child under the Nuclear Installations Act 1965 as extended by section 3, unless (in either case) the child lives for at least 48 hours.

(5) This Act applies in respect of births after (but not before) its passing, and in respect of any such birth it replaces any law in force before its passing, whereby a per-

son could be liable to a child in respect of disabilities with which it might be born; but in section 1(3) of this Act the expression "liable in tort" does not include any reference to liability by virtue of this Act, or to liability by virtue of any such law.

(6) References to the Nuclear Installations Act 1965 are to that Act as amended; and for the purposes of section 28 of that Act (power by Order in Council to extend the Act to territories outside the United Kingdom) section 3 of this Act is to be treated as if it were a provision of that Act.

[120C]

NOTES
Commencement: 22 July 1976.
Sub-s (2)-(4): words in square brackets added, inserted or substituted by the Human Fertilisation and Embryology Act 1990, s 44(2).

6 Citation and extent

(1) This Act may be cited as the Congenital Disabilities (Civil Liability) Act 1976.

(2) This Act extends to Northern Ireland but not to Scotland.

[121]

NOTE
Commencement: 22 July 1976.

FATAL ACCIDENTS ACT 1976

(C 30)

An Act to consolidate the Fatal Accidents Acts.

[22 July 1976]

[1 Right of action for wrongful act causing death

(1) If death is caused by any wrongful act, neglect or default which is such as would (if death had not ensued) have entitled the person injured to maintain an action and recover damages in respect thereof, the person who would have been liable if death had not ensued shall be liable to an action for damages, notwithstanding the death of the person injured.

(2) Subject to section 1A(2) below, every such action shall be for the benefit of the dependants of the person ("the deceased") whose death has been so caused.

(3) In this Act "dependant" means—
   (a) the wife or husband or former wife or husband of the deceased;
   (b) any person who—
      (i) was living with the deceased in the same household immediately before the date of the death; and
      (ii) had been living with the deceased in the same household for at least two years before that date; and
      (iii) was living during the whole of that period as the husband or wife of the deceased;
   (c) any parent or other ascendant of the deceased;

(d) any person who was treated by the deceased as his parent;
(e) any child or other descendant of the deceased;
(f) any person (not being a child of the deceased) who, in the case of any marriage to which the deceased was at any time a party, was treated by the deceased as a child of the family in relation to that marriage;
(g) any person who is, or is the issue of, a brother, sister, uncle or aunt of the deceased.

(4) The reference to the former wife or husband of the deceased in subsection (3)(a) above includes a reference to a person whose marriage to the deceased has been annulled or declared void as well as a person whose marriage to the deceased has been dissolved.

(5) In deducing any relationship for the purposes of subsection (3) above—
(a) any relationship of affinity shall be treated as a relationship by consanguinity, any relationship of the half blood as a relationship of the whole blood, and the stepchild of any person as his child, and
(b) an illegitimate person shall be treated as the legitimate child of his mother and reputed father.

(6) Any reference in this Act to injury includes any disease and any impairment of a person's physical or mental condition.]

[122]

NOTES
Commencement: 1 January 1983.
Substituted by the Administration of Justice Act 1982, s 3.

[1A Bereavement

(1) An action under this Act may consist of or include a claim for damages for bereavement.

(2) A claim for damages for bereavement shall only be for the benefit—
(a) of the wife or husband of the deceased; and
(b) where the deceased was a minor who was never married—
   (i) of his parents, if he was legitimate; and
   (ii) of his mother, if he was illegitimate.

(3) Subject to subsection (5) below, the sum to be awarded as damages under this section shall be [£7,500].

(4) Where there is a claim for damages under this section for the benefit of both the parents of the deceased, the sum awarded shall be be divided equally between them (subject to any deduction falling to be made in respect of costs not recovered from the defendant).

(5) The Lord Chancellor may by order made by statutory instrument, subject to annulment in pursuance of a resolution of either House of Parliament, amend this section by varying the sum for the time being specified in subsection (3) above.]

[123]

NOTES
Commencement: 1 January 1983.
Added by the Administration of Justice Act 1982, s 3.
Sub-s (3): sum in square brackets substituted by SI 1990/2575, art 2.

[2 Persons entitled to bring the action

(1) The action shall be brought by and in the name of the executor or administrator of the deceased.

(2) If—
    (a) there is no executor or administrator of the deceased, or
    (b) no action is brought within six months after the death by and in the name of an executor or administrator of the deceased,

the action may be brought by and in the name of all or any of the persons for whose benefit an executor or administrator could have brought it.

(3) Not more than one action shall lie for and in respect of the same subject matter of complaint.

(4) The plaintiff in the action shall be required to deliver to the defendant or his solicitor full particulars of the persons for whom and on whose behalf the action is brought and of the nature of the claim in respect of which damages are sought to be recovered.]

NOTES
Commencement: 1 January 1983.
Substituted by the Administration of Justice Act 1982, s 3.

[3 Assessment of damages

(1) In the action such damages, other than damages for bereavement, may be awarded as are proportioned to the injury resulting from the death to the dependants respectively.

(2) After deducting the costs not recovered from the defendant any amount recovered otherwise than as damages for bereavement shall be divided among the dependants in such shares as may be directed.

(3) In an action under this Act where there fall to be assessed damages payable to a widow in respect of the death of her husband there shall not be taken account the re-marriage of the widow or her prospects of re-marriage.

(4) In an action under this Act where there fall to be assessed damages payable to a person who is a dependant by virtue of section 1(3)(b) above in respect of the death of the person with whom the dependant was living as husband or wife there shall be taken into account (together with any other matter that appears to the court to be relevant to the action) the fact that the dependant had no enforceable right to financial support by the deceased as a result of their living together.

(5) If the dependants have incurred funeral expenses in respect of the deceased, damages may be awarded in respect of those expenses.

(6) Money paid into court in satisfaction of a cause of action under this Act may be in one sum without specifying any person's share.]

NOTES
Commencement: 1 January 1983.
Substituted by the Administration of Justice Act 1982, s 3.

[4 Assessment of damages: disregard of benefits

In assessing damages in respect of a person's death in an action under this Act, benefits which have accrued or will or may accrue to any person from his estate or otherwise as a result of his death shall be disregarded.]

[126]

NOTES
Commencement: 1 January 1983.
Substituted by the Administration of Justice Act 1982, s 3.

5 Contributory negligence

Where any person dies as the result partly of his own fault and partly of the fault of any other person or persons, and accordingly if an action were brought for the benefit of the estate under the Law Reform (Miscellaneous Provisions) Act 1934 the damages recoverable would be reduced under section 1(1) of the Law Reform (Contributory Negligence) Act 1945, any damages recoverable in an action ... under this Act shall be reduced to a proportionate extent.

[127]

NOTES
Commencement: 1 September 1976.
Words omitted repealed by the Administration of Justice Act 1982, s 3, s 75, Sch 9, Pt I.

7 Short title, etc

(1) This Act may be cited as the Fatal Accidents Act 1976.

(2) This Act shall come into force on 1st September 1976, but shall not apply to any cause of action arising on a death before it comes into force.

(3) This Act shall not extend to Scotland or Northern Ireland.

[128]

RESALE PRICES ACT 1976

(C 53)

An Act to consolidate those provisions of the Resale Prices Act 1964 still having effect, Part II of the Restrictive Trade Practices Act 1956, and related enactments; and to repeal the provisions of the Resale Prices Act 1964 and the Restrictive Trade Practices Act 1968 which have ceased to have any effect

[26 October 1976]

PART I
PROHIBITION OF COLLECTIVE RESALE PRICE MAINTENANCE

1 Collective agreement by suppliers

(1) It is unlawful for any two or more persons carrying on business in the United Kingdom as suppliers of any goods to make or carry out any agreement or arrangement by which they undertake—
    (a) to withhold supplies of goods for delivery in the United Kingdom from dealers (whether party to the agreement or arrangement or not) who resell

or have resold goods in breach of any condition as to the price at which those goods may be resold;
  (b) to refuse to supply goods for delivery in the United Kingdom to such dealers except on terms and conditions which are less favourable than those applicable in the case of other dealers carrying on business in similar circumstances; or
  (c) to supply goods only to persons who undertake or have undertaken—
    (i) to withhold supplies of goods as described in paragraph (a) above; or
    (ii) to refuse to supply goods as described in paragraph (b) above.

(2) It is unlawful for any two or more such persons to make or carry out any agreement or arrangement authorising—
  (a) the recovery of penalties (however described) by or on behalf of the parties to the agreement or arrangement from dealers who resell or have resold goods in breach of any such condition as is described in paragraph (a) of subsection (1) above; or
  (b) the conduct of any domestic proceedings in connection therewith.

[129]

NOTE
Commencement: 15 December 1976.

PART III
GENERAL AND SUPPLEMENTAL

30 Short title, extent and commencement

(1) This Act may be cited as the Resale Prices Act 1976.

(2) This Act extends to Northern Ireland.

(3) This Act shall come into operation on such day as the Secretary of State may appoint by order made by statutory instrument.

[130]

NOTE
Commencement: 15 December 1976.

TORTS (INTERFERENCE WITH GOODS) ACT 1977

(C 32)

An Act to amend the law concerning conversion and other torts affecting goods

[22 July 1977]

Preliminary

1 Definition of "wrongful interference with goods"

In this Act "wrongful interference", or "wrongful interference with goods", means—
  (a) conversion of goods (also called trover),
  (b) trespass to goods,

(c) negligence so far as it results in damage to goods or to an interest in goods,
(d) subject to section 2, any other tort so far as it results in damage to goods or to an interest in goods,

[and references in this Act (however worded) to proceedings for wrongful interference or to a claim or right to claim for wrongful interference shall include references to proceedings by virtue of Part I of the Consumer Protection Act 1987 (product liability) in respect of any damage to goods or to an interest in goods or, as the case may be, to a claim or right to claim by virtue of that Part in respect of any such damage.]

[131]

NOTES
Commencement: 1 June 1978 (England & Wales); 1 January 1981 (Northern Ireland).
Words in square brackets added by the Consumer Protection Act 1987, s 48, Sch 4.

Detention of goods

2 Abolition of detinue

(1) Detinue is abolished.

(2) An action lies in conversion for loss or destruction of goods which a bailee has allowed to happen in breach of his duty to his bailor (that is to say it lies in a case which is not otherwise conversion, but would have been detinue before detinue was abolished).

[132]

NOTE
Commencement: 1 June 1978 (England & Wales); 1 January 1981 (Northern Ireland).

3 Form of judgment where goods are detained

(1) In proceedings for wrongful interference against a person who is in possession or in control of the goods relief may be given in accordance with this section, so far as appropriate.

(2) The relief is—
   (a) an order for delivery of the goods, and for payment of any consequential damages, or
   (b) an order for delivery of the goods, but giving the defendant the alternative of paying damages by reference to the value of the goods, together in either alternative with payment of any consequential damages, or
   (c) damages.

(3) Subject to rules of court—
   (a) relief shall be given under only one of paragraphs (a), (b) and (c) of subsection (2),
   (b) relief under paragraph (a) of subjection (2) is at the discretion of the court, and the claimant may choose between the others.

(4) If it is shown to the satisfaction of the court that an order under subsection (2)(a) has not been complied with, the court may—
   (a) revoke the order, or the relevant part of it, and

(b) make an order for payment of damages by reference to the value of the goods.

(5) Where an order is made under subsection (2)(b) the defendant may satisfy the order by returning the goods at any time before execution of judgment, but without prejudice to liability to pay any consequential damages.

(6) An order for delivery of the goods under subsection (2)(a) or (b) may impose such conditions as may be determined by the court, or pursuant to rules of court, and in particular, where damages by reference to the value of the goods would not be the whole of the value of the goods, may require an allowance to be made by the claimant to reflect the difference.

For example, a bailor's action against the bailee may be one in which the measure of damages is not the full value of the goods, and then the court may order delivery of the goods, but require the bailor to pay the bailee a sum reflecting the difference.

(7) Where under subsection (1) or subsection (2) of section 6 an allowance is to be made in respect of an improvement of the goods, and an order is made under subsection (2)(a) or (b), the court may assess the allowance to be made in respect of the improvement, and by the order require, as a condition for delivery of the goods, that allowance to be made by the claimant.

(8) This section is without prejudice—
(a) to the remedies afforded by section 133 of the Consumer Credit Act 1974, or
(b) to the remedies afforded by sections 35, 42 and 44 of the Hire-Purchase Act 1965, or to those sections of the Hire-Purchase Act (Northern Ireland) 1966 (so long as those sections respectively remain in force), or
(c) to any jurisdiction to afford ancillary or incidental relief.

[133]

NOTE
Commencement: 1 June 1978 (England & Wales); 1 January 1981 (Northern Ireland).

4 Interlocutory relief where goods are detained

(1) In this section "proceedings" means proceedings for wrongful interference.

(2) On the application of any person in accordance with rules of court, the High Court shall, in such circumstances as may be specified in the rules, have power to make an order providing for the delivery up of any goods which are or may become the subject matter of subsequent proceedings in the court, or as to which any question may arise in proceedings.

(3) Delivery shall be, as the order may provide, to the claimant or to a person appointed by the court for the purpose, and shall be on such terms and conditions as may be specified in the order.

(4) The power to make rules of court under section [84 of the Supreme Court Act 1981] or under section 7 of the Northern Ireland Act 1962 shall include power to make rules of court as to the manner in which an application for such an order can be made, and as to the circumstances in which such an order can be made; and any such rules may include such incidental, supplementary and consequential provisions as the authority making the rules may consider necessary or expedient.

(5) The preceding provisions of this section shall have effect in relation to county courts as they have effect in relation to the High Court, and as if in those provisions references to rules of court and to section [84] of the said Act of [1981] or section 7 of the Northern Ireland Act 1962 included references to county court rules and to [section 75 of the County Courts Act 1984] or [Article 47 of the County Courts (Northern Ireland) Order 1980].

[134]

NOTES
Commencement: 1 June 1978 (England & Wales); 1 January 1981 (Northern Ireland).
Sub-s (4): amended by the Supreme Court Act 1981, s 152 (1), Sch 5.
Sub-s (5): first and second amendments made by the Supreme Court Act 1981, s 152 (1), Sch 5; third amendment made by the County Courts Act 1984, s 148(1), Sch 2, para 64; final amendment made by the County Courts (Northern Ireland) Order 1980, SI 1980 No 397, art 68 (2), Sch 1, Pt II.

Damages

5 Extinction of title on satisfaction of claim for damages

(1) Where damages for wrongful interference are, or would fall to be, assessed on the footing that the claimant is being compensated—
   (a) for the whole of his interest in the goods, or
   (b) for the whole of his interest in the goods subject to a reduction for contributory negligence,

payment of the assessed damages (under all heads), or as the case may be settlement of a claim for damages for the wrong (under all heads), extinguishes the claimant's title to that interest.

(2) In subsection (1) the reference to the settlement of the claim includes—
   (a) where the claim is made in court proceedings, and the defendant has paid a sum into court to meet the whole claim, the taking of that sum by the claimant, and
   (b) where the claim is made in court proceedings, and the proceedings are settled or compromised, the payment of what is due in accordance with the settlement or compromise, and
   (c) where the claim is made out of court and is settled or compromised, the payment of what is due in accordance with the settlement or compromise.

(3) It is hereby declared that subsection (1) does not apply where damages are assessed on the footing that the claimant is being compensated for the whole of his interest in the goods, but the damages paid are limited to some lesser amount by virtue of any enactment or rule of law.

(4) Where under section 7(3) the claimant accounts over to another person (the "third party") so as to compensate (under all heads) the third party for the whole of his interest in the goods, the third party's title to that interest is extinguished.

(5) This section has effect subject to any agreement varying the respective rights of the parties to the agreement, and where the claim is made in court proceedings has effect subject to any order of the court.

[135]

NOTE
Commencement: 1 June 1978 (England & Wales); 1 January 1981 (Northern Ireland).

6 Allowance for improvement of the goods

(1) If in proceedings for wrongful interference against a person (the "improver") who has improved the goods, it is shown that the improver acted in the mistaken but honest belief that he had a good title to them, an allowance shall be made for the extent to which, at the time as at which the goods fall to be valued in assessing damages, the value of the goods is attributable to the improvement.

(2) If, in proceedings for wrongful interference against a person ("the purchaser") who has purported to purchase the goods—
   (a) from the improver, or
   (b) where after such a purported sale the goods passed by a further purported sale on one or more occasions, on any such occasion,

it is shown that the purchaser acted in good faith, an allowance shall be made on the principle set out in subsection (1).

For example, where a person in good faith buys a stolen car from the improver and is sued in conversion by the true owner the damages may be reduced to reflect the improvement, but if the person who bought the stolen car from the improver sues the improver for failure of consideration, and the improver acted in good faith, subsection (3) below will ordinarily make a comparable reduction in the damages he recovers from the improver.

(3) If in a case within subsection (2) the person purporting to sell the goods acted in good faith, then in proceedings by the purchaser for recovery of the purchase price because of failure of consideration, or in any other proceedings founded on that failure of consideration, an allowance shall, where appropriate, be made on the principle set out in subsection (1).

(4) This section applies, with the necessary modifications, to a purported bailment or other disposition of goods as it applies to a purported sale of goods.

[136]

NOTE
Commencement: 1 June 1978 (England & Wales); 1 January 1981 (Northern Ireland).

Liability to two or more claimants

7 Double liability

(1) In this section "double liability" means the double liability of the wrongdoer which can arise—
   (a) where one of two or more rights of action for wrongful interference is founded on a possessory title, or
   (b) where the measure of damages in an action for wrongful interference founded on a proprietary title is or includes the entire value of the goods, although the interest is one of two or more interests in the goods.

(2) In proceedings to which any two or more claimants are parties, the relief shall be such as to avoid double liability of the wrongdoer as between those claimants.

(3) On satisfaction, in whole or in part, of any claim for an amount exceeding that recoverable if subsection (2) applied, the claimant is liable to account over to the other person having a right to claim to such extent as will avoid double liability.

(4) Where, as the result of enforcement of a double liability, any claimant is unjustly enriched to any extent, he shall be liable to reimburse the wrongdoer to that extent.

For example, if a converter of goods pays damages first to a finder of the goods, and then to the true owner, the finder is unjustly enriched unless he accounts over to the true owner under subsection (3); and then the true owner is unjustly enriched and becomes liable to reimburse the converter of the goods.

[137]

NOTE
Commencement: 1 June 1978 (England & Wales); 1 January 1981 (Northern Ireland).

8 Competing rights to the goods

(1) The defendant in an action for wrongful interference shall be entitled to show, in accordance with rules of court, that a third party has a better right than the plaintiff as respects all or any part of the interest claimed by the plaintiff, or in right of which he sues, and any rule of law (sometimes called jus tertii) to the contrary is abolished.

(2) Rules of court relating to proceedings for wrongful interference may—
    (a) require the plaintiff to give particulars of his title,
    (b) require the plaintiff to identify any person who, to his knowledge, has or claims any interest in the goods,
    (c) authorise the defendant to apply for directions as to whether any person should be joined with a view to establishing whether he has a better right than the plaintiff, or has a claim as a result of which the defendant might be doubly liable,
    (d) where a party fails to appear on an application within paragraph (c), or to comply with any direction given by the court on such an application, authorise the court to deprive him of any right of action against the defendant for the wrong either unconditionally, or subject to such terms or conditions as may be specified.

(3) Subsection (2) is without prejudice to any other power of making rules of court.

[138]

NOTE
Commencement: 1 June 1978 (England & Wales); 1 January 1981 (Northern Ireland).

9 Concurrent actions

(1) This section applies where goods are the subject of two or more claims for wrongful interference (whether or not the claims are founded on the same wrongful act, and whether or not any of the claims relates also to other goods).

(2) Where goods are the subject of two or more claims under section 6 this section shall apply as if any claim under section 6(3) were a claim for wrongful interference.

(3) If proceedings have been brought in a county court on one of those claims, county court rules may waive, or allow a court to waive, any limit (financial or territorial) on the jurisdiction of county courts in [the County Courts Act 1984] or the County Courts [(Northern Ireland) Order 1980] so as to allow another of those claims to be brought in the same county court.

(4) If proceedings are brought on one of the claims in the High Court, and proceedings on any other are brought in a county court, whether prior to the High Court proceedings or not, the High Court may, on the application of the defendant, after notice has been given to the claimant in the county court proceedings—
  (a) order that the county court proceedings be transferred to the High Court, and
  (b) order security for costs or impose such other terms as the court thinks fit.

[139]

NOTES
Commencement: 1 June 1978 (England & Wales); 1 January 1981 (Northern Ireland).
Sub-s (3): first amendment made by the County Courts Act 1984, s 148(1), Sch 2, para 65; second amendment made by the County Courts (Northern Ireland) Order 1980, SI 1980 No 397, art 68 (2), Sch 1, Pt II.

Conversion and trespass to goods

10 Co-owners

(1) Co-ownership is no defence to an action founded on conversion or trespass to goods where the defendant without the authority of the other co-owner—
  (a) destroys the goods, or disposes of the goods in a way giving a good title to the entire property in the goods, or otherwise does anything equivalent to the destruction of the other's interest in the goods, or
  (b) purports to dispose of the goods in a way which would give a good title to the entire property in the goods if he was acting with the authority of all co-owners of the goods.

(2) Subsection (1) shall not effect the law concerning execution or enforcement of judgments, or concerning any form of distress.

(3) Subsection (1)(a) is by way of restatement of existing law so far as it relates to conversion.

[140]

NOTE
Commencement: 1 June 1978 (England & Wales); 1 January 1981 (Northern Ireland).

11 Minor amendments

(1) Contributory negligence is no good defence in proceedings founded on conversion, or on intentional trespass to goods.

(2) Receipt of goods by way of pledge is conversion if the delivery of the goods is conversion.

(3) Denial of title is not of itself conversion.

[141]

NOTE
Commencement: 1 June 1978 (England & Wales); 1 January 1981 (Northern Ireland).

Uncollected goods

12 Bailee's power of sale

(1) This section applies to goods in the possession or under the control of a bailee where—

(a) the bailor is in breach of an obligation to take delivery of the goods or, if the terms of the bailment so provide, to give directions as to their delivery, or
(b) the bailee could impose such an obligation by giving notice to the bailor, but is unable to trace or communicate with the bailor, or
(c) the bailee can reasonably expect to be relieved of any duty to safeguard the goods on giving notice to the bailor, but is unable to trace or communicate with the bailor.

(2) In the cases in Part I of Schedule 1 to this Act a bailee may, for the purposes of subsection (1), impose an obligation on the bailor to take delivery of the goods, or as the case may be to give directions as to their delivery, and in those cases the said Part I sets out the methods of notification.

(3) If the bailee—
(a) has in accordance with Part II of Schedule 1 to this Act given notice to the bailor of his intention to sell the goods under this subsection, or
(b) has failed to trace or communicate with the bailor with a view to giving him such a notice, after having taken reasonable steps for the purpose,

and is reasonably satisfied that the bailor owns the goods, he shall be entitled, as against the bailor, to sell the goods.

(4) Where subsection (3) applies but the bailor did not in fact own the goods, a sale under this section, or under section 13, shall not give a good title as against the owner, or as against a person claiming under the owner.

(5) A bailee exercising his powers under subsection (3) shall be liable to account to the bailor for the proceeds of sale, less any costs of sale, and—
(a) the account shall be taken on the footing that the bailee should have adopted the best method of sale reasonably available in the circumstances, and
(b) where subsection (3)(a) applies, any sum payable in respect of the goods by the bailor to the bailee which accrued due before the bailee gave notice of intention to sell the goods shall be deductible from the proceeds of sale.

(6) A sale duly made under this section gives a good title to the purchaser as against the bailor.

(7) In this section, section 13, and Schedule 1 to this Act,
(a) "bailor" and "bailee" include their respective successors in title, and
(b) references to what is payable, paid or due to the bailee in respect of the goods include references to what would be payable by the bailor to the bailee as a condition of delivery of the goods at the relevant time.

(8) This section, and Schedule 1 to this Act, have effect subject to the terms of the bailment.

(9) This section shall not apply where the goods were bailed before the commencement of this Act.

NOTE
Commencement: 1 January 1978.

13 Sale authorised by the court

(1) If a bailee of the goods to which section 12 applies satisfies the court that he is entitled to sell the goods under section 12, or that he would be so entitled if he had

given any notice required in accordance with Schedule 1 to this Act, the court—
  (a) may authorise the sale of the goods subject to such terms and conditions, if any, as may be specified in the order, and
  (b) may authorise the bailee to deduct from the proceeds of sale any costs of sale and any amount due from the bailor to the bailee in respect of the goods, and
  (c) may direct the payment into court of the net proceeds of sale, less any amount deducted under paragraph (b), to be held to the credit of the bailor.

(2) A decision of the court authorising a sale under this section shall, subject to any right of appeal, be conclusive, as against the bailor, of the bailee's entitlement to sell the goods, and gives a good title to the purchaser as against the bailor.

(3) In this section "the court" means the High Court or a county court, [and a county court shall have jurisdiction in the proceedings save that, in Northern Ireland, a county court shall only have jurisdiction in proceedings if the value of the goods does not exceed the county court limit mentioned in Article 10(1) of the County Courts (Northern Ireland) Order 1980.]

[143]

NOTES
Commencement: 1 January 1978.
Sub-s (3): words in square brackets substituted by SI 1991/724, art 2(1)(i), (8), Schedule, Pt I; for transitional provisions in relation to Crown proceedings, and savings, see arts 11, 12 thereof.

Supplemental

14 Interpretation

(1) In this Act, unless the context otherwise requires—
  ...
  "enactment" includes an enactment contained in an Act of the Parliament of Northern Ireland or an Order in Council made under the Northern Ireland (Temporary Provisions) Act 1972, or in a Measure of the Northern Ireland Assembly,
  "goods" includes all chattels personal other than things in action and money,
  "High Court" includes the High Court of Justice in Northern Ireland.

(2) References in this Act to any enactment include references to that enactment as amended, extended or applied by or under that or any other enactment.

[144]

NOTES
Commencement: 1 January 1978.
Sub-s (1): words omitted repealed by SI 1991/724, art 2(8), Schedule, Pt I; for transitional provisions in relation to Crown proceedings, and savings, see arts 11, 12 thereof.

16 Extent and application to the Crown

(1) ...

(2) This Act, except section 15, extends to Northern Ireland.

(3) This Act shall bind the Crown, but as regards the Crown's liability in tort shall not bind the Crown further than the Crown is made liable in tort by the Crown Proceedings Act 1947.

[145]

NOTES
Commencement: 1 January 1978.
Sub-s (1): applies to Scotland only.

17 Short title, etc

(1) This Act may be cited as the Torts (Interference with Goods) Act 1977.

(2) This Act shall come into force on such day as the Lord Chancellor may by order contained in a statutory instrument appoint, and such an order may appoint different dates for different provisions or for different purposes.

(3) Schedule 2 to this Act contains transitional provisions.

NOTE
Commencement: 1 January 1978 (sub-ss (1),(2)); 1 June 1978 (sub-s (3), (England & Wales); 1 January 1978 (Northern Ireland).

SCHEDULE 1

Uncollected Goods

Section 12

Part I
Power to Impose Obligation to Collect Goods

1 (1) For the purposes of section 12(1) a bailee may, in the circumstances specified in this Part of this Schedule, by notice given to the bailor impose on him an obligation to take delivery of the goods.

(2) The notice shall be in writing, and may be given either—
  (a) by delivering it to the bailor, or
  (b) by leaving it at his proper address, or
  (c) by post.

(3) The notice shall—
  (a) specify the name and address of the bailee, and give sufficient particulars of the goods and the address or place where they are held, and
  (b) state that the goods are ready for delivery to the bailor, or where combined with a notice terminating the contract of bailment, will be ready for delivery when the contract is terminated, and
  (c) specify the amount, if any, which is payable by the bailor to the bailee in respect of the goods and which became due before the giving of the notice.

(4) Where the notice is sent by post it may be combined with a notice under Part II of this Schedule if the notice is sent by post in a way complying with paragraph 6(4).

(5) References in this Part of this Schedule to taking delivery of the goods include, where the terms of the bailment admit, references to giving directions as to their delivery.

(6) This Part of this Schedule is without prejudice to the provisions of any contract requiring the bailor to take delivery of the goods.

Goods accepted for repair or other treatment

2 If a bailee has accepted goods for repair or other treatment on the terms (expressed or implied) that they will be re-delivered to the bailor when the repair or other treatment has been carried out, the notice may be given at any time after the repair or other treatment has been carried out.

Goods accepted for valuation or appraisal

3   If a bailee has accepted goods in order to value or appraise them, the notice may be given at any time after the bailee has carried out the valuation or appraisal.

Storage, warehousing, etc.

4   (1)   If a bailee is in possession of goods which he has held as custodian, and his obligation as custodian has come to an end, the notice may be given at any time after the ending of the obligation, or may be combined with any notice terminating his obligation as custodian.

(2)   This paragraph shall not apply to goods held by a person as mercantile agent, that is to say by a person having in the customary course of his business as a mercantile agent authority either to sell goods or to consign goods for the purpose of sale, or to buy goods, or to raise money on the security of goods.

Supplemental

5   Paragraphs 2, 3 and 4 apply whether or not the bailor has paid any amount due to the bailee in respect of the goods, and whether or not the bailment is for reward, or in the course of business, or gratuitous.

PART II
NOTICE OF INTENTION TO SELL GOODS

6   (1)   A notice under section 12(3) shall
   (a)   specify the name and address of the bailee, and give sufficient particulars of the goods and the address or place where they are held, and
   (b)   specify the date on or after which the bailee proposes to sell the goods, and
   (c)   specify the amount, if any, which is payable by the bailor to the bailee in respect of the goods, and which became due before the giving of the notice.

(2)   The period between giving of the notice and the date specified in the notice as that on or after which the bailee proposes to exercise the power of sale shall be such as will afford the bailor a reasonable opportunity of taking delivery of the goods.

(3)   If any amount is payable in respect of the goods by the bailor to the bailee, and became due before giving of the notice, the said period shall be not less than three months.

(4)   The notice shall be in writing and shall be sent by post in a registered letter, or by the recorded delivery service.

7   (1)   The bailee shall not give a notice under section 12(3), or exercise his right to sell the goods pursuant to such a notice, at a time when he has notice that, because of a dispute concerning the goods, the bailor is questioning or refusing to pay all or any part of what the bailee claims to be due to him in respect of the goods.

(2)   This paragraph shall be left out of account in determining under section 13(1) whether a bailee of goods is entitled to sell the goods under section 12, or would be so entitled if he had given any notice required in accordance with this Schedule.

Supplemental

8   For the purposes of this Schedule, and of section 26 of the Interpretation Act 1889 in its application to this Schedule, the proper address of the person to whom a notice is to be given shall be—
   (a)   in the case of a body corporate, a registered or principal office of the body corporate, and
   (b)   in any other case, the last known address of the person.

NOTE
Commencement: 1 January 1978.

SCHEDULE 2

TRANSITIONAL

Section 17

1 This Act shall not affect any action or arbitration brought before the commencement of this Act or any proceedings brought to enforce a decision in the action or arbitration.

2 Subject to paragraph 1, this Act applies to acts or omissions before it comes into force as well as to later ones, and for the purposes of the Limitation Act 1939, the Statute of Limitations (Northern Ireland) 1958, or any other limitation enactment, the cause of action shall be treated as having accrued at the time of the act or omission even if proceedings could not have been brought before the commencement of this Act.

3 For the purposes of this Schedule, any claim by way of set-off or counterclaim shall be deemed to be a separate action, and to have been brought on the same date as the action in which the set-off or counterclaim is pleaded.

[149]-[150]

NOTE
Commencement: 1 June 1978 (England & Wales); 1 January 1981 (Northern Ireland).

UNFAIR CONTRACT TERMS ACT 1977

(C 50)

An Act to impose further limits on the extent to which under the law of England and Wales and Northern Ireland civil liability for breach of contract, or for negligence or other breach of duty, can be avoided by means of contract terms and otherwise, and under the law of Scotland civil liability can be avoided by means of contract terms

[26 October 1977]

PART I
AMENDMENT OF LAW FOR ENGLAND AND WALES AND NORTHERN IRELAND

Introductory

1 Scope of Part I

(1) For the purposes of this Part of this Act, "negligence" means the breach—
   (a) of any obligation, arising from the express or implied terms of a contract, to take reasonable care or to exercise reasonable skill in the performance of the contract;
   (b) of any common law duty to take reasonable care or exercise reasonable skill (but not any stricter duty);
   (c) of the common duty of care imposed by the Occupiers' Liability Act 1957 or the Occupiers' Liability Act (Northern Ireland) 1957.

(2) This Part of this Act is subject to Part III; and in relation to contracts, the operation of sections 2 to 4 and 7 is subject to the exceptions made by Schedule 1.

(3) In the case of both contract and tort, sections 2 to 7 apply (except where the contrary is stated in section 6(4)) only to business liability, that is liability for breach of obligations or duties arising—
   (a) from things done or to be done by a person in the course of a business (whether his own business or another's); or
   (b) from the occupation of premises used for business purposes of the occupier;

and references to liability are to be read accordingly [but liability of an occupier of premises for breach of an obligation or duty towards a person obtaining access to the premises for recreational or educational purposes, being liability for loss or damage suffered by reason of the dangerous state of the premises, is not a business liability of the occupier unless granting that person such access for the purposes concerned falls within the business purposes of the occupier].

(4) In relation to any breach of duty or obligation, it is immaterial for any purpose of this Part of this Act whether the breach was inadvertent or intentional, or whether liability for it arises directly or vicariously.

[151]

NOTES
Commencement: 1 February 1978.
Sub-s (3): words in square brackets added by the Occupiers' Liability Act 1984, s 2.

Avoidance of liability for negligence, breach of contract, etc

2 Negligence liability

(1) A person cannot by reference to any contract term or to a notice given to persons generally or to particular persons exclude or restrict his liability for death or personal injury resulting from negligence.

(2) In the case of other loss or damage, a person cannot so exclude or restrict his liability for negligence except in so far as the term or notice satisfies the requirement of reasonableness.

(3) Where a contract term or notice purports to exclude or restrict liability for negligence a person's agreement to or awareness of it is not of itself to be taken as indicating his voluntary acceptance of any risk.

[152]

NOTE
Commencement: 1 February 1978.

3 Liability arising in contract

(1) This section applies as between contracting parties where one of them deals as consumer or on the other's written standard terms of business.

(2) As against that party, the other cannot by reference to any contract term—
   (a) when himself in breach of contract, exclude or restrict any liability of his in respect of the breach; or
   (b) claim to be entitled—
      (i) to render a contractual performance substantially different from that which was reasonably expected of him, or

(ii) in respect of the whole or any part of his contractual obligation, to render no performance at all,

except in so far as (in any of the cases mentioned above in this subsection) the contract term satisfies the requirement of reasonableness.

[153]

NOTE
Commencement: 1 February 1978.

4 Unreasonable indemnity clauses

(1) A person dealing as consumer cannot by reference to any contract term be made to indemnify another person (whether a party to the contract or not) in respect of liability that may be incurred by the other for negligence or breach of contract, except in so far as the contract term satisfies the requirement of reasonableness.

(2) This section applies whether the liability in question—
  (a) is directly that of the person to be indemnified or is incurred by him vicariously;
  (b) is to the person dealing as consumer or to someone else.

[154]

NOTE
Commencement: 1 February 1978.

Liability arising from sale or supply of goods

5 "Guarantee" of consumer goods

(1) In the case of goods of a type ordinarily supplied for private use or consumption, where loss or damage—
  (a) arises from the goods proving defective while in consumer use; and
  (b) results from the negligence of a person concerned in the manufacture or distribution of the goods,

liability for the loss or damage cannot be excluded or restricted by reference to any contract term or notice contained in or operating by reference to a guarantee of the goods.

(2) For these purposes—
  (a) goods are to be regarded as "in consumer use" when a person is using them, or has them in his possession for use, otherwise than exclusively for the purposes of a business; and
  (b) anything in writing is a guarantee if it contains or purports to contain some promise or assurance (however worded or presented) that defects will be made good by complete or partial replacement, or by repair, monetary compensation or otherwise.

(3) This section does not apply as between the parties to a contract under or in pursuance of which possession or ownership of the goods passed.

[155]

NOTE
Commencement: 1 February 1978.

6 Sale and hire-purchase

(1) Liability for breach of the obligations arising from—
   (a) [section 12 of the Sale of Goods Act 1979] (seller's implied undertakings as to title, etc.);
   (b) section 8 of the Supply of Goods (Implied Terms) Act 1973 (the corresponding thing in relation to hire-purchase).

cannot be excluded or restricted by reference to any contract term.

(2) As against a person dealing as consumer, liability for breach of the obligations arising from—
   (a) [section 13, 14 or 15 of the 1979 Act] (seller's implied undertakings as to conformity of goods with description or sample, or as to their quality or fitness for a particular purpose);
   (b) section 9, 10 or 11 of the 1973 Act (the corresponding things in relation to hire-purchase),

cannot be excluded or restricted by reference to any contract term.

(3) As against a person dealing otherwise than as consumer, the liability specified in subsection (2) above can be excluded or restricted by reference to a contract term, but only in so far as the term satisfies the requirement of reasonableness.

(4) The liabilities referred to in this section are not only the business liabilities defined by section 1(3), but include those arising under any contract of sale of goods or hire-purchase agreement.

[156]

NOTES
Commencement: 1 February 1978.
Sub-ss (1), (2): words in square brackets substituted by the Sale of Goods Act 1979, s 63, Sch 2, para 19.

7 Miscellaneous contracts under which goods pass

(1) Where the possession or ownership of goods passes under or in pursuance of a contract not governed by the law of sale of goods or hire-purchase, subsections (2) to (4) below apply as regards the effect (if any) to be given to contract terms excluding or restricting liability for breach of obligation arising by implication of law from the nature of the contract.

(2) As against a person dealing as consumer, liability in respect of the goods' correspondence with description or sample, or their quality or fitness for any particular purpose, cannot be excluded or restricted by reference to any such term.

(3) As against a person dealing otherwise than as consumer, that liability can be excluded or restricted by reference to such a term, but only in so far as the term satisfies the requirement of reasonableness.

[(3A) Liability for breach of the obligations arising under section 2 of the Supply of Goods and Services Act 1982 (implied terms about title etc in certain contracts for the transfer of the property in goods) cannot be excluded or restricted by references to any such term.]

(4) Liability in respect of—
   (a) the right to transfer ownership of the goods, or give possession; or

(b) the assurance of quiet possession to a person taking goods in pursuance of the contract,

cannot [(in a case to which subsection (3A) above does not apply)] be excluded or restricted by reference to any such term except in so far as the term satisfies the requirement of reasonableness.

(5) This section does not apply in the case of goods passing on a redemption of trading stamps within the Trading Stamps Act 1964 or the Trading Stamps Act (Northern Ireland) 1965.

[157]

NOTES

Commencement: 4 January 1983 (sub-s (3A)); 1 February 1978 (remainder).
Sub-s (3A): added by the Supply of Goods and Services Act 1982, s 17(2), (3).
Sub-s (4): words in square brackets added by the Supply of Goods and Services Act 1982, s 17(2), (3).

Other provisions about contracts

9 Effect of breach

(1) Where for reliance upon it a contract term has to satisfy the requirement of reasonableness, it may be found to do so and be given effect accordingly notwithstanding that the contract has been terminated either by breach or by a party electing to treat it as repudiated.

(2) Where on a breach the contract is nevertheless affirmed by a party entitled to treat it as repudiated, this does not of itself exclude the requirement of reasonableness in relation to any contract term.

[158]

NOTE

Commencement: 1 February 1978.

10 Evasion by means of secondary contract

A person is not bound by any contract term prejudicing or taking away rights of his which arise under, or in connection with the performance of, another contract, so far as those rights extend to the enforcement of another's liability which this Part of this Act prevents that other from excluding or restricting.

[159]

NOTE

Commencement: 1 February 1978.

Explanatory provisions

11 The "reasonableness" test

(1) In relation to a contract term, the requirement of reasonableness for the purposes of this Part of this Act, section 3 of the Misrepresentation Act 1967 and section 3 of the Misrepresentation Act (Northern Ireland) 1967 is that the term shall have been a fair and reasonable one to be included having regard to the circumstances which

were, or ought reasonably to have been, known to or in the contemplation of the parties when the contract was made.

(2) In determining for the purposes of section 6 or 7 above whether a contract term satisfies the requirement of reasonableness, regard shall be had in particular to the matters specified in Schedule 2 to this Act; but this subsection does not prevent the court or arbitrator from holding, in accordance with any rule of law, that a term which purports to exclude or restrict any relevant liability is not a term of the contract.

(3) In relation to a notice (not being a notice having contractual effect), the requirement of reasonableness under this Act is that it should be fair and reasonable to allow reliance on it, having regard to all the circumstances obtaining when the liability arose or (but for the notice) would have arisen.

(4) Where by reference to a contract term or notice a person seeks to restrict liability to a specified sum of money, and the question arises (under this or any other Act) whether the term or notice satisfies the requirement of reasonableness, regard shall be had in particular (but without prejudice to subsection (2) above in the case of contract terms) to—
   (a) the resources which he could expect to be available to him for the purpose of meeting the liability should it arise; and
   (b) how far it was open to him to cover himself by insurance.

(5) It is for those claiming that a contract term or notice satisfies the requirement of reasonableness to show that it does.

[160]

NOTE
Commencement: 1 February 1978.

12 "Dealing as consumer"

(1) A party to a contract "deals as consumer" in relation to another party if—
   (a) he neither makes the contract in the course of a business nor holds himself out as doing so; and
   (b) the other party does make the contract in the course of a business; and
   (c) in the case of a contract governed by the law of sale of goods or hire-purchase, or by section 7 of this Act, the goods passing under or in pursuance of the contract are of a type ordinarily supplied for private use or consumption.

(2) But on a sale by auction or by competitive tender the buyer is not in any circumstances to be regarded as dealing as consumer.

(3) Subject to this, it is for those claiming that a party does not deal as consumer to show that he does not.

[161]

NOTE
Commencement: 1 February 1978.

13 Varieties of exemption clause

(1) To the extent that this Part of this Act prevents the exclusion or restriction of any liability it also prevents—

(a) making the liability or its enforcement subject to restrictive or onerous conditions;
(b) excluding or restricting any right or remedy in respect of the liability, or subjecting a person to any prejudice in consequence of his pursuing any such right or remedy;
(c) excluding or restricting rules of evidence or procedure;

and (to that extent) sections 2 and 5 to 7 also prevent excluding or restricting liability by reference to terms and notices which exclude or restrict the relevant obligation or duty.

(2) But an agreement in writing to submit present or future differences to arbitration is not to be treated under this Part of this Act as excluding or restricting any liability.

NOTE
Commencement: 1 February 1978.

14 Interpretation of Part I

In this Part of this Act—
"business" includes a profession and the activities of any government department or local or public authority;
"goods" has the same meaning as in [the Sale of Goods Act 1979]:
"hire-purchase agreement" has the same meaning as in the Consumer Credit Act 1974;
"negligence" has the meaning given by section 1(1);
"notice" includes an announcement, whether or not in writing, and any other communication or pretended communication; and
"personal injury" includes any disease and any impairment of physical or mental condition.

NOTES
Commencement: 1 February 1978.
Words in square brackets in definition "goods" substituted by the Sale of Goods Act 1979, s 63, Sch 2, para 20.

Part III
Provisions applying to whole of United Kingdom

Miscellaneous

26 International supply contracts

(1) The limits imposed by this Act on the extent to which a person may exclude or restrict liability by reference to a contract term do not apply to liability arising under such a contract as is described in subsection (3) below.

(2) The terms of such a contract are not subject to any requirement of reasonableness under section 3 or 4 ...

(3) Subject to subsection (4), that description of contract is one whose characteristics are the following—

(a) either it is a contract of sale of goods or it is one under or in pursuance of which the possession or ownership of goods passes; and
(b) it is made by parties whose places of business (or, if they have none, habitual residences) are in the territories of different States (the Channel Islands and the Isle of Man being treated for this purpose as different States from the United Kingdom).

(4) A contract falls within subsection (3) above only if either—
(a) the goods in question are, at the time of the conclusion of the contract, in the course of carriage, or will be carried, from the territory of one State to the territory of another; or
(b) the acts constituting the offer and acceptance have been done in the territories of different States; or
(c) the contract provides for the goods to be delivered to the territory of a State other than that within whose territory those acts were done.

[164]

NOTES
Commencement: 1 February 1978.
Sub-s (2): words omitted apply to Scotland only.

27 Choice of law clauses

(1) Where the [law applicable to] a contract is the law of any part of the United Kingdom only by choice of the parties (and apart from that choice would be the law of some country outside the United Kingdom) sections 2 to 7 and 16 to 21 of this Act do not operate as part [of the law applicable to the contract].

(2) This Act has effect notwithstanding any contract term which applies or purports to apply the law of some country outside the United Kingdom, where (either or both)—
(a) the term appears to the court, or arbitrator or arbiter to have been imposed wholly or mainly for the purpose of enabling the party imposing it to evade the operation of this Act; or
(b) in the making of the contract one of the parties dealt as consumer, and he was then habitually resident in the United Kingdom, and the essential steps necessary for the making of the contract were taken there, whether by him or by others on his behalf.

(3) ...

[165]

NOTES
Commencement: 1 February 1978.
Sub-s (1): words in square brackets substituted by the Contracts (Applicable Law) Act 1990, s 5, Sch 4.
Sub-s (3): applies to Scotland only.

29 Saving for other relevant legislation

(1) Nothing in this Act removes or restricts the effect of, or prevents reliance upon, any contractual provision which—
(a) is authorised or required by the express terms or necessary implication of an enactment; or

(b) being made with a view to compliance with an international agreement to which the United Kingdom is a party, does not operate more restrictively than is contemplated by the agreement.

(2) A contract term is to be taken—
   (a) for the purposes of Part I of this Act, as satisfying the requirement of reasonableness; and
   (b) ...

if it is incorporated or approved by, or incorporated pursuant to a decision or ruling of, a competent authority acting in the exercise of any statutory jurisdiction or function and is not a term in a contract to which the competent authority is itself a party.

(3) In this section—
   "competent authority" means any court, arbitrator or arbiter, government department or public authority;
   "enactment" means any legislation (including subordinate legislation) of the United Kingdom or Northern Ireland and any instrument having effect by virtue of such legislation; and
   "statutory" means conferred by an enactment.

NOTES
Commencement: 1 February 1978.
Sub-s (2): words omitted apply to Scotland only.

General

31 Commencement; amendments; repeals

(1) This Act comes into force on 1st February 1978.

(2) Nothing in this Act applies to contracts made before the date on which it comes into force; but subject to this, it applies to liability for any loss or damage which is suffered on or after that date.

(3) The enactments specified in Schedule 3 to this Act are amended as there shown.

(4) The enactments specified in Schedule 4 to this Act are repealed to the extent specified in column 3 of that Schedule.

NOTE
Commencement: 1 February 1978.

32 Citation and extent

(1) This Act may be cited as the Unfair Contract Terms Act 1977.

(2) Part I of this Act extends to England and Wales and to Northern Ireland; but it does not extend to Scotland.

(3) ...

(4) This Part of this Act extends to the whole of the United Kingdom.

NOTES
Commencement: 1 February 1978.

Sub-s (3): applies to Scotland only.

SCHEDULE 1
SCOPE OF SECTIONS 2 TO 4 AND 7

Section 1 (2)

1 Sections 2 to 4 of this Act do not extend to—
   (a) any contract of insurance (including a contract to pay an annuity on human life);
   (b) any contract so far as it relates to the creation or transfer of an interest in land, or to the termination of such an interest, whether by extinction, merger, surrender, forfeiture or otherwise;
   (c) any contract so far as it relates to the creation or transfer of a right or interest in any patent, trade mark, copyright [or design right], registered design, technical or commercial information or other intellectual property, or relates to the termination of any such right or interest;
   (d) any contract so far as it relates—
       (i) to the formation or dissolution of a company (which means any body corporate or unincorporated association and includes a partnership), or
       (ii) to its constitution or the rights or obligations of its corporators or members;
   (e) any contract so far as it relates to the creation or transfer of securities or of any right or interest in securities.

2 Section 2(1) extends to—
   (a) any contract of marine salvage or towage;
   (b) any charterparty of a ship or hovercraft; and
   (c) any contract for the carriage of goods by ship or hovercraft;

but subject to this sections 2 to 4 and 7 do not extend to any such contract except in favour of a person dealing as consumer.

3 Where goods are carried by ship or hovercraft in pursuance of a contract which either—
   (a) specifies that as the means of carriage over part of the journey to be covered, or
   (b) makes no provision as to the means of carriage and does not exclude that means,

then sections 2(2), 3 and 4 do not, except in favour of a person dealing as consumer, extend to the contract as it operates for and in relation to the carriage of the goods by that means.

4 Section 2(1) and (2) do not extend to a contract of employment, except in favour of the employee.

5 Section 2(1) does not affect the validity of any discharge and indemnity given by a person, on or in connection with an award to him of compensation for pneumoconiosis attributable to employment in the coal industry, in respect of any further claim arising from his contracting that disease.

[169]

NOTES
Commencement: 1 February 1978.
Para 1: in sub-para (c) the reference to a trade mark includes reference to a service mark, by virtue of the Patents, Designs and Marks Act 1986, s 2(3), Sch 2, Pt I, words in square brackets added by the Copyright, Designs and Patents Act 1988, s 303(1), Sch 7, para 24.

SCHEDULE 2
"GUIDELINES" FOR APPLICATION OF REASONABLENESS TEST

Sections 11(2), 24(2)

The matters to which regard is to be had in particular for the purposes of sections 6(3), 7(3) and (4), 20 and 21 are any of the following which appear to be relevant—

(a) the strength of the bargaining positions of the parties relative to each other, taking into account (among other things) alternative means by which the customer's requirements could have been met;
(b) whether the customer received an inducement to agree to the term, or in accepting it had an opportunity of entering into a similar contract with other persons, but without having to accept a similar term;
(c) whether the customer knew or ought reasonably to have known of the existence and extent of the term (having regard, among other things, to any custom of the trade and any previous course of dealing between the parties);
(d) where the term excludes or restricts any relevant liability if some condition is not complied with, whether it was reasonable at the time of the contract to expect that compliance with that condition would be practicable;
(e) whether the goods were manufactured, processed or adapted to the special order of the customer.

[170]

NOTE
Commencement: 1 February 1978.

CIVIL LIABILITY (CONTRIBUTION) ACT 1978

(C 47)

An Act to make new provision for contribution between persons who are jointly or severally, or both jointly and severally, liable for the same damage and in certain other similar cases where two or more persons have paid or may be required to pay compensation for the same damage; and to amend the law relating to proceedings against persons jointly liable for the same debt or jointly or severally, or both jointly and severally, liable for the same damage

[31 July 1978]

Proceedings for contribution

1 Entitlement to contribution

(1) Subject to the following provisions of this section, any person liable in respect of any damage suffered by another person may recover contribution from any other person liable in respect of the same damage (whether jointly with him or otherwise).

(2) A person shall be entitled to recover contribution by virtue of subsection (1) above notwithstanding that he has ceased to be liable in respect of the damage in question since the time when the damage occurred, provided that he was so liable immediately before he made or was ordered or agreed to make the payment in respect of which the contribution is sought.

(3) A person shall be liable to make contribution by virtue of subsection (1) above notwithstanding that he has ceased to be liable in respect of the damage in question since the time when the damage occurred, unless he ceased to be liable by virtue of the expiry of a period of limitation or prescription which extinguished the right on which the claim against him in respect of the damage was based.

(4) A person who has made or agreed to make any payment in bona fide settlement or compromise of any claim made against him in respect of any damage (including a payment into court which has been accepted) shall be entitled to recover contribution in accordance with this section without regard to whether or not he himself is or ever was liable in respect of the damage, provided, however, that he would have been liable assuming that the factual basis of the claim against him could be established.

(5) A judgment given in any action brought in any part of the United Kingdom by or on behalf of the person who suffered the damage in question against any person from whom contribution is sought under this section shall be conclusive in the proceedings for contribution as to any issue determined by that judgment in favour of the person from whom the contribution is sought.

(6) References in this section to a person's liability in respect of any damage are references to any such liability which has been or could be established in an action brought against him in England and Wales by or on behalf of the person who suffered the damage; but it is immaterial whether any issue arising in any such action was or would be determined (in accordance with the rules of private international law) by reference to the law of a country outside England and Wales.

[171]

NOTE
Commencement: 1 January 1979.

2 Assessment of contribution

(1) Subject to subsection (3) below, in any proceedings for contribution under section 1 above the amount of the contribution recoverable from any person shall be such as may be found by the court to be just and equitable having regard to the extent of that person's responsibility for the damage in question.

(2) Subject to subsection (3) below, the court shall have power in any such proceedings to exempt any person from liability to make contribution, or to direct that the contribution to be recovered from any person shall amount to a complete indemnity.

(3) Where the amount of the damages which have or might have been awarded in respect of the damage in question in any action brought in England and Wales by or on behalf of the person who suffered it against the person from whom the contribution is sought was or would have been subject to—
   (a) any limit imposed by or under any enactment or by any agreement made before the damage occurred;
   (b) any reduction by virtue of section 1 of the Law Reform (Contributory Negligence) Act 1945 or section 5 of the Fatal Accidents Act 1976; or
   (c) any corresponding limit or reduction under the law of a country outside England and Wales;

the person from whom the contribution is sought shall not by virtue of any contribution awarded under section 1 above be required to pay in respect of the damage a greater amount than the amount of those damages as so limited or reduced.

[172]

NOTE
Commencement: 1 January 1979.

Proceedings for the same debt or damage

3 Proceedings against persons jointly liable for the same debt or damage

Judgment recovered against any person liable in respect of any debt or damage shall not be a bar to an action, or to the continuance of an action, against any other person who is (apart from any such bar) jointly liable with him in respect of the same debt or damage.

[173]

NOTE
Commencement: 1 January 1979.

4 Successive actions against persons liable (jointly or otherwise) for the same damage

If more than one action is brought in respect of any damage by or on behalf of the person by whom it was suffered against persons liable in respect of the damage (whether jointly or otherwise) the plaintiff shall not be entitled to costs in any of those actions, other than that in which judgment is first given, unless the court is of the opinion that there was reasonable ground for bringing the action.

[174]

NOTE
Commencement: 1 January 1979.

Supplemental

5 Application to the Crown

Without prejudice to section 4(1) of the Crown Proceedings Act 1947 (indemnity and contribution), this Act shall bind the Crown, but nothing in this Act shall be construed as in any way affecting Her Majesty in Her private capacity (including in right of Her Duchy of Lancaster) or the Duchy of Cornwall.

[175]

NOTE
Commencement: 1 January 1979.

6 Interpretation

(1) A person is liable in respect of any damage for the purposes of this Act if the person who suffered it (or anyone representing his estate or dependants) is entitled to recover compensation from him in respect of that damage (whatever the legal basis of his liability, whether tort, breach of contract, breach of trust or otherwise).

(2) References in this Act to an action brought by or on behalf of the person who suffered any damage include references to an action brought for the benefit of his estate or dependants.

(3) In this Act "dependants" has the same meaning as in the Fatal Accidents Act 1976.

(4) In this Act, except in section 1(5) above, "action" means an action brought in England and Wales.

[176]

NOTE
Commencement: 1 January 1979.

7 Savings

(1) Nothing in this Act shall affect any case where the debt in question became due or (as the case may be) the damage in question occurred before the date on which it comes into force.

(2) A person shall not be entitled to recover contribution or liable to make contribution in accordance with section 1 above by reference to any liability based on breach of any obligation assumed by him before the date on which this Act comes into force.

(3) The right to recover contribution in accordance with section 1 above supersedes any right, other than an express contractual right, to recover contribution (as distinct from indemnity) otherwise than under this Act in corresponding circumstances; but nothing in this Act shall affect—
   (a) any express or implied contractual or other right to indemnity; or
   (b) any express contractual provision regulating or excluding contribution;

which would be enforceable apart from this Act (or render enforceable any agreement for indemnity or contribution which would not be enforceable apart from this Act).

[177]

NOTE
Commencement: 1 January 1979.

8 Application to Northern Ireland

In the application of this Act to Northern Ireland—
   (a) the reference in section 2(3)(b) to section 1 of the Law Reform (Contributory Negligence) Act 1945 or section 5 of the Fatal Accidents Act 1976 shall be construed as a reference to section 2 of the Law Reform (Miscellaneous Provisions) Act (Northern Ireland) 1948 or Article 7 of the Fatal Accidents (Northern Ireland) Order 1977;
   (b) the reference in section 5 to section 4(1) of the Crown Proceedings Act 1947 shall be construed as a reference to section 4(1) of that Act as it applies in Northern Ireland;
   (c) the reference in section 6(3) to the Fatal Accidents Act 1976 shall be construed as a reference to the Fatal Accidents (Northern Ireland) Order 1977;
   (d) references to England and Wales shall be construed as references to Northern Ireland; and
   (e) any reference to an enactment shall be construed as including a reference to an enactment of the Parliament of Northern Ireland and a Measure of the Northern Ireland Assembly.

[178]

NOTE
Commencement: 1 January 1979.

10 Short title, commencement and extent

(1) This Act may be cited as the Civil Liability (Contribution) Act 1978.

(2) This Act shall come into force on 1st January next following the date on which it is passed.

(3) ...

[179]

NOTES
Commencement: 1 January 1979.
Sub-s (3): applies to Scotland only.

SALE OF GOODS ACT 1979

(C 54)

An Act to consolidate the law relating to the sale of goods

[6 December 1979]

Part II
Formation of the Contract

Contract of sale

2 Contract of sale

(1) A contract of sale of goods is a contract by which the seller transfers or agrees to transfer the property in goods to the buyer for a money consideration, called the price.

(2) There may be a contract of sale between one part owner and another.

(3) A contract of sale may be absolute or conditional.

(4) Where under a contract of sale the property in the goods is transferred from the seller to the buyer the contract is called a sale.

(5) Where under a contract of sale the transfer of the property in the goods is to take place at a future time or subject to some condition later to be fulfilled the contract is called an agreement to sell.

(6) An agreement to sell becomes a sale when the time elapses or the conditions are fulfilled subject to which the property in the goods is to be transferred.

NOTE
Commencement: 1 January 1980.

Subject matter of contract

7 Goods perishing before sale but after agreement to sell

Where there is an agreement to sell specific goods and subsequently the goods, without any fault on the part of the seller or buyer, perish before the risk passes to the buyer, the agreement is avoided.

NOTE
Commencement: 1 January 1980.

The price

8 Ascertainment of price

(1) The price in a contract of sale may be fixed by the contract, or may be left to be fixed in a manner agreed by the contract, or may be determined by the course of dealing between the parties.

(2) Where the price is not determined as mentioned in subsection (1) above the buyer must pay a reasonable price.

(3) What is a reasonable price is a question of fact dependent on the circumstances of each particular case.

[182]

NOTE
Commencement: 1 January 1980.

9 Agreement to sell at valuation

(1) Where there is an agreement to sell goods on the terms that the price is to be fixed by the valuation of a third party, and he cannot or does not make the valuation, the agreement is avoided; but if the goods or any part of them have been delivered to and appropriated by the buyer he must pay a reasonable price for them.

(2) Where the third party is prevented from making the valuation by the fault of the seller or buyer, the party not at fault may maintain an action for damages against the party at fault.

[183]

NOTE
Commencement: 1 January 1980.

Conditions and warranties

10 Stipulations about time

(1) Unless a different intention appears from the terms of the contract, stipulations as to the time of payment are not of the essence of a contract of sale.

(2) Whether any other stipulation as to time is or is not of the essence of the contract depends on the terms of the contract.

(3) In a contract of sale "month" prima facie means calendar month.

[183A]

NOTE
Commencement: 1 January 1980.

11 When conditions to be treated as warranty

(1) ...

(2) Where a contract of sale is subject to a condition to be fulfilled by the seller, the buyer may waive the condition, or may elect to treat the breach of the condition as a breach of warranty and not as a ground for treating the contract as repudiated.

(3) Whether a stipulation in a contract of sale is a condition, the breach of which may give rise to a right to treat the contract as repudiated, or a warranty, the breach of which may give rise to a claim for damages but not to a right to reject the goods and treat the contract as repudiated, depends in each case on the construction of the contract; and a stipulation may be a condition, though called a warranty in the contract.

(4) Where a contract of sale is not severable and the buyer has accepted the goods or part of them, the breach of a condition to be fulfilled by the seller can only be treated as a breach of warranty, and not as a ground for rejecting the goods and treating the contract as repudiated, unless there is an express or implied term of the contract to that effect.

(5) ...

(6) Nothing in this section affects a condition or warranty whose fulfilment is excused by reason of impossibility or otherwise.

(7) Paragraph 2 of Schedule 1 below applies in relation to a contract made before 22 April 1967 or (in the application of this Act to Northern Ireland) 28 July 1967.

[183B]

NOTES
Commencement: 1 January 1980.
Sub-ss (1), (5): apply to Scotland only.

12 Implied terms about title, etc

(1) In a contract of sale, other than one to which subsection(3) below applies, there is an implied condition on the part of the seller that in the case of a sale he has a right to sell the goods, and in the case of an agreement to sell he will have such a right at the time when the property is to pass.

(2) In a contract of sale, other than one to which subsection (3) below applies, there is also an implied warranty that—
  (a) the goods are free, and will remain free until the time when the property is to pass, from any charge or encumbrance not disclosed or known to the buyer before the contract is made, and
  (b) the buyer will enjoy quiet possession of the goods except so far as it may be disturbed by the owner or other person entitled to the benefit of any charge or encumbrance so disclosed or known.

(3) This subsection applies to a contract of sale in the case of which there appears from the contract or is to be inferred from its circumstances an intention that the seller should transfer only such title as he or a third person may have.

(4) In a contract to which subsection (3) above applies there is an implied warranty that all charges or encumbrances known to the seller and not known to the buyer have been disclosed to the buyer before the contract is made.

(5) In a contract to which subsection (3) above applies there is also an implied warranty that none of the following will disturb the buyer's quiet possession of the goods, namely—
  (a) the seller;
  (b) in a case where the parties to the contract intend that the seller should transfer only such title as a third person may have, that person;
  (c) anyone claiming through or under the seller or that third person otherwise than under a charge or encumbrance disclosed or known to the buyer before the contract is made.

(6) Paragraph 3 of Schedule 1 below applies in relation to a contract made before 18 May 1973.

NOTE
Commencement: 1 January 1980.

13 Sale by description

(1) Where there is a contract for the sale of goods by description, there is an implied condition that the goods will correspond with the description.

(2) If the sale is by sample as well as by description it is not sufficient that the bulk of the goods corresponds with the sample if the goods do not also correspond with the description.

(3) A sale of goods is not prevented from being a sale by description by reason only that, being exposed for sale or hire, they are selected by the buyer.

(4) Paragraph 4 of Schedule 1 below applies in relation to a contract made before 18th May 1973.

[185]

NOTE
Commencement: 1 January 1980.

14 Implied terms about quality or fitness

(1) Except as provided by this section and section 15 below and subject to any other enactment, there is no implied condition or warranty about the quality or fitness for any particular purpose of goods supplied under a contract of sale.

(2) Where the seller sells goods in the course of a business, there is an implied condition that the goods supplied under the contract are of merchantable quality, except that there is no such condition—
- (a) as regards defects specifically drawn to the buyer's attention before the contract is made; or
- (b) if the buyer examines the goods before the contract is made, as regards defects which that examination ought to reveal.

(3) Where the seller sells goods in the course of a business and the buyer, expressly or by implication, makes known—
- (a) to the seller, or
- (b) where the purchase price or part of it is payable by instalments and the goods were previously sold by a credit-broker to the seller, to that credit-broker,

any particular purpose for which the goods are being bought, there is an implied condition that the goods supplied under the contract are reasonably fit for that purpose, whether or not that is a purpose for which such goods are commonly supplied, except where the circumstances show that the buyer does not rely, or that it is unreasonable for him to rely, on the skill or judgment of the seller or credit-broker.

(4) An implied condition or warranty about quality or fitness for a particular purpose may be annexed to a contract of sale by usage.

(5) The preceding provisions of this section apply to a sale by a person who in the course of a business is acting as agent for another as they apply to a sale by a principal in the course of a business, except where that other is not selling in the course of a business and either the buyer knows that fact or reasonable steps are taken to bring it to the notice of the buyer before the contract is made.

(6) Goods of any kind are of merchantable quality within the meaning of subsection (2) above if they are as fit for the purpose or purposes for which goods of that kind are commonly bought as it is reasonable to expect having regard to any description applied to them, the price (if relevant) and all the other relevant circumstances.

(7) Paragraph 5 of Schedule 1 below applies in relation to a contract made on or after 18 May 1973 and before the appointed day, and paragraph 6 in relation to one made before 18th May 1973.

(8) In subsection (7) above and paragraph 5 of Schedule 1 below references to the appointed day are to the day appointed for the purposes of those provisions by an order of the Secretary of State made by statutory instrument.

[186]

NOTE
Commencement: 1 January 1980.

Sale by sample

15 Sale by sample

(1) A contract of sale is a contract for sale by sample where there is an express or implied term to that effect in the contract.

(2) In the case of a contract for sale by sample there is an implied condition—
   (a) that the bulk will correspond with the sample in quality;
   (b) that the buyer will have a reasonable opportunity of comparing the bulk with the sample;
   (c) that the goods will be free from any defect, rendering them unmerchantable, which would not be apparent on reasonable examination of the sample.

(3) In subsection (2)(c) above "unmerchantable" is to be construed in accordance with section 14 (6) above.

(4) Paragraph 7 of Schedule 1 below applies in relation to a contract made before 18 May 1973.

[187]

NOTE
Commencement: 1 January 1980.

Part IV
Performance of the Contract

34 Buyer's right of examining the goods

(1) Where goods are delivered to the buyer, and he has not previously examined them, he is not deemed to have accepted them until he has had a reasonable opportunity of examining them for the purposes of ascertaining whether they are in conformity with the contract.

(2) Unless otherwise agreed, when the seller tenders delivery of goods to the buyer, he is bound on request to afford the buyer a reasonable opportunity of examining the goods for the purposes of ascertaining whether they are in conformity with the contract.

[187A]

35 Acceptance

(1) The buyer is deemed to have accepted the goods when he intimates to the seller that he has accepted them, or (except where section 34 above or otherwise provides) when the goods have been delivered to him and he does any act in relation to them which is inconsistent with the ownership of the seller, or when after the lapse of a reasonable time he retains the goods without intimating to the seller that he has rejected them.

(2) Paragraph 10 of Schedule 1 below applies in relation to a contract made before 22nd April 1967 or (in the application of this Act of Northern Ireland) 28th July 1967.

[187B]

NOTES
Commencement: 1 January 1980.

Part VI
Actions for Breach of the Contract

Seller's remedies

49 Action for price

(1) Where, under a contract of sale, the property in the goods has passed to the buyer and he wrongfully neglects or refuses to pay for the goods according to the terms of the contract, the seller may maintain an action against him for the price of the goods.

(2) Where, under a contract of sale, the price is payable on a day certain irrespective of delivery and the buyer wrongfully neglects or refuses to pay such price, the seller may maintain an action for the price, although the property in the goods has not passed and the goods have not been appropriated to the contract.

(3) ...

[188]

NOTES
Commencement: 1 January 1980.
Sub-s (3): applies to Scotland only.

50 Damages for non-acceptance

(1) Where the buyer wrongfully neglects or refuses to accept and pay for the goods, the seller may maintain an action against him for damages for non-acceptance.

(2) The measure of damages is the estimated loss directly and naturally resulting, in the ordinary course of events, from the buyer's breach of contract.

(3) Where there is an available market for the goods in question the measure of damages is prima facie to be ascertained by the difference between the contract price and the market or current price at the time or times when the goods ought to have been accepted or (if no time was fixed for acceptance) at the time of the refusal to accept.

[189]

NOTES
Commencement: 1 January 1980.

Buyer's remedies

51 Damages for non-delivery

(1) Where the seller wrongfully neglects or refuses to deliver the goods to the buyer, the buyer may maintain an action against the seller for damages for non-delivery.

(2) The measure of damages is the estimated loss directly and naturally resulting, in the ordinary course of events, from the seller's breach of contract.

(3) Where there is an available market for the goods in question the measure of damages is prima facie to be ascertained by the difference between the contract price and the market or current price of the goods at the time or times when they ought to have been delivered or (if no time was fixed) at the time of the refusal to deliver.

NOTES
Commencement: 1 January 1980.

52 Specific performance

(1) In any action for breach of contract to deliver specific or ascertained goods the court may, if it thinks fit, on the plaintiff's application, by its judgment or decree direct that the contract shall be performed specifically, without giving the defendant the option of retaining the goods on payment of damages.

(2) The plaintiff's application may be made at any time before judgment or decree.

(3) The judgment or decree may be unconditional, or on such terms and conditions as to damages, payment of the price and otherwise as seem just to the court.

(4) ...

NOTES
Commencement: 1 January 1980.
Sub-s (4): applies to Scotland only.

53 Remedy for breach of warranty

(1) Where there is a breach of warranty by the seller, or where the buyer elects (or is compelled) to treat any breach of a condition on the part of the seller as a breach of warranty, the buyer is not by reason only of such breach of warranty entitled to reject the goods; but he may—
    (a) set up against the seller the breach of warranty in diminution or extinction of the price, or
    (b) maintain an action against the seller for damages for the breach of warranty.

(2) The measure of damages for breach of warranty is the estimated loss directly and naturally resulting, in the ordinary course of events, from the breach of warranty.

(3) In the case of breach of warranty of quality such loss is prima facie the difference between the value of the goods at the time of delivery to the buyer and the value they would have had if they had fulfilled the warranty.

(4) The fact that the buyer has set up the breach of warranty in diminution or extinction of the price does not prevent him from maintaining an action for the same breach of warranty if he has suffered further damage.

(5) ...

NOTES
Commencement: 1 January 1980.
Sub-s (5): applies to Scotland only.

PART VII
SUPPLEMENTARY

61 Interpretation

(1) In this Act, unless the context or subject matter otherwise requires—

"action" includes counterclaim and set-off, and in Scotland condescendence and claim and compensation;

"business" includes a profession and the activities of any government department (including a Northern Ireland department) or local or public authority;

"buyer" means a person who buys or agrees to buy goods;

"contract of sale" includes an agreement to sell as well as a sale;

"credit-broker" means a person acting in the course of a business of credit brokerage carried on by him, that is a business of effecting introductions of individuals desiring to obtain credit—
  (a) to persons carrying on any business so far as it relates to the provision of credit, or
  (b) to other persons engaged in credit brokerage;

...

"delivery" means voluntary transfer of possession from one person to another;

"document of title to goods" has the same meaning as it has in the Factors Acts;

"Factors Acts" means the Factors Act 1889, the Factors (Scotland) Act 1890, and any enactment amending or substituted for the same;

"fault" means wrongful act or default;

"future goods" means goods to be manufactured or acquired by the seller after the making of the contract of sale;

"goods" includes all personal chattels other than things in action and money, and in Scotland all corporeal moveables except money; and in particular "goods" includes emblements, industrial growing crops, and things attached to or forming part of the land which are agreed to be severed before sale or under the contract of sale;

"plaintiff" includes pursuer, complainer, claimant in a multiplepoinding and defendant or defender counter-claiming;

"property" means the general property in goods, and not merely a special property;

"quality", in relation to goods, includes their state or condition;

"sale" includes a bargain and sale as well as a sale and delivery;

"seller" means a person who sells or agrees to sell goods;

"specific goods" means goods identified and agreed on at the time a contract of sale is made;

"warranty" (as regards England and Wales and Northern Ireland) means an agreement with reference to goods which are the subject of a contract of sale, but collateral to the main purpose of such contract, the breach of which gives rise to a claim for damages, but not to a right to reject the goods and treat the contract as repudiated.

(2) ...

(3) A thing is deemed to be done in good faith within the meaning of this Act when it is in fact done honestly, whether it is done negligently or not.

(4) A person is deemed to be insolvent within the meaning of this Act if he has either ceased to pay his debts in the ordinary course of business or he cannot pay his debts as they become due ... .

(5) Goods are in a deliverable state within the meaning of this Act when they are in such a state that the buyer would under the contract be bound to take delivery of them.

(6) As regards the definition of "business" in subsection (1) above, paragraph 14 of Schedule 1 below applies in relation to a contract made on or after 18th May 1973 and before 1st February 1978, and paragraph 15 in relation to one made before 18th May 1973.

NOTES
Commencement: 1 January 1980.
Sub-s (4): words omitted repealed by the Insolvency Act 1985, s 235, Sch 10, Part III, and the Insolvency Act 1986, s 437, Sch 11.
Other words omitted apply to Scotland only.

64 Short title and commencement

(1) This Act may be cited as the Sale of Goods Act 1979.

(2) This Act comes into force on 1st January 1980.

NOTE
Commencement: 1 January 1980.

LIMITATION ACT 1980

(C 58)

An Act to consolidate the Limitation Acts 1939 to 1980.

Part I
Ordinary Time Limits for Different Classes of Action

Time limits under Part I subject to extension or exclusion under Part II

1 Time limits under Part I subject to extension or exclusion under Part II

(1) This Part of this Act gives the ordinary time limits for bringing actions of the various classes mentioned in the following provisions of this Part.

(2) The ordinary time limits given in this Part of this Act are subject to extension or exclusion in accordance with the provisions of Part II of this Act.

[195]

NOTE
Commencement: 1 May 1981.

Actions founded on tort

2 Time limit for actions founded on tort

An action founded on tort shall not be brought after the expiration of six years from the date on which the cause of action accrued.

[196]

NOTE
Commencement: 1 May 1981.

3 Time limit in case of successive conversions and extinction of title of owner of converted goods

(1) Where any cause of action in respect of the conversion of a chattel has accrued to any person and, before he recovers possession of the chattel, a further conversion takes place, no action shall be brought in respect of the further conversion after the expiration of six years from the accrual of the cause of action in respect of the original conversion.

(2) Where any such cause of action has accrued to any person and the period prescribed for bringing that action has expired and he has not during that period recovered possession of the chattel, the title of that person to the chattel shall be extinguished.

[197]

NOTE
Commencement: 1 May 1981.

4 Special time limit in case of theft

(1) The right of any person from whom a chattel is stolen to bring an action in respect of the theft shall not be subject to the time limits under sections 2 and 3(1) of this Act, but if his title to the chattel is extinguished under section 3(2) of this Act he may not bring an action in respect of a theft preceding the loss of his title, unless the theft in question preceded the conversion from which time began to run for the purposes of section 3(2).

(2) Subsection (1) above shall apply to any conversion related to the theft of a chattel as it applies to the theft of a chattel; and, except as provided below, every conversion following the theft of a chattel before the person from whom it is stolen recovers possession of it shall be regarded for the purposes of this section as related to the theft.

If anyone purchases the stolen chattel in good faith neither the purchase nor any conversion following it shall be regarded as related to the theft.

(3) Any cause of action accruing in respect of the theft or any conversion related to the theft of a chattel to any person from whom the chattel is stolen shall be disregarded for the purpose of applying section 3(1) or (2) of this Act to his case.

(4) Where in any action brought in respect of the conversion of a chattel it is proved that the chattel was stolen from the plaintiff or anyone through whom he claims it shall be presumed that any conversion following the theft is related to the theft unless the contrary is shown.

(5) In this section "theft" includes—
   (a) any conduct outside England and Wales which would be theft if committed in England and Wales; and
   (b) obtaining any chattel (in England and Wales or elsewhere) in the circumstances described in section 15(1) of the Theft Act 1968 (obtaining by deception) or by blackmail within the meaning of section 21 of that Act;

and references in this section to a chattel being "stolen" shall be construed accordingly.

[198]

NOTE
Commencement: 1 May 1981.

[4A Time limit for actions for libel or slander

The time limit under section 2 of this Act shall not apply to an action for libel or slander, but no such action shall be brought after the expiration of three years from the date on which the cause of action accrued.]

[199]

NOTES
Commencement: 30 December 1985 (for effect, see s 69(5), Sch 9, para 14).
Added by the Administration of Justice Act 1985, s 57(2).

Actions founded on simple contract

5 Time limit for actions founded on simple contract

An action founded on simple contract shall not be brought after the expiration of six years from the date on which the cause of action accrued.

[200]

NOTE
Commencement: 1 May 1981.

6 Special time limit for actions in respect of certain loans

(1) Subject to subsection (3) below, section 5 of this Act shall not bar the right of action on a contract of loan to which this section applies.

(2) This section applies to any contract of loan which—
   (a) does not provide for repayment of the debt on or before a fixed or determinable date; and
   (b) does not effectively (whether or not it purports to do so) make the obligation to repay the debt conditional on a demand for repayment made by or on behalf of the creditor or on any other matter;

except where in connection with taking the loan the debtor enters into any collateral obligation to pay the amount of the debt or any part of it (as, for example, by delivering a promissory note as security for the debt) on terms which would exclude the application of this section to the contract of loan if they applied directly to repayment of the debt.

(3) Where a demand in writing for repayment of the debt under a contract of loan to which this section applies is made by or on behalf of the creditor (or, where there are joint creditors, by or on behalf of any one of them) section 5 of this Act shall thereupon apply as if the cause of action to recover the debt had accrued on the date on which the demand was made.

(4) In this section "promissory note" has the same meaning as in the Bills of Exchange Act 1882.

[201]

NOTE
Commencement: 1 May 1981.

7 Time limit for actions to enforce certain awards

An action to enforce an award, where the submission is not by an instrument under seal, shall not be brought after the expiration of six years from the date on which the cause of action accrued.

[202]

NOTE
Commencement: 1 May 1981.

General rule for actions on a specialty

8 Time limit for actions on a specialty

(1) An action upon a specialty shall not be brought after the expiration of twelve years from the date on which the cause of action accrued.

(2) Subsection (1) above shall not affect any action for which a shorter period of limitation is prescribed by any other provision of this Act.

[203]

NOTE
Commencement: 1 May 1981.

Actions for sums recoverable by statute

9 Time limit for actions for sums recoverable by statute

(1) An action to recover any sum recoverable by virtue of any enactment shall not be brought after the expiration of six years from the date on which the cause of action accrued.

(2) Subsection (1) above shall not affect any action to which section 10 of this Act applies.

[204]

NOTE
Commencement: 1 May 1981.

10 Special time limit for claiming contribution

(1) Where under section 1 of the Civil Liability (Contribution) Act 1978 any person becomes entitled to a right to recover contribution in respect of any damage from any other person, no action to recover contribution by virtue of that right shall be brought after the expiration of two years from the date on which that right accrued.

(2) For the purposes of this section the date on which a right to recover contribution in respect of any damage accrues to any person (referred to below in this section as "the relevant date") shall be ascertained as provided in subsections (3) and (4) below.

(3) If the person in question is held liable in respect of that damage—
   (a) by a judgment given in any civil proceedings; or
   (b) by an award made on any arbitration;

the relevant date shall be the date on which the judgment is given, or the date of the award (as the case may be).

For the purposes of this subsection no account shall be taken of any judgment or award given or made on appeal in so far as it varies the amount of damages awarded against the person in question.

(4) If, in any case not within subsection (3) above, the person in question makes or agrees to make any payment to one or more persons in compensation for that damage (whether he admits any liability in respect of the damage or not), the relevant date shall be the earliest date on which the amount to be paid by him is agreed between him (or his representative) and the person (or each of the persons, as the case may be) to whom the payment is to be made.

(5) An action to recover contribution shall be one to which sections 28, 32 and 35 of this Act apply, but otherwise Parts II and III of this Act (except sections 34, 37 and 38) shall not apply for the purposes of this section.

[205]

NOTE
Commencement: 1 May 1981.

Actions in respect of wrongs causing personal injuries or death

11 Special time limit for actions in respect of personal injuries

(1) This section applies to any action for damages for negligence, nuisance or breach of duty (whether the duty exists by virtue of a contract or of provision made by or under a statute or independently of any contract or any such provision) where the damages claimed by the plaintiff for the negligence, nuisance or breach of duty consist of or include damages in respect of personal injuries to the plaintiff or any other person.

(2) None of the time limits given in the preceding provisions of this Act shall apply to an action to which this section applies.

(3) An action to which this section applies shall not be brought after the expiration of the period applicable in accordance with subsection (4) or (5) below.

(4) Except where subsection (5) below applies, the period applicable is three years from—

(a) the date on which the cause of action accrued; or
(b) the date of knowledge (if later) of the person injured.

(5) If the person injured dies before the expiration of the period mentioned in subsection (4) above, the period applicable as respects the cause of action surviving for the benefit of his estate by virtue of section 1 of the Law Reform (Miscellaneous Provisions) Act 1934 shall be three years from—
(a) the date of death; or
(b) the date of the personal representative's knowledge;

whichever is the later.

(6) For the purposes of this section "personal representative" includes any person who is or has been a personal representative of the deceased, including an executor who has not proved the will (whether or not he has renounced probate) but not anyone appointed only as a special personal representative in relation to settled land; and regard shall be had to any knowledge acquired by any such person while a personal representative or previously.

(7) If there is more than one personal representative, and their dates of knowledge are different, subsection (5)(b) above shall be read as referring to the earliest of those dates.

[206]

NOTE
Commencement: 1 May 1981.

[11A Actions in respect of defective products

(1) This section shall apply to an action for damages by virtue of any provision of Part I of the Consumer Protection Act 1987.

(2) None of the time limits given in the preceding provisions of this Act shall apply to an action to which this section applies.

(3) An action to which this section applies shall not be brought after the expiration of the period of ten years from the relevant time, within the meaning of section 4 of the said Act of 1987; and this subsection shall operate to extinguish a right of action and shall do so whether or not that right of action had accrued, or time under the following provisions of this Act had begun to run, at the end of the said period of ten years.

(4) Subject to subsection (4) below, an action to which this section applies in which the damages claimed by the plaintiff consist of or include damages in respect of personal injuries to the plaintiff or any other person or loss of or damage to any property, shall not be brought after the expiration of the period of three years from whichever is the later of—
(a) the date on which the cause of action accrued; and
(b) the date of knowledge of the injured person or, in the case of loss of damage to property, the date of knowledge of the plaintiff or (if earlier) of any person in whom his cause of action was previously vested.

(5) If in a case where the damages claimed by the plaintiff consist of or include damages in respect of personal injuries to the plaintiff or any other person the injured person died before the expiration of the period mentioned in subsection (4) above, that subsection shall have effect as respects the cause of action surviving for the benefit of his

estate by virtue of section 1 of the Law Reform (Miscellaneous Provisions) Act 1934 as if for the reference to that period there were substituted a reference to the period of three years from whichever is the later of—
   (a) the date of death; and
   (b) the date of the personal representative's knowledge.

(6) For the purposes of this section "personal representative" includes any person who is or has been a personal representative of the deceased, including an executor who has not proved the will (whether or not he has renounced probate) but not anyone appointed only as a special personal representative in relation to settled land; and regard shall be had to any knowledge acquired by any such person while a personal representative or previously.

(7) If there is more than one personal representative and their dates of knowledge are different, subsection (5)(b) above shall be read as referring to the earliest of those dates.

(8) Expressions used in this section or section 14 of this Act and in Part I of the Consumer Protection Act 1987 have the same meanings in this section or that section as in that Part; and section 1(1) of that Act (Part I to be construed as enacted for the purpose of complying with the product liability Directive) shall apply for the purpose of construing this section and the following provisions of this Act so far as they relate to an action by virtue of any provision of that Part as it applies for the purpose of construing that Part.]

NOTES
   Commencement: 1 May 1981.
   Added by the Consumer Protection Act 1987, s 6, Sch 1, Pt I, para 1.

12 Special time limit for actions under Fatal Accidents legislation

(1) An action under the Fatal Accidents Act 1976 shall not be brought if the death occurred when the person injured could no longer maintain an action and recover damages in respect of the injury (whether because of a time limit in this Act or in any other Act, or for any other reason).

Where any such action by the injured person would have been barred by the time limit in section 11 [or 11A] of this Act, no account shall be taken of the possibility of that time limit being overridden under section 33 of this Act.

(2) None of the time limits given in the preceding provisions of this Act shall apply to an action under the Fatal Accidents Act 1976, but no such action shall be brought after the expiration of three years from—
   (a) the date of death; or
   (b) the date of knowledge of the person for whose benefit the action is brought;
whichever is the later.

(3) An action under the Fatal Accidents Act 1976 shall be one to which sections 28, 33 and 35 of this Act apply, and the application to any such action of the time limit under subsection (2) above shall be subject to section 39; but otherwise Parts II and III of this Act shall not apply to any such action.

NOTES
Commencement: 1 May 1981.
Sub-s (1): words in square brackets added by the Consumer Protection Act 1987, s 6, Sch 1, Pt I, para 2.

13 Operation of time limit under section 12 in relation to different dependants

(1) Where there is more than one person for whose benefit an action under the Fatal Accidents Act 1976 is brought, section 12(2)(b) of this Act shall be applied separately to each of them.

(2) Subject to subsection (3) below, if by virtue of subsection (1) above the action would be outside the time limit given by section 12(2) as regards one or more, but not all, of the persons for whose benefit it is brought, the court shall direct that any person as regards whom the action would be outside that limit shall be excluded from those for whom the action is brought.

(3) The court shall not give such a direction if it is shown that if the action were brought exclusively for the benefit of the person in question it would not be defeated by a defence of limitation (whether in consequence of section 28 of this Act or an agreement between the parties not to raise the defence, or otherwise).

[209]

NOTE
Commencement: 1 May 1981.

14 Definition of date of knowledge for purposes of sections 11 and 12

(1) [Subject to subsection (1A) below,] In sections 11 and 12 of this Act references to a person's date of knowledge are references to the date on which he first had knowledge of the following facts—
   (a) that the injury in question was significant; and
   (b) that the injury was attributable in whole or in part to the act or omission which is alleged to constitute negligence, nuisance or breach of duty; and
   (c) the identity of the defendant; and
   (d) if it is alleged that the act or omission was that of a person other than the defendant, the identity of that person and the additional facts supporting the bringing of an action against the defendant;

and knowledge that any acts or omissions did or did not, as a matter of law, involve negligence, nuisance or breach of duty is irrelevant.

[(1A) In section 11A of this Act and in section 12 of this Act so far as that section applies to an action by virtue of section 6(1)(a) of the Consumer Protection Act 1987 (death caused by defective product) references to a person's date of knowledge are references to the date on which he first had knowledge of the following facts—
   (a) such facts about the damage caused by the defect as would lead a reasonable person who had suffered such damage to consider it sufficiently serious to justify his instituting proceedings for damages against a defendant who did not dispute liability and was able to satisfy a judgment; and
   (b) that the damage was wholly or partly attributable to the facts and circumstances alleged to constitute the defect; and
   (c) the identity of the defendant;

but, in determining the date on which a person first had such knowledge there shall be disregarded both the extent (if any) of that person's knowledge on any date of whether particular facts or circumstances would or would not, as a matter of law, constitute a defect and, in a case relating to loss of or damage to property, any knowledge which that person had on a date on which he had no right of action by virtue of Part I of that Act in respect of the loss or damage.]

(2) For the purposes of this section an injury is significant if the person whose date of knowledge is in question would reasonably have considered it sufficiently serious to justify his instituting proceedings for damages against a defendant who did not dispute liability and was able to satisfy a judgment.

(3) For the purposes of this section a person's knowledge includes knowledge which he might reasonably have been expected to acquire—
- (a) from facts observable or ascertainable by him; or
- (b) from facts ascertainable by him with the help of medical or other appropriate expert advice which it is reasonable for him to seek;

but a person shall not be fixed under this subsection with knowledge of a fact ascertainable only with the help of expert advice so long as he has taken all reasonable steps to obtain (and, where appropriate, to act on) that advice.

[210]

NOTES
Commencement: 1 March 1988 (para (1A)); 1 May 1981 (remainder)
Sub-s (1): words in square brackets added by the Consumer Protection Act 1987, s 6, Sch 1, Pt I, para 3.
Sub-s (1A): added by the Consumer Protection Act 1987, s 6, Sch 1, Pt I, para 3.

Actions in respect of latent damage not involving personal injuries

[14A Special time limit for negligence actions where facts relevant to cause of action are not known at date of accrual

(1) This section applies to any action for damages for negligence, other than one to which section 11 of this Act applies, where the starting date for reckoning the period of limitation under subsection (4)(b) below falls after the date on which the cause of action accrued.

(2) Section 2 of this Act shall not apply to an action to which this section applies.

(3) An action to which this section applies shall not be brought after the expiration of the period applicable in accordance with subsection (4) below.

(4) That period is either—
- (a) six years from the date on which the cause of action accrued; or
- (b) three years from the starting date as defined by subsection (5) below, if that period expires later than the period mentioned in paragraph (a) above.

(5) For the purposes of this section, the starting date for reckoning the period of limitation under subsection (4)(b) above is the earliest date on which the plaintiff or any person in whom the cause of action was vested before him first had both the knowledge required for bringing an action for damages in respect of the relevant damage and a right to bring such an action.

(6) In subsection (5) above "the knowledge required for bringing an action for damages in respect of the relevant damage" means knowledge both—
- (a) of the material facts about the damage in respect of which damages are claimed; and

(b) of the other facts relevant to the current action mentioned in subsection (8) below.

(7) For the purposes of subsection (6)(a) above, the material facts about the damage are such facts about the damage as would lead a reasonable person who had suffered such damage to consider it sufficiently serious to justify his instituting proceedings for damages against a defendant who did not dispute liability and was able to satisfy a judgment.

(8) The other facts referred to in subsection (6)(b) above are—
   (a) that the damage was attributable in whole or in part to the act or omission which is alleged to constitute negligence; and
   (b) the identity of the defendant; and
   (c) if it is alleged that the act or omission was that of a person other than the defendant, the identity of that person and the additional facts supporting the bringing of an action against the defendant.

(9) Knowledge that any acts or omissions did or did not, as a matter of law, involve negligence is irrelevant for the purposes of subsection (5) above.

(10) For the purposes of this section a person's knowledge includes knowledge which he might reasonably have been expected to acquire—
   (a) from facts observable or ascertainable by him; or
   (b) from facts ascertainable by him with the help of appropriate expert advice which it is reasonable for him to seek;

but a person shall not be taken by virtue of this subsection to have knowledge of a fact ascertainable only with the help of expert advice so long as he has taken all reasonable steps to obtain (and, where appropriate, to act on) that advice.]

NOTES
Commencement: 18 September 1986.
Added by the Latent Damage Act 1986, s 1.

[14B Overriding time limit for negligence actions not involving personal injuries

(1) An action for damages for negligence, other than one to which section 11 of this Act applies, shall not be brought after the expiration of fifteen years from the date (or, if more than one, from the last of the dates) on which there occurred any act or omission—
   (a) which is alleged to constitute negligence; and
   (b) to which the damage in respect of which damages are claimed is alleged to be attributable (in whole or in part).

(2) This section bars the right of action in a case to which subsection (1) above applies notwithstanding that—
   (a) the cause of action has not yet accrued; or
   (b) where section 14A of this Act applies to the action, the date which is for the purposes of that section the starting date for reckoning the period mentioned in subsection (4)(b) of that section has not yet occurred;

before the end of the period of limitation prescribed by this section.]

NOTES
Commencement: 18 September 1986.
Added by the Latent Damage Act 1986, s 1.

Part II
Extension or Exclusion of Ordinary Time Limits

Disability

28 Extension of limitation period in case of disability

(1) Subject to the following provisions of this section, if on the date when any right of action accrued for which a period of limitation is prescribed by this Act, the person to whom it accrued was under a disability, the action may be brought at any time before the expiration of six years from the date when he ceased to be under a disability or died (whichever first occurred) notwithstanding that the period of limitation has expired.

(2) This section shall not affect any case where the right of action first accrued to some person (not under a disability) through whom the person under a disability claims.

(3) When a right of action which has accrued to a person under a disability accrues, on the death of that person while still under a disability, to another person under a disability, no further extension of time shall be allowed by reason of the disability of the second person.

(4) No action to recover land or money charged on land shall be brought by virtue of this section by any person after the expiration of thirty years from the date on which the right of action accrued to that person or some person through whom he claims.

[(4A) If the action is one to which section 4A of this Act applies, subsection (1) above shall have effect as if for the words from "at any time" to "occurred)" there were substituted the words "by him at any time before the expiration of three years from the date when he ceased to be under a disability".]

(5) If the action is one to which section 10 of this Act applies, subsection (1) above shall have effect as if for the words "six years" there were substituted the words "two years".

(6) If the action is one to which section 11 or 12(2) of this Act applies, subsection (1) above shall have effect as if for the words "six years" there were substituted the words "three years".

[(7) If the action is one to which section 11A of this Act applies or one by virtue of section 6(1)(a) of the Consumer Protection Act 1987 (death caused by defective product), subsection (1) above—
(a) shall not apply to the time limit prescribed by subsection (3) of the said section 11A or to that time limit as applied by virtue of section 12(1) of this Act; and
(b) in relation to any other time limit prescribed by this Act shall have effect as if for the word "six years" there were substituted the words "three years".]

NOTES

Commencement: 1 March 1988 (sub-s (7)); 30 December 1985 (sub-s (4A)); 1 May 1981 (remainder).

Sub-s (4A): added with savings by the Administration of Justice Act 1985, ss 57(3), 69(5), Sch 9, para 14.

Sub-s (7): added by the Consumer Protection Act 1987, s 6, Sch 1, Pt I, para 4.

[28A Extension for cases where the limitation period is the period under section 14A(4)(b)

(1) Subject to subsection (2) below, if in the case of any action for which a period of limitation is prescribed by section 14A of this Act—
   (a) the period applicable in accordance with subsection (4) of that section is the period mentioned in paragraph (b) of that subsection;
   (b) on the date which is for the purposes of that section the starting date for reckoning that period the person by reference to whose knowledge that date fell to be determined under subsection (5) of that section was under a disability; and
   (c) section 28 of this Act does not apply to the action;

the action may be brought at any time before the expiration of three years from the date when he ceased to be under a disability or died (whichever first occurred) notwithstanding that the period mentioned above has expired.

(2) An action may not be brought by virtue of subsection (1) above after the end of the period of limitation prescribed by section 14B of this Act.]

NOTES
Commencement: 18 September 1986.
Added by the Latent Damage Act 1986, s 2(1).

Acknowledgment and part payment

29 Fresh accrual of action on acknowledgment or part payment

(1) Subsections (2) and (3) below apply where any right of action (including a foreclosure action) to recover land or an advowson or any right of a mortgagee of personal property to bring a foreclosure action in respect of the property has accrued.

(2) If the person in possession of the land, benefice or personal property in question acknowledges the title of the person to whom the right of action has accrued—
   (a) the right shall be treated as having accrued on and not before the date of the acknowledgment; and
   (b) in the case of a right of action to recover land which has accrued to a person entitled to an estate or interest taking effect on the determination of an entailed interest against whom time is running under section 27 of this Act, section 27 shall thereupon cease to apply to the land.

(3) In the case of a foreclosure or other action by a mortgagee, if the person in possession of the land, benefice or personal property in question or the person liable for the mortgage debt makes any payment in respect of the debt (whether of principal or interest) the right shall be treated as having accrued on and not before the date of the payment.

(4) Where a mortgagee is by virtue of the mortgage in possession of any mortgaged land and either—

    (a) receives any sum in respect of the principal or interest of the mortgage debt; or

    (b) acknowledges the title of the mortgagor, or his equity of redemption;

an action to redeem the land in his possession may be brought at any time before the expiration of twelve years from the date of the payment or acknowledgment.

(5) Subject to subsection (6) below, where any right of action has accrued to recover—

    (a) any debt or other liquidated pecuniary claim; or

    (b) any claim to the personal estate of a deceased person or to any share or interest in any such estate;

and the person liable or accountable for the claim acknowledges the claim or makes any payment in respect of it the right shall be treated as having accrued on and not before the date of the acknowledgment or payment.

(6) A payment of a part of the rent or interest due at any time shall not extend the period for claiming the remainder then due, but any payment of interest shall be treated as a payment in respect of the principal debt.

(7) Subject to subsection (6) above, a current period of limitation may be repeatedly extended under this section by further acknowledgments or payments, but a right of action, once barred by this Act, shall not be revived by any subsequent acknowledgment or payment.

[215]

NOTES
Commencement: 1 May 1981.
This section derived from the Limitation Act 1939, s 23.

30 Formal provisions as to acknowledgments and part payments

(1) To be effective for the purposes of section 29 of this Act, an acknowledgment must be in writing and signed by the person making it.

(2) For the purposes of section 29, any acknowledgment or payment—

    (a) may be made by the agent of the person by whom it is required to be made under that section; and

    (b) shall be made to the person, or to an agent of the person, whose title or claim is being acknowledged or, as the case may be, in respect of whose claim the payment is being made.

[216]

NOTE
Commencement: 1 May 1981.

31 Effect of acknowledgment or part payment on persons other than the maker or recipient

(1) An acknowledgment of the title to any land, benefice, or mortgaged personalty by any person in possession of it shall bind all other persons in possession during the ensuing period of limitation.

(2) A payment in respect of a mortgage debt by the mortgagor or any other person liable for the debt, or by any person in possession of the mortgaged property, shall, so far as any right of the mortgagee to foreclose or otherwise to recover the property is concerned, bind all other persons in possession of the mortgaged property during the ensuing period of limitation.

(3) Where two or more mortgagees are by virtue of the mortgage in possession of the mortgaged land, an acknowledgment of the mortgagor's title or of his equity of redemption by one of the mortgagees shall only bind him and his successors and shall not bind any other mortgagee or his successors.

(4) Where in a case within subsection (3) above the mortgagee by whom the acknowledgment is given is entitled to a part of the mortgaged land and not to any ascertained part of the mortgage debt the mortgagor shall be entitled to redeem that part of the land on payment, with interest, of the part of the mortgage debt which bears the same proportion to the whole of the debt as the value of the part of the land bears to the whole of the mortgaged land.

(5) Where there are two or more mortgagors, and the title or equity of redemption of one of the mortgagors is acknowledged as mentioned above in this section, the acknowledgment shall be treated as having been made to all the mortgagors.

(6) An acknowledgment of any debt or other liquidated pecuniary claim shall bind the acknowledgor and his successors but not any other person.

(7) A payment made in respect of any debt or other liquidated pecuniary claim shall bind all persons liable in respect of the debt or claim.

(8) An acknowledgment by one of several personal representatives of any claim to the personal estate of a deceased person or to any share or interest in any such estate, or a payment by one of several personal representatives in respect of any such claim, shall bind the estate of the deceased person.

(9) In this section "successor", in relation to any mortgagee or person liable in respect of any debt or claim, means his personal representatives and any other person on whom the rights under the mortgage or, as the case may be, the liability in respect of the debt or claim devolve (whether on death or bankruptcy or the disposition of property or the determination of a limited estate or interest in settled property or otherwise).

[217]

NOTE
Commencement: 1 May 1981.

Fraud, concealment and mistake

32 Postponement of limitation period in case of fraud, concealment or mistake

(1) Subject to [subsections (3) and (4A)] below, where in the case of any action for which a period of limitation is prescribed by this Act, either—
  (a) the action is based upon the fraud of the defendant; or
  (b) any fact relevant to the plaintiff's right of action has been deliberately concealed from him by the defendant; or
  (c) the action is for relief from the consequences of a mistake;

the period of limitation shall not begin to run until the plaintiff has discovered the fraud, concealment or mistake (as the case may be) or could with reasonable diligence have discovered it.

References in this subsection to the defendant include references to the defendant's agent and to any person through whom the defendant claims and his agent.

(2) For the purposes of subsection (1) above, deliberate commission of a breach of duty in circumstances in which it is unlikely to be discovered for some time amounts to deliberate concealment of the facts involved in that breach of duty.

(3) Nothing in this section shall enable any action—
   (a) to recover, or recover the value of, any property; or
   (b) to enforce any charge against, or set aside any transaction affecting, any property;

to be brought against the purchaser of the property or any person claiming through him in any case where the property has been purchased for valuable consideration by an innocent third party since the fraud or concealment or (as the case may be) the transaction in which the mistake was made took place.

(4) A purchaser is an innocent third party for the purposes of this section—
   (a) in the case of fraud or concealment of any fact relevant to the plaintiff's right of action, if he was not a party to the fraud or (as the case may be) to the concealment of that fact and did not at the time of the purchase know or have reason to believe that the fraud or concealment had taken place; and
   (b) in the case of mistake, if he did not at the time of the purchase know or have reason to believe that the mistake had been made.

[(4A) Subsection (1) above shall not apply in relation to the time limit prescribed by section 11A(3) of this Act or in relation to that time limit as applied by virtue of section 12(1) of this Act].

[(5) Sections 14A and 14B of this Act shall not apply to any action to which subsection (1)(b) above applies (and accordingly the period of limitation referred to in that subsection, in any case to which either of those sections would otherwise apply, is the period applicable under section 2 of this Act).]

[218]

NOTES
    Commencement: 1 March 1988 (sub-s (4A)); 18 September 1986 (sub-s (5)); 1 May 1981 (remainder).
    Sub-s (1): words in square brackets substituted by the Consumer Protection Act 1987, s 6, Sch 1, Pt I, para 5.
    Sub-s (4A): inserted by the Consumer Protection Act 1987, s 6, Sch 1, Pt I, para 5.
    Sub-s (5): added by the Latent Damage Act 1986, s 2(2).

Discretionary extension of time limit for actions for libel or slander

[32A Discretionary extension of time limit for actions for libel or slander

Where a person to whom a cause of action for libel or slander has accrued has not brought such an action within the period of three years mentioned in section 4A of this Act (or, where applicable, the period allowed by section 28(1) as modified by

section 28(4A)) because all or any of the facts relevant to that cause of action did not become known to him until after the expiration of that period, such an action—
(a) may be brought by him at any time before the expiration of one year from the earliest date on which he knew all the facts relevant to that cause of action; but
(b) shall not be so brought without the leave of the High Court.]

[219]

NOTES
Commencement: 30 December 1985 (for effect, see s 69(5), Sch 9, para 14).
Added by the Administration of Justice Act 1985, s 57(4).

Discretionary exclusion of time limit for actions in respect of personal injuries or death

33 Discretionary exclusion of time limit for actions in respect of personal injuries or death

(1) If it appears to the court that it would be equitable to allow an action to proceed having regard to the degree to which—
(a) the provisions of section 11 [or 11A] or 12 of this Act prejudice the plaintiff or any person whom he represents; and
(b) any decision of the court under this subsection would prejudice the defendant or any person whom he represents;

the court may direct that those provisions shall not apply to the action, or shall not apply to any specified cause of action to which the action relates.

[(1A) The court shall not under this section disapply—
(a) subsection (3) of section 11A; or
(b) where the damages claimed by the plaintiff are confined to damages for loss of or damage to any property, any other provision in its application to an action by virtue of Part I of the Consumer Protection Act 1987.]

(2) The court shall not under this section disapply section 12(1) except where the reason why the person injured could no longer maintain an action was because of the time limit in section 11 [or subsection (4) of section 11A].

If, for example, the person injured could at his death no longer maintain an action under the Fatal Accidents Act 1976 because of the time limit in Article 29 in Schedule 1 to the Carriage by Air Act 1961, the court has no power to direct that section 12(1) shall not apply.

(3) In acting under this section the court shall have regard to all the circumstances of the case and in particular to—
(a) the length of, and the reasons for, the delay on the part of the plaintiff;
(b) the extent to which, having regard to the delay, the evidence adduced or likely to be adduced by the plaintiff or the defendant is or is likely to be less cogent than if the action had been brought within the time allowed by section 11 [, by section 11A] or (as the case may be) by section 12;
(c) the conduct of the defendant after the cause of action arose, including the extent (if any) to which he responded to requests reasonably made by the plaintiff for information or inspection for the purpose of ascertaining facts which were or might be relevant to the plaintiff's cause of action against the defendant;

(d) the duration of any disability of the plaintiff arising after the date of the accrual of the cause of action;

(e) the extent to which the plaintiff acted promptly and reasonably once he knew whether or not the act or omission of the defendant, to which the injury was attributable, might be capable at that time of giving rise to an action for damages;

(f) the steps, if any, taken by the plaintiff to obtain medical, legal or other expert advice and the nature of any such advice he may have received.

(4) In a case where the person injured died when, because of section 11 [or subsection (4) of section 11A], he could no longer maintain an action and recover damages in respect of the injury, the court shall have regard in particular to the length of, and the reasons for, the delay on the part of the deceased.

(5) In a case under subsection (4) above, or any other case where the time limit, or one of the time limits, depends on the date of knowledge of a person other than the plaintiff, subsection (3) above shall have effect with appropriate modifications, and shall have effect in particular as if references to the plaintiff included references to any person whose date of knowledge is or was relevant in determining a time limit.

(6) A direction by the court disapplying the provisions of section 12(1) shall operate to disapply the provisions to the same effect in section 1(1) of the Fatal Accidents Act 1976.

(7) In this section "the court" means the court in which the action has been brought.

(8) References in this section to section 11 [or 11A] include references to that section as extended by any of the preceding provisions of this Part of this Act or by any provision of Part III of this Act.

[220]

NOTES

Commencement: 1 March 1988 (sub-s (1A)); 1 May 1981 (remainder).

Sub-ss (1), (3), (4), (8): words in square brackets added by the Consumer Protection Act 1987, s 6, Sch 1, Pt I, para 6.

Sub-s (1A): inserted by the Consumer Protection Act 1987, s 6, Sch 1, Part I, para 6.

Part III
Miscellaneous and General

36 Equitable jurisdiction and remedies

(1) The following time limits under this Act, that is to say—

(a) the time limit under section 2 for actions founded on tort;

[(aa) the time limit under section 4A for actions for libel or slander;]

(b) the time limit under section 5 for actions founded on simple contract;

(c) the time limit under section 7 for actions to enforce awards where the submission is not by an instrument under seal;

(d) the time limit under section 8 for actions on a specialty;

(e) the time limit under section 9 for actions to recover a sum recoverable by virtue of any enactment; and

(f) the time limit under section 24 for actions to enforce a judgment;

shall not apply to any claim for specific performance of a contract or for an injunction or for other equitable relief, except in so far as any such time limit may be applied by the court by analogy in like manner as the corresponding time limit under any enactment repealed by the Limitation Act 1939 was applied before 1st July 1940.

(2) Nothing in this Act shall affect any equitable jurisdiction to refuse relief on the ground of acquiescence or otherwise.

[221]

NOTES
Commencement: 1 May 1981.
Sub-s (1): para (aa) inserted with savings by the Administration of Justice Act 1985, ss 57(5), 69(5), Sch 9, para 14.

38 Interpretation

(1) In this Act, unless the context otherwise requires—
"action" includes any proceeding in a court of law, including an ecclesiastical court;
"land" includes corporeal hereditaments, tithes and rentcharges and any legal or equitable estate or interest therein, including an interest in the proceeds of the sale of land held upon trust for sale, but except as provided above in this definition does not include any incorporeal hereditament;
"personal estate" and "personal property" do not include chattels real;
"personal injuries" includes any disease and any impairment of a person's physical or mental condition, and "injury" and cognate expressions shall be construed accordingly;
"rent" includes a rentcharge and a rentservice; "rentcharge" means any annuity or periodical sum of money charged upon or payable out of land, except a rent service or interest on a mortgage on land;
"settled land", "statutory owner" and "tenant for life" have the same meanings respectively as in the Settled Land Act 1925;
"trust" and "trustee" have the same meanings respectively as in the Trustee Act 1925; and
"trust for sale" has the same meaning as in the Law of Property Act 1925.

(2) For the purposes of this Act a person shall be treated as under a disability while he is an infant, or of unsound mind.

(3) For the purposes of subsection (2) above a person is of unsound mind if he is a person who, by reason of mental disorder within the meaning of the [Mental Health Act 1983], is incapable of managing and administering his property and affairs.

(4) Without prejudice to the generality of subsection (3) above, a person shall be conclusively presumed for the purposes of subsection (2) above to be of unsound mind—
  (a) while he is liable to be detained or subject to guardianship under [the Mental Health Act 1983 (otherwise than by virtue of section 35 or 89)]; and
  [(b) while he is receiving treatment as an in-patient in any hospital within the meaning of the Mental Health Act 1983 or mental nursing home within the meaning of the Nursing Homes Act 1975 without being liable to be detained under the said Act of 1983 (otherwise than by virtue of section 35 or 89), being treatment which follows without any interval a period during which he was liable to be detained or subject to guardianship under the Mental Health Act 1959, or the said Act of 1983 (otherwise than by virtue of section 35 or 89) or by virtue of any enactment repealed or excluded by the Mental Health Act 1959].

(5) Subject to subsection (6) below, a person shall be treated as claiming through another person if he became entitled by, through, under, or by the act of that other person to the right claimed, and any person whose estate or interest might have been barred by a person entitled to an entailed interest in possession shall be treated as claiming through the person so entitled.

(6) A person becoming entitled to any estate or interest by virtue of a special power of appointment shall not be treated as claiming through the appointor.

(7) References in this Act to a right of action to recover land shall include references to a right to enter into possession of the land or, in the case of rentcharges and tithes, to distrain for arrears of rent or tithe, and references to the bringing of such an action shall include references to the making of such an entry or distress.

(8) References in this Act to the possession of land shall, in the case of tithes and rentcharges, be construed as references to the receipt of the tithe or rent, and references to the date of dispossession or discontinuance of possession of land shall, in the case of rent charges, be construed as references to the date of the last receipt of rent.

(9) References in Part II of this Act to a right of action shall include references to—
    (a) a cause of action;
    (b) a right to receive money secured by a mortgage or charge on any property;
    (c) a right to recover proceeds of the sale of land; and
    (d) a right to receive a share or interest in the personal estate of a deceased person.

(10) References in Part II to the date of the accrual of a right of action shall be construed—
    (a) in the case of an action upon a judgment, as references to the date on which the judgment became enforceable; and
    (b) in the case of an action to recover arrears of rent or interest, or damages in respect of arrears of rent or interest, as references to the date on which the rent or interest became due.

NOTES
Commencement: 1 May 1981.
Amended by the Mental Health Act 1983, s 148, Sch 4, para 55.

41 Short title, commencement and extent

(1) This Act may be cited as the Limitation Act 1980.

(2) This Act, except section 35, shall come into force on 1st May 1981.

(3) Section 35 of this Act shall come into force on 1st May 1981 to the extent (if any) that the section substituted for section 28 of the Limitation Act 1939 by section 8 of the Limitation Amendment Act 1980 is in force immediately before that date; but otherwise section 35 shall come into force on such day as the Lord Chancellor may by order made by statutory instrument appoint, and different days may be appointed for different purposes of that section (including its application in relation to different courts or proceedings).

(4) The repeal by this Act of section 14(1) of the Limitation Act 1963 and the corresponding saving in paragraph 2 of Schedule 2 to this Act shall extend to Northern Ireland, but otherwise this Act does not extend to Scotland or to Northern Ireland.

NOTE
Commencement: 1 May 1981.

HIGHWAYS ACT 1980

(C 66)

An Act to consolidate the Highways Acts 1959 to 1971 and related enactments, with amendments to give effect to recommendations of the Law Commission

[13 November 1980]

PART IV

MAINTENANCE OF HIGHWAYS: ENFORCEMENT OF LIABILITY FOR MAINTENANCE

58 Special defence in action against a highway authority for damages for non-repair of highway

(1) In an action against a highway authority in respect of damage resulting from their failure to maintain a highway maintainable at the public expense it is a defence (without prejudice to any other defence or the application of the law relating to contributory negligence) to prove that the authority had taken such care as in all the circumstances was reasonably required to secure that the part of the highway to which the action relates was not dangerous for traffic.

(2) For the purposes of a defence under subsection (1) above, the court shall in particular have regard to the following matters:—
  (a) the character of the highway, and the traffic which was reasonably to be expected to use it;
  (b) the standard of maintenance appropriate for a highway of that character and used by such traffic;
  (c) the state of repair in which a reasonable person would have expected to find the highway;
  (d) whether the highway authority knew, or could reasonably have been expected to know, that the condition of the part of the highway to which the action relates was likely to cause danger to users of the highway;
  (e) where the highway authority could not reasonably have been expected to repair that part of the highway before the cause of action arose, what warning notices of its condition had been displayed;

but for the purposes of such a defence it is not relevant to prove that the highway authority had arranged for a competent person to carry out or supervise the maintenance of the part of the highway to which the action relates unless it is also proved that the authority had given him proper instructions with regard to the maintenance of the highway and that he had carried out the instructions.

(3) This section binds the Crown.

(4) ...

NOTES
Commencement: 1 January 1981.
Sub-s (4): repealed by the New Roads and Street Works Act 1991, s 168(2), Sch 9.

PART XIV
MISCELLANEOUS AND SUPPLEMENTARY PROVISIONS: SAVINGS ETC

345 Short title, commencement and extent

(1) This Act may be cited as the Highways Act 1980.

(2) This Act shall come into force on 1st January 1981.

(3) This Act (except paragraph 18(c) of Schedule 24) extends to England and Wales only.

NOTE
Commencement: 1 January 1981.

CONTEMPT OF COURT ACT 1981

(C 49)

An Act to amend the law relating to contempt of court and related matters

[27 July 1981]

STRICT LIABILITY

3 Defence of innocent publication or distribution

(1) A person is not guilty of contempt of court under the strict liability rule as the publisher of any matter to which that rule applies if at the time of publication (having taken all reasonable care) he does not know and has no reason to suspect that relevant proceedings are active.

(2) A person is not guilty of contempt of court under the strict liability rule as the distributor of a publication containing any such matter if at the time of distribution (having taken all reasonable care) he does not know that it contains such matter and has no reason to suspect that it is likely to do so.

(3) The burden of proof of any fact tending to establish a defence afforded by this section to any person lies upon that person.

(4) ...

NOTES
Commencement: 27 August 1981.
Sub-s (4): words omitted repeal the Administration of Justice Act 1960, s 11.

4 Contemporary reports of proceedings

(1) Subject to this section a person is not guilty of contempt of court under the strict liability rule in respect of a fair and accurate report of legal proceedings held in public, published contemporaneously and in good faith.

(2) In any such proceedings the court may, where it appears to be necessary for avoiding a substantial risk of prejudice to the administration of justice in those proceedings, or in any other proceedings pending or imminent, order that the publication of any report of the proceedings, or any part of the proceedings, be postponed for such period as the court thinks necessary for that purpose.

(3) For the purposes of subsection (1) of this section and of section 3 of the Law of Libel Amendment Act 1888 (privilege) a report of proceedings shall be treated as published contemporaneously—
    (a) in the case of a report of which publication is postponed pursuant to an order under subsection (2) of this section, if published as soon as practicable after that order expires;
    (b) in the case of a report of committal proceedings of which publication is permitted by virtue only of subsection (3) of section 8 of the Magistrates' Courts Act 1980, if published as soon as practicable after publication is so permitted.

(4) Subsection (9) of the said section 8 is repealed.

NOTE
Commencement: 27 August 1981.

SUPPLEMENTAL

21 Short title, commencement and extent

(1) This Act may be cited as the Contempt of Court Act 1981.

(2) The provisions of this Act relating to legal aid in England and Wales shall come into force on such day as the Lord Chancellor may appoint by order made by statutory instrument; and the provisions of this Act relating to legal aid in Scotland and Northern Ireland shall come into force on such day or days as the Secretary of State may so appoint.

Different days may be appointed under this subsection in relation to different courts.

(3) Subject to subsection (2), this Act shall come into force at the expiration of the period of one month beginning with the day on which it is passed.

(4) Sections 7, 8(3), 12, 13(1) to (3), 14, 16, 17 and 18, Parts I and III of Schedule 2 and Schedules 3 and 4 of this Act do not extend to Scotland.

(5) This Act, except sections 15 and 17 and Schedules 2 and 3, extends to Northern Ireland.

CIVIL AVIATION ACT 1982

(C 16)

[27 May 1982]

An Act to Consolidate certain enactments relating to civil aviation.

Part III
Regulation of Civil Aviation

Trespass by Aircraft and Aircraft Nuisance, Noise, etc

76 Liability of aircraft in respect of trespass, nuisance and surface damage

(1) No action shall lie in respect of trespass or in respect of nuisance, by reason only of the flight of an aircraft over any property at a height above the ground which, having regard to wind, weather and all the circumstances of the case is reasonable, or the ordinary incidents of such flight, so long as the provisions of any Air Navigation Order and of any orders under section 62 above have been duly complied with and there has been no breach of section 81 below.

(2) Subject to subsection (3) below, where material loss or damage is caused to any person or property on land or water by, or by a person in, or an article, animal or person falling from, an aircraft while in flight, taking off or landing, then unless the loss or damage was caused or contributed to by the negligence of the person by whom it was suffered, damages in respect of the loss or damage shall be recoverable without proof of negligence or intention or other cause of action, as if the loss or damage had been caused by the wilful act, neglect, or default of the owner of the aircraft.

(3) Where material loss or damage is caused as aforesaid in circumstances in which—
    (a) damages are recoverable in respect of the said loss or damage by virtue only of subsection (2) above, and
    (b) a legal liability is created in some person other than the owner to pay damages in respect of the said loss or damage,

the owner shall be entitled to be indemnified by that other person against any claim in respect of the said loss or damage.

(4) Where the aircraft concerned has been bona fide demised, let or hired out for any period exceeding fourteen days to any other person by the owner thereof, and no pilot, commander, navigator or operative member of the crew of the aircraft is in the employment of the owner, this section shall have effect as if for references to the owner there were substituted references to the person to whom the aircraft has been so demised, let or hired out.

NOTE
Commencement: 27 August 1982.

Part V
Miscellaneous and General

110 Citation and commencement

(1) This Act may be cited as the Civil Aviation Act 1982.

(2) This Act shall come into force at the expiration of the period of three months beginning with its passing.

NOTE
Commencement: 27 August 1982.

SUPPLY OF GOODS AND SERVICES ACT 1982

(C 29)

An Act to amend the law with respect to the terms to be implied in certain contracts for the transfer of the property in goods, in certain contracts for the hire of goods and in certain contracts for the supply of a service; and for connected purposes.

[13 July 1982]

PART I
SUPPLY OF GOODS

Contracts for the transfer of property in goods

1 The contracts concerned

(1) In this Act a "contract for the transfer of goods" means a contract under which one person transfers or agrees to transfer to another the property in goods, other than an excepted contract.

(2) For the purposes of this section an excepted contract means any of the following:—
   (a) a contract of sale of goods;
   (b) a hire-purchase agreement;
   (c) a contract under which the property in goods is (or is to be) transferred in exchange for trading stamps on their redemption;
   (d) a transfer or agreement to transfer which is made by deed and for which there is no consideration other than the presumed consideration imported by the deed;
   (e) a contract intended to operate by way of mortgage, pledge, charge or other security.

(3) For the purposes of this Act a contract is a contract for the transfer of goods whether or not services are also provided or to be provided under the contract, and (subject to subsection (2) above) whatever is the nature of the consideration for the transfer or agreement to transfer.

NOTE
Commencement: 4 January 1983.

2 Implied terms about title, etc

(1) In a contract for the transfer of goods, other than one to which subsection (3) below applies, there is an implied condition on the part of the transferor that in the

case of a transfer of the property in the goods he has a right to transfer the property and in the case of an agreement to transfer the property in the goods he will have such a right at the time when the property is to be transferred.

(2) In a contract for the transfer of goods, other than one to which subsection (3) below applies, there is also an implied warranty that—
- (a) the goods are free, and will remain free until the time when the property is to be transferred, from any charge or encumbrance not disclosed or known to the transferee before the contract is made, and
- (b) the transferee will enjoy quiet possession of the goods except so far as it may be disturbed by the owner or other person entitled to the benefit of any charge or encumbrance so disclosed or known.

(3) This subsection applies to a contract for the transfer of goods in the case of which there appears from the contract or is to be inferred from its circumstances an intention that the transferor should transfer only such title as he or a third person may have.

(4) In a contract to which subsection (3) above applies there is an implied warranty that all charges or encumbrances known to the transferor and not known to the transferee have been disclosed to the transferee before the contract is made.

(5) In a contract to which subsection (3) above applies there is also an implied warranty that none of the following will disturb the transferee's quiet possession of the goods, namely—
- (a) the transferor;
- (b) in a case where the parties to the contract intend that the transferor should transfer only such title as a third person may have, that person;
- (c) anyone claiming through or under the transferor or that third person otherwise than under a charge or encumbrance disclosed or known to the transferee before the contract is made.

[232]

NOTE
Commencement: 4 January 1983.

3 Implied terms where transfer is by description

(1) This section applies where, under a contract for the transfer of goods, the transferor transfers or agrees to transfer the property in the goods by description.

(2) In such a case there is an implied condition that the goods will correspond with the description.

(3) If the transferor transfers or agrees to transfer the property in the goods by sample as well as by description it is not sufficient that the bulk of the goods corresponds with the sample if the goods do not also correspond with the description.

(4) A contract is not prevented from falling within subsection (1) above by reason only that, being exposed for supply, the goods are selected by the transferee.

[233]

NOTE
Commencement: 4 January 1983.

4 Implied terms about quality or fitness

(1) Except as provided by this section and section 5 below and subject to the provisions of any other enactment, there is no implied condition or warranty about the

quality or fitness for any particular purpose of goods supplied under a contract for the transfer of goods.

(2) Where, under such a contract, the transferor transfers the property in goods in the course of a business, there is (subject to subsection (3) below) an implied condition that the goods supplied under the contract are of merchantable quality.

(3) There is no such condition as is mentioned in subsection (2) above—
  (a) as regards defects specifically drawn to the transferee's attention before the contract is made; or
  (b) if the transferee examines the goods before the contract is made, as regards defects which that examination ought to reveal.

(4) Subsection (5) below applies where, under a contract for the transfer of goods, the transferor transfers the property in goods in the course of a business and the transferee, expressly or by implication, makes known—
  (a) to the transferor, or
  (b) where the consideration or part of the consideration for the transfer is a sum payable by instalments and the goods were previously sold by a credit-broker to the transferor, to that credit-broker,

any particular purpose for which the goods are being acquired.

(5) In that case there is (subject to subsection (6) below) an implied condition that the goods supplied under the contract are reasonably fit for that purpose, whether or not that is a purpose for which such goods are commonly supplied.

(6) Subsection (5) above does not apply where the circumstances show that the transferee does not rely, or that it is unreasonable for him to rely, on the skill or judgment of the transferor or credit-broker.

(7) An implied condition or warranty about quality or fitness for a particular purpose may be annexed by usage to a contract for the transfer of goods.

(8) The preceding provisions of this section apply to a transfer by a person who in the course of a business is acting as agent for another as they apply to a transfer by a principal in the course of a business, except where that other is not transferring in the course of a business and either the transferee knows that fact or reasonable steps are taken to bring it to the transferee's notice before the contract concerned is made.

(9) Goods of any kind are of merchantable quality within the meaning of subsection (2) above if they are as fit for the purpose or purposes for which goods of that kind are commonly supplied as it is reasonable to expect having regard to any description applied to them, the price (if relevant) and all the other relevant circumstances.

[234]

NOTE
Commencement: 4 January 1983.

5 Implied terms where transfer is by sample

(1) This section applies where, under a contract for the transfer of goods, the transferor transfers or agrees to transfer the property in the goods by reference to a sample.

(2) In such a case there is an implied condition—
  (a) that the bulk will correspond with the sample in quality; and
  (b) that the transferee will have a reasonable opportunity of comparing the bulk with the sample; and

(c) that the goods will be free from any defect, rendering them unmerchantable, which would not be apparent on reasonable examination of the sample.

(3) In subsection (2)(c) above "unmerchantable" is to be construed in accordance with section 4(9) above.

(4) For the purposes of this section a transferor transfers or agrees to transfer the property in goods by reference to a sample where there is an express or implied term to that effect in the contract concerned.

[235]

NOTE
Commencement: 4 January 1983.

Contracts for the hire of goods

6 The contracts concerned

(1) In this Act a "contract for the hire of goods" means a contract under which one person bails or agrees to bail goods to another by way of hire, other than an excepted contract.

(2) For the purposes of this section an excepted contract means any of the following:—
    (a) a hire-purchase agreement;
    (b) a contract under which goods are (or are to be) bailed in exchange for trading stamps on their redemption.

(3) For the purposes of this Act a contract is a contract for the hire of goods whether or not services are also provided or to be provided under the contract, and (subject to subsection (2) above) whatever is the nature of the consideration for the bailment or agreement to bail by way of hire.

[236]

NOTE
Commencement: 4 January 1983.

7 Implied terms about right to transfer possession, etc

(1) In a contract for the hire of goods there is an implied condition on the part of the bailor that in the case of a bailment he has a right to transfer possession of the goods by way of hire for the period of the bailment and in the case of an agreement to bail he will have such a right at the time of the bailment.

(2) In a contract for the hire of goods there is also an implied warranty that the bailee will enjoy quiet possession of the goods for the period of the bailment except so far as the possession may be disturbed by the owner or other person entitled to the benefit of any charge or encumbrance disclosed or known to the bailee before the contract is made.

(3) The preceding provisions of this section do not affect the right of the bailor to repossess the goods under an express or implied term of the contract.

[237]

NOTE
Commencement: 4 January 1983.

8 Implied terms where hire is by description

(1) This section applies where, under a contract for the hire of goods, the bailor bails or agrees to bail the goods by description.

(2) In such a case there is an implied condition that the goods will correspond with the description.

(3) If under the contract the bailor bails or agrees to bail the goods by reference to a sample as well as a description it is not sufficient that the bulk of the goods corresponds with the sample if the goods do not also correspond with the description.

(4) A contract is not prevented from falling within subsection (1) above by reason only that, being exposed for supply, the goods are selected by the bailee.

[238]

NOTE
Commencement: 4 January 1983.

9 Implied terms about quality or fitness

(1) Except as provided by this section and section 10 below and subject to the provisions of any other enactment, there is no implied condition or warranty about the quality or fitness for any particular purpose of goods bailed under a contract for the hire of goods.

(2) Where, under such a contract, the bailor bails goods in the course of a business, there is (subject to subsection (3) below) an implied condition that the goods supplied under the contract are of merchantable quality.

(3) There is no such condition as is mentioned in subsection (2) above—
 (a) as regards defects specifically drawn to the bailee's attention before the contract is made; or
 (b) if the bailee examines the goods before the contract is made, as regards defects which that examination ought to reveal.

(4) Subsection (5) below applies where, under a contract for the hire of goods, the bailor bails goods in the course of a business and the bailee, expressly or by implication, makes known—
 (a) to the bailor in the course of negotiations conducted by him in relation to the making of the contract, or
 (b) to a credit-broker in the course of negotiations conducted by that broker in relation to goods sold by him to the bailor before forming the subject matter of the contract,
any particular purpose for which the goods are being bailed.

(5) In that case there is (subject to subsection (6) below) an implied condition that the goods supplied under the contract are reasonably fit for that purpose, whether or not that is a purpose for which such goods are commonly supplied.

(6) Subsection (5) above does not apply where the circumstances show that the bailee does not rely, or that it is unreasonable for him to rely, on the skill or judgment of the bailor or credit-broker.

(7) An implied condition or warranty about quality or fitness for a particular purpose may be annexed by usage to a contract for the hire of goods.

(8) The preceding provisions of this section apply to a bailment by a person who in the course of a business is acting as agent for another as they apply to a bailment by a

principal in the course of a business, except where that other is not bailing in the course of a business and either the bailee knows that fact or reasonable steps are taken to bring it to the bailee's notice before the contract concerned is made.

(9) Goods of any kind are of merchantable quality within the meaning of subsection (2) above if they are as fit for the purpose or purposes for which goods of that kind are commonly supplied as it is reasonable to expect having regard to any description applied to them, the consideration for the bailment (if relevant) and all the other relevant circumstances.

[239]

NOTE
Commencement: 4 January 1983.

10 Implied terms where hire is by sample

(1) This section applies where, under a contract for the hire of goods, the bailor bails or agrees to bail the goods by reference to a sample.

(2) In such a case there is an implied condition—
  (a) that the bulk will correspond with the sample in quality; and
  (b) that the bailee will have a reasonable opportunity of comparing the bulk with the sample; and
  (c) that the goods will be free from any defect, rendering them unmerchantable, which would not be apparent on reasonable examination of the sample.

(3) In subsection (2)(c) above "unmerchantable" is to be construed in accordance with section 9(9) above.

(4) For the purposes of this section a bailor bails or agrees to bail goods by reference to a sample where there is an express or implied term to that effect in the contract concerned.

[240]

NOTE
Commencement: 4 January 1983.

Exclusion of implied terms, etc

11 Exclusion of implied terms, etc

(1) Where a right, duty or liability would arise under a contract for the transfer of goods or a contract for the hire of goods by implication of law, it may (subject to subsection (2) below and the 1977 Act) be negatived or varied by express agreement, or by the course of dealing between the parties, or by such usage as binds both parties to the contract.

(2) An express condition or warranty does not negative a condition or warranty implied by the preceding provisions of this Act unless inconsistent with it.

(3) Nothing in the preceding provisions of this Act prejudices the operation of any other enactment or any rule of law whereby any condition or warranty (other than one relating to quality or fitness) is to be implied in a contract for the transfer of goods or a contract for the hire of goods.

[241]

NOTES
Commencement: 4 January 1983.
1977 Act: the Unfair Contract Terms Act 1977.

PART II
SUPPLY OF SERVICES

12 The contracts concerned

(1) In this Act a "contract for the supply of a service" means, subject to subsection (2) below, a contract under which a person ("the supplier") agrees to carry out a service.

(2) For the purposes of this Act, a contract of service or apprenticeship is not a contract for the supply of a service.

(3) Subject to subsection (2) above, a contract is a contract for the supply of a service for the purposes of this Act whether or not goods are also—
   (a) transferred or to be transferred, or
   (b) bailed or to be bailed by way of hire,

under the contract, and whatever is the nature of the consideration for which the service is to be carried out.

(4) The Secretary of State may by order provide that one or more of sections 13 to 15 below shall not apply to services of a description specified in the order, and such an order may make different provision for different circumstances.

(5) The power to make an order under subsection (4) above shall be exercisable by statutory instrument subject to annulment in pursuance of a resolution of either House of Parliament.

[242]

NOTE
Commencement: 4 January 1983.

13 Implied term about care and skill

In a contract for the supply of a service where the supplier is acting in the course of a business, there is an implied term that the supplier will carry out the service with reasonable care and skill.

[243]

NOTE
Commencement: 4 January 1983.

14 Implied term about time for performance

(1) Where, under a contract for the supply of a service by a supplier acting in the course of a business, the time for the service to be carried out is not fixed by the contract, left to be fixed in a manner agreed by the contract or determined by the course of dealing between the parties, there is an implied term that the supplier will carry out the service within a reasonable time.

(2) What is a reasonable time is a question of fact.

[244]

NOTE
Commencement: 4 January 1983.

15 Implied term about consideration

(1) Where, under a contract for the supply of a service, the consideration for the service is not determined by the contract, left to be determined in a manner agreed by the contract or determined by the course of dealing between the parties, there is an implied term that the party contracting with the supplier will pay a reasonable charge.

(2) What is a reasonable charge is a question of fact.

[245]

NOTE
Commencement: 4 July 1983.

16 Exclusion of implied terms, etc

(1) Where a right, duty or liability would arise under a contract for the supply of a service by virtue of this Part of this Act, it may (subject to subsection (2) below and the 1977 Act) be negatived or varied by express agreement, or by the course of dealing between the parties, or by such usage as binds both parties to the contract.

(2) An express term does not negative a term implied by this Part of this Act unless inconsistent with it.

(3) Nothing in this Part of this Act prejudices—
   (a) any rule of law which imposes on the supplier a duty stricter than that imposed by section 13 or 14 above; or
   (b) subject to paragraph (a) above, any rule of law whereby any term not inconsistent with this Part of this Act is to be implied in a contract for the supply of a service.

(4) This Part of this Act has effect subject to any other enactment which defines or restricts the rights, duties or liabilities arising in connection with a service of any description.

[246]

NOTE
Commencement: 4 July 1983.

PART III
SUPPLEMENTARY

17 Minor and consequential amendments

(Sub-s (1) amends the Supply of Goods (Implies Terms) Act 1973, s 10(2); sub-ss (2), (3) amend the Unfair Contract Terms Act 1977, s 7.)

18 Interpretation: general

(1) In the preceding provisions of this Act and this section—
   "bailee", in relation to a contract for the hire of goods means (depending on the context) a person to whom the goods are bailed under the contract, or a person to whom they are to be so bailed, or a person to whom the rights under the contract of either of those persons have passed;

"bailor", in relation to a contract for the hire of goods, means (depending on the context) a person who bails the goods under the contract, or a person who agrees to do so, or a person to whom the duties under the contract of either of those persons have passed;

"business" includes a profession and the activities of any government department or local or public authority;

"credit-broker" means a person acting in the course of a business of credit brokerage carried on by him;

"credit brokerage" means the effecting of introductions—
  (a) of individuals desiring to obtain credit to persons carrying on any business so far as it relates to the provision of credit; or
  (b) of individuals desiring to obtain goods on hire to persons carrying on a business which comprises or relates to the bailment of goods under a contract for the hire of goods; or
  (c) of individuals desiring to obtain credit, or to obtain goods on hire, to other credit-brokers;

"enactment" means any legislation (including subordinate legislation) of the United Kingdom or Northern Ireland;

"goods" include all personal chattels (including emblements, industrial growing crops, and things attached to or forming part of the land which are agreed to be severed before the transfer or bailment concerned or under the contract concerned), other than things in action and money;

"hire-purchase agreement" has the same meaning as in the 1974 Act;

"property", in relation to goods, means the general property in them and not merely a special property;

"quality", in relation to goods, includes their state or condition;

"redemption", in relation to trading stamps, has the same meaning as in the Trading Stamps Act 1964 or, as respects Northern Ireland, the Trading Stamps Act (Northern Ireland) 1965;

"trading stamps" has the same meaning as in the said Act of 1964 or, as respects Northern Ireland, the said Act of 1965;

"transferee", in relation to a contract for the transfer of goods, means (depending on the context) a person to whom the property in the goods is transferred under the contract, or a person to whom the property is to be so transferred, or a person to whom the rights under the contract of either of those persons have passed;

"transferor", in relation to a contract for the transfer of goods, means (depending on the context) a person who transfers the property in the goods under the contract, or a person who agrees to do so, or a person to whom the duties under the contract of either of those persons have passed.

(2) In subsection (1) above, in the definitions of bailee, bailor, transferee and transferor, a reference to rights or duties passing is to their passing by assignment, operation of law or otherwise.

[247]

NOTE
Commencement: 4 January 1983 (certain purposes); 4 July 1983 (certain purposes); to be appointed (remainder).

19 Interpretation: references to Acts

In this Act—

"the 1973 Act" means the Supply of Goods (Implied Terms) Act 1973;
"the 1974 Act" means the Consumer Credit Act 1974;
"the 1977 Act" means the Unfair Contract Terms Act 1977; and
"the 1979 Act" means the Sale of Goods Act 1979.

[248]

NOTE
Commencement: 4 January 1983 (certain purposes); 4 July 1983 (certain purposes); to be appointed (remainder).

20 Citation, transitional provisions, commencement and extent

(1) This Act may be cited as the Supply of Goods and Services Act 1982.

(2) The transitional provisions in the Schedule to this Act shall have effect.

(3) Part I of this Act together with section 17 and so much of sections 18 and 19 above as relates to that Part shall not come into operation until 4th January 1983; and Part II of this Act together with so much of sections 18 and 19 above as relates to that Part shall not come into operation until such day as may be appointed by an order made by the Secretary of State.

(4) The power to make an order under subsection (3) above shall be exercisable by statutory instrument.

(5) No provision of this Act applies to a contract made before the provision comes into operation.

(6) This Act extends to Northern Ireland but not to Scotland.

[249]

NOTE
Commencement: 13 July 1982.

ADMINISTRATION OF JUSTICE ACT 1982

(C 53)

An Act to make further provision with respect to the administration of justice and matters connected therewith; to amend the law relating to actions for damages for personal injuries, including injuries resulting in death, and to abolish certain actions for loss of services; to amend the law relating to wills; to make further provision with respect to funds in court, statutory deposits and schemes for the common investment of such funds and deposits and certain other funds; to amend the law relating to deductions by employers under attachment of earnings orders; to make further provision with regard to penalties that may be awarded by the Solicitors' Disciplinary Tribunal under section 47 of the Solicitors Act 1974; to make further provision for the appointment of justices of the peace in England and Wales and in relation to temporary vacancies in the membership of the Law Commission; to enable the title register kept by the Chief Land Registrar to be kept otherwise than in documentary form; and to authorise the payment of travelling, subsistence and financial loss allowances for justices of the peace in Northern Ireland

[28 October 1982]

Part I
Damages for Personal Injuries etc
Abolition of certain claims for damages etc

1 Abolition of right to damages for loss of expectation of life

(1) In an action under the law of England and Wales or the law of Northern Ireland for damages for personal injuries—
   (a) no damages shall be recoverable in respect of any loss of expectation of life caused to the injured person by the injuries; but
   (b) if the injured person's expectation of life has been reduced by the injuries, the court, in assessing damages in respect of pain and suffering caused by the injuries, shall take account of any suffering caused or likely to be caused to him by awareness that his expectation of life has been so reduced.

(2) The references in subsection (1)(a) above to damages in respect of loss of expectation of life does not include damages in respect of loss of income.

[250]

NOTE
Commencement: 1 January 1983.

2 Abolition of actions for loss of services etc

No person shall be liable in tort under the law of England and Wales or the law of Northern Ireland—
   (a) to a husband on the ground only of his having deprived him of the services or society of his wife;
   (b) to a parent (or person standing in the place of a parent) on the ground only of his having deprived him of the services of a child; or
   (c) on the ground only—
      (i) of having deprived another of the services of his menial servant;
      (ii) of having deprived another of the services of his female servant by raping or seducing her; or
      (iii) of enticement of a servant or harbouring a servant.

[251]

NOTE
Commencement: 1 January 1983.

5 Maintenance at public expense to be taken into account in assessment of damages

In an action under the law of England and Wales or the law of Northern Ireland for damages for personal injuries (including any such action arising out of a contract) any saving to the injured person which is attributable to his maintenance wholly or partly at public expense in a hospital, nursing home or other institution shall be set off against any income lost by him as a result of his injuries.

[252]

NOTE
Commencement: 1 January 1983.

Part IX
General and Supplementary

77 Extent

(1) Subject to subsection (6) below, the following provisions of this Act—
   (a) sections 3, 4 and 6;
   (b) Part III;
   (c) sections 17 to 22;
   (d) Part V;
   (e) sections 49 to 57;
   (f) sections 65 to 67,

extend to England and Wales only.

(2) Sections 1, 2, 5, 39, 42 to 47, 64 and 74 above extend to England and Wales and Northern Ireland.

(3) Part II of this Act and section 26 above extend to Scotland only and Part VI of this Act applies to Scotland only to the extent specified in section 48 above.

(4) Part VIII of this Act extends to Northern Ireland only.

(5) The repeal of the Wills Act Amendment Act 1852 by section 75 above does not extend to Northern Ireland.

(6) Subject to subsection (5) above, where any enactment repealed or amended or instrument revoked by this Act extends to any part of the United Kingdom, the repeal, amendment or revocation extends to that part.

NOTE
Commencement: 1 January 1983.

78 Citation

This Act may be cited as the Administration of Justice Act 1982.

NOTE
Commencement: 28 October 1982.

OCCUPIERS' LIABILITY ACT 1984
(C 3)

An Act to amend the law of England and Wales as to the liability of persons as occupiers of premises for injury suffered by persons other than their visitors; and to amend the Unfair Contract Terms Act 1977, as it applies to England and Wales, in relation to persons obtaining access to premises for recreational or educational purposes.

[13 March 1984]

1 Duty of occupier to persons other than his visitors

(1) The rules enacted by this section shall have effect, in place of the rules of the common law, to determine—

(a) whether any duty is owed by a person as occupier of premises to persons other than his visitors in respect of any risk of their suffering injury on the premises by reason of any danger due to the state of the premises or to things done or omitted to be done on them; and
(b) if so, what that duty is.

(2) For the purposes of this section, the persons who are to be treated respectively as an occupier of any premises (which, for those purposes, include any fixed or movable structure) and as his visitors are—
(a) any person who owes in relation to the premises the duty referred to in section 2 of the Occupiers' Liability Act 1957 (the common duty of care), and
(b) those who are his visitors for the purposes of that duty.

(3) An occupier of premises owes a duty to another (not being his visitor) in respect of any such risk as is referred to in subsection (1) above if—
(a) he is aware of the danger or has reasonable grounds to believe that it exists;
(b) he knows or has reasonable grounds to believe that the other is in the vicinity of the danger concerned or that he may come into the vicinity of the danger (in either case, whether the other has lawful authority for being in that vicinity or not); and
(c) the risk is one against which, in all the circumstances of the case, he may reasonably be expected to offer the other some protection.

(4) Where, by virtue of this section, an occupier of premises owes a duty to another in respect of such a risk, the duty is to take such care as is reasonable in all the circumstances of the case to see that he does not suffer injury on the premises by reason of the danger concerned.

(5) Any duty owed by virtue of this section in respect of a risk may, in an appropriate case, be discharged by taking such steps as are reasonable in all the circumstances of the case to give warning of the danger concerned or to discourage persons from incurring the risk.

(6) No duty is owed by virtue of this section to any person in respect of risks willingly accepted as his by that person (the question whether a risk was so accepted to be decided on the same principles as in other cases in which one person owes a duty of care to another).

(7) No duty is owed by virtue of this section to persons using the highway, and this section does not affect any duty owed to such persons.

(8) Where a person owes a duty by virtue of this section, he does not, by reason of any breach of the duty, incur any liability in respect of any loss of or damage to property.

(9) In this section—
"highway" means any part of a highway other than a ferry or waterway;
"injury" means anything resulting in death or personal injury, including any disease and any impairment of physical or mental condition; and
"movable structure" includes any vessel, vehicle or aircraft.

NOTE
Commencement: 13 May 1984.

3 Application to Crown

Section 1 of this Act shall bind the Crown, but as regards the Crown's liability in tort shall not bind the Crown further than the Crown is made liable in tort by the Crown Proceedings Act 1947.

[256]

NOTE
Commencement: 13 May 1984.

4 Short title, commencement and extent

(1) This Act may be cited as the Occupiers' Liability Act 1984.

(2) This Act shall come into force at the end of the period of two months beginning with the day on which it is passed.

(3) This Act extends to England and Wales only.

[257]

NOTE
Commencement: 13 May 1984.

DATA PROTECTION ACT 1984

(C 35)

An Act to regulate the use of automatically processed information relating to individuals and the provision of services in respect of such information.

[12 July 1984]

Part III
Rights of Data Subjects

22 Compensation for inaccuracy

(1) An individual who is the subject of personal data held by a data user and who suffers damage by reason of the inaccuracy of the data shall be entitled to compensation from the data user for that damage and for any distress which the individual has suffered by reason of the inaccuracy.

(2) In the case of data which accurately record information received or obtained by the data user from the data subject or a third party, subsection (1) above does not apply if the following requirements have been complied with—
   (a) the data indicate that the information was received or obtained as aforesaid or the information has not been extracted from the data except in a form which includes an indication to that effect; and
   (b) if the data subject has notified the data user that he regards the information as incorrect or misleading, an indication to that effect has been included in the data or the information has not been extracted from the data except in a form which includes an indication to that effect.

(3) In proceedings brought against any person by virtue of this section it shall be a defence to prove that he had taken such care as in all the circumstances was reasonably required to ensure the accuracy of the data at the material time.

(4) Data are inaccurate for the purposes of this section if incorrect or misleading as to any matter of fact.

[258]

NOTE
Commencement: 12 July 1984.

23 Compensation for loss or unauthorised disclosure

(1) An individual who is the subject of personal data held by a data user or in respect of which services are provided by a person carrying on a computer bureau and who suffers damage by reason of—
  (a) the loss of the data;
  (b) the destruction of the data without the authority of the data user or, as the case may be, of the person carrying on the bureau; or
  (c) subject to subsection (2) below, the disclosure of the data, or access having been obtained to the data, without such authority as aforesaid,

shall be entitled to compensation from the data user or, as the case may be, the person carrying on the bureau for that damage and for any distress which the individual has suffered by reason of the loss, destruction, disclosure or access.

(2) In the case of a registered data user, subsection (1)(c) above does not apply to disclosure to, or access by, any person falling within a description specified pursuant to section 4(3)(d) above in an entry in the register relating to that data user.

(3) In proceedings brought against any person by virtue of this section it shall be a defence to prove that he had taken such care as in all the circumstances was reasonably required to prevent the loss, destruction, disclosure or access in question.

[259]

NOTE
Commencement: 12 July 1984.

Part V
General

43 Short title and extent

(1) This Act may be cited as the Data Protection Act 1984.

(2) This Act extends to Northern Ireland.

(3) Her Majesty may by Order in Council direct that this Act shall extend to any of the Channel Islands with such exceptions and modifications as may be specified in the Order.

[260]

NOTE
Commencement: 12 July 1984.

BUILDING ACT 1984

(C 55)

An Act to consolidate certain enactments concerning building and buildings and related matters
[31 October 1984]

Part I
Building Regulations

Power to make building regulations

1 Power to make building regulations

(1) The Secretary of State may, for any of the purposes of—
  (a) securing the health, safety, welfare and convenience of persons in or about buildings and of others who may be affected by buildings or matters connected with buildings,
  (b) furthering the conservation of fuel and power, and
  (c) preventing waste, undue consumption, misuse or contamination of water,

make regulations with respect to the design and construction of buildings and the provision of services, fittings and equipment in or in connection with buildings.

(2) Regulations made under subsection (1) above are known as building regulations.

(3) Schedule 1 to this Act has effect with respect to the matters as to which building regulations may provide.

(4) The power to make building regulations is exercisable by statutory instrument, which is subject to annulment in pursuance of a resolution of either House of Parliament.

NOTES
Commencement: 1 December 1984.
Sub-ss (1), (2) derived from the Public Health Act 1936, s 61(1), (2), and the Health and Safety at Work etc Act 1974, s 61(1); sub-s (4) derived from the Public Health Act 1961, s 4(7).

Breach of building regulations

38 Civil liability

(1) Subject to this section—
  (a) breach of a duty imposed by building regulations, so far as it causes damage, is actionable, except in so far as the regulations provide otherwise, and
  (b) as regards such a duty, building regulations may provide for a prescribed defence to be available in an action for breach of that duty brought by virtue of this subsection.

(2) Subsection (1) above, and any defence provided for in regulations made by virtue of it, do not apply in the case of a breach of such a duty in connection with a building erected before the date on which that subsection comes into force unless the regulations imposing the duty apply to or in connection with the building by virtue of section 2(2) above or paragraph 8 of Schedule 1 to this Act.

(3) This section does not affect the extent (if any) to which breach of—
   (a) a duty imposed by or arising in connection with this Part of this Act or any other enactment relating to building regulations, or
   (b) a duty imposed by building regulations in a case to which subsection (1) above does not apply,

is actionable, or prejudice a right of action that exists apart from the enactments relating to building regulations.

(4) In this section, "damage" includes the death of, or injury to, any person (including any disease and any impairment of a person's physical or mental condition).

NOTE
Commencement: 1 December 1984 (so far as enables regulations to be made); to be appointed (remainder).

PART V
SUPPLEMENTARY

135 Short title and extent

(1) This Act may be cited as the Building Act 1984.

(2) This Act does not extend to Scotland or to Northern Ireland.

NOTES
Commencement: 1 December 1984.
See further, in relation to statutory undertakers: the Water Act 1989, s 190, Sch 25, para 1 and the Electricity Act 1989, s 112(1), Sch 16, para 1.

POLICE AND CRIMINAL EVIDENCE ACT 1984

(C 60)

An Act to make further provision in relation to the powers and duties of the police, persons in police detention, criminal evidence, police discipline and complaints against the police; to provide for arrangements for obtaining the views of the community on policing and for a rank of deputy chief constable; to amend the law relating to the Police Federations and Police Forces and Police Cadets in Scotland; and for connected purposes

[31 October 1984]

PART II
POWERS OF ENTRY, SEARCH AND SEIZURE

Entry and search without search warrant

17 Entry for purpose of arrest etc

(1) Subject to the following provisions of this section, and without prejudice to any other enactment, a constable may enter and search any premises for the purpose—

(a) of executing—
   (i) a warrant of arrest issued in connection with or arising out of criminal proceedings; or
   (ii) a warrant of commitment issued under section 76 of the Magistrates' Courts Act 1980;
(b) of arresting a person for an arrestable offence;
(c) of arresting a person for an offence under—
   (i) section 1 (prohibition of uniforms in connection with political objects), ... of the Public Order Act 1936;
   (ii) any enactment contained in sections 6 to 8 or 10 of the Criminal Law Act 1977 (offences relating to entering and remaining on property);
   [(iii) section 4 of the Public Order Act 1986 (fear or provocation of violence);]
(d) of recapturing a person who is unlawfully at large and whom he is pursuing; or
(e) of saving life or limb or preventing serious damage to property.

(2) Except for the purpose specified in paragraph (e) of subsection (1) above, the powers of entry and search conferred by this section—
(a) are only exercisable if the constable has reasonable grounds for believing that the person whom he is seeking is on the premises; and
(b) are limited, in relation to premises consisting of two or more separate dwellings, to powers to enter and search—
   (i) any parts of the premises which the occupiers of any dwelling comprised in the premises use in common with the occupiers of any other such dwelling; and
   (ii) any such dwelling in which the constable has reasonable grounds for believing that the person whom he is seeking may be.

(3) The powers of entry and search conferred by this section are only exercisable for the purposes specified in subsection (1)(c)(ii) above by a constable in uniform.

(4) The power of search conferred by this section is only a power to search to the extent that is reasonably required for the purpose for which the power of entry is exercised.

(5) Subject to subsection (6) below, all the rules of common law under which a constable has power to enter premises without a warrant are hereby abolished.

(6) Nothing in subsection (5) above affects any power of entry to deal with or prevent a breach of the peace.

NOTES
Commencement: 1 January 1986.
Sub-s (1): in para (c), in sub-para (i) words omitted repealed by the Public Order Act 1986, s 40(2), (3), Sch 2, para 7, Sch 3; sub-para (iii) added by the Public Order 1986, s 40(2), Sch 2, para 7.

Seizure etc

19 General power of seizure etc

(1) The powers conferred by subsections (2), (3) and (4) below are exercisable by a constable who is lawfully on any premises.

(2) The constable may seize anything which is on the premises if he has reasonable grounds for believing—

(a) that it has been obtained in consequence of the commission of an offence; and
(b) that it is necessary to seize it in order to prevent it being concealed, lost, damaged, altered or destroyed.

(3) The constable may seize anything which is on the premises if he has reasonable grounds for believing—
(a) that it is evidence in relation to an offence which he is investigating or any other offence; and
(b) that it is necessary to seize it in order to prevent the evidence being concealed, lost, altered or destroyed.

(4) The constable may require any information which is contained in a computer and is accessible from the premises to be produced in a form in which it can be taken away and in which it is visible and legible if he has reasonable grounds for believing—
(a) that—
  (i) it is evidence in relation to an offence which he is investigating or any other offence; or
  (ii) it has been obtained in consequence of the commission of an offence; and
(b) that it is necessary to do so in order to prevent it being concealed, lost, tampered with or destroyed.

(5) The powers conferred by this section are in addition to any power otherwise conferred.

(6) No power of seizure conferred on a constable under any enactment (including an enactment contained in an Act passed after this Act) is to be taken to authorise the seizure of an item which the constable exercising the power has reasonable grounds for believing to be subject to legal privilege.

[265]

NOTES
Commencement: 1 January 1986.

22 Retention

(1) Subject to subsection (4) below, anything which has been seized by a constable or taken away by a constable following a requirement made by virtue of section 19 or 20 above may be retained so long as is necessary in all the circumstances.

(2) Without prejudice to the generality of subsection (1) above—
(a) anything seized for the purposes of a criminal investigation may be retained, except as provided by subsection (4) below,—
  (i) for use as evidence at a trial for an offence; or
  (ii) for forensic examination or for investigation in connection with an offence; and
(b) anything may be retained in order to establish its lawful owner, where there are reasonable grounds for believing that it has been obtained in consequence of the commission of an offence.

(3) Nothing seized on the ground that it may be used—
(a) to cause physical injury to any person;
(b) to damage property;
(c) to interfere with evidence; or
(d) to assist in escape from police detention or lawful custody,

may be retained when the person from whom it was seized is no longer in police detention or the custody of a court or is in the custody of a court but has been released on bail.

(4) Nothing may be retained for either of the purposes mentioned in subsection (2)(a) above if a photograph or copy would be sufficient for that purpose.

(5) Nothing in this section affects any power of a court to make an order under section 1 of the Police (Property) Act 1897.

[266]

NOTES
Commencement: 1 January 1986.

PART III
ARREST

24 Arrest without warrant for arrestable offences

(1) The powers of summary arrest conferred by the following subsections shall apply—
- (a) to offences for which the sentence is fixed by law;
- (b) to offences for which a person of 21 years of age or over (not previously convicted) may be sentenced to imprisonment for a term of five years (or might be so sentenced but for the restrictions imposed by section 33 of the Magistrates' Courts Act 1980); and
- (c) to the offences to which subsection (2) below applies,

and in this Act "arrestable offence" means any such offence.

(2) The offences to which this subsection applies are—
- (a) offences for which a person may be arrested under the customs and excise Acts, as defined in section 1(1) of the Customs and Excise Management Act 1979;
- (b) offences under [the Official Secrets Act 1920] that are not arrestable offences by virtue of the term of imprisonment for which a person may be sentenced in respect of them;
- [(bb) offences under any provision of the Official Secrets Act 1989 except section 8(1), (4) or (5);]
- (c) offences under section ... , 22 (causing prostitution of women) or 23 (procuration of girl under 21) of the Sexual Offences Act 1956;
- (d) offences under section 12(1) (taking motor vehicle or other conveyance without authority etc.) or 25(1) (going equipped for stealing, etc.) of the Theft Act 1968; and
- [(e) any offence under the Football (Offences) Act 1991.]

(3) Without prejudice to section 2 of the Criminal Attempts Act 1981, the powers of summary arrest conferred by the following subsections shall also apply to the offences of—
- (a) conspiring to commit any of the offences mentioned in subsection (2) above;
- (b) attempting to commit any such offence [other than an offence under section 12(1) of the Theft Act 1968];
- (c) inciting, aiding, abetting, counselling or procuring the commission of any such offence;

and such offences are also arrestable offences for the purposes of this Act.

(4) Any person may arrest without a warrant—
   (a) anyone who is in the act of committing an arrestable offence;
   (b) anyone whom he has reasonable grounds for suspecting to be committing such an offence.

(5) Where an arrestable offence has been committed, any person may arrest without a warrant—
   (a) anyone who is guilty of the offence;
   (b) anyone whom he has reasonable grounds for suspecting to be guilty of it.

(6) Where a constable has reasonable grounds for suspecting that an arrestable offence has been committed, he may arrest without a warrant anyone whom he has reasonable grounds for suspecting to be guilty of the offence.

(7) A constable may arrest without a warrant—
   (a) anyone who is about to commit an arrestable offence;
   (b) anyone whom he has reasonable grounds for suspecting to be about to commit an arrestable offence.

[267]

NOTES

Commencement: 1 January 1986.

Sub-s (2): words in square brackets in sub-para (b) substituted, and sub-para (bb) added, by the Official Secrets Act 1989, s 11(1); in para (c) words omitted repealed by the Sexual Offences Act 1985, s 5(3), Schedule; original para (e) repealed by the Criminal Justice Act 1988, s 170(2), Sch 16; current para (e) added by the Football Offences Act 1991, s 5(1).

Sub-s (3): para (b) amended by the Criminal Justice Act 1988, s 170(1), Sch 15, paras 97, 98.

25 General arrest conditions

(1) Where a constable has reasonable grounds for suspecting that any offence which is not an arrestable offence has been committed or attempted, or is being committed or attempted, he may arrest the relevant person if it appears to him that service of a summons is impracticable or inappropriate because any of the general arrest conditions is satisfied.

(2) In this section "the relevant person" means any person whom the constable has reasonable grounds to suspect of having committed or having attempted to commit the offence or of being in the course of committing or attempting to commit it.

(3) The general arrest conditions are—
   (a) that the name of the relevant person is unknown to, and cannot be readily ascertained by, the constable;
   (b) that the constable has reasonable grounds for doubting whether a name furnished by the relevant person as his name is his real name;
   (c) that—
       (i) the relevant person has failed to furnish a satisfactory address for service; or
       (ii) the constable has reasonable grounds for doubting whether an address furnished by the relevant person is a satisfactory address for service;
   (d) that the constable has reasonable grounds for believing that arrest is necessary to prevent the relevant person—
       (i) causing physical injury to himself or any other person;
       (ii) suffering physical injury;
       (iii) causing loss of or damage to property;

(iv) committing an offence against public decency; or
(v) causing an unlawful obstruction of the highway;
(e) that the constable has reasonable grounds for believing that arrest is necessary to protect a child or other vulnerable person from the relevant person.

(4) For the purposes of subsection (3) above an address is a satisfactory address for service if it appears to the constable—
(a) that the relevant person will be at it for a sufficiently long period for it to be possible to serve him with a summons; or
(b) that some other person specified by the relevant person will accept service of a summons for the relevant person at it.

(5) Nothing in subsection (3)(d) above authorises the arrest of a person under subparagraph (iv) of that paragraph except where members of the public going about their normal business cannot reasonably be expected to avoid the person to be arrested.

(6) This section shall not prejudice any power of arrest conferred apart from this section.

NOTE
Commencement: 1 January 1986.

Part XI
Miscellaneous and Supplementary

120 Extent

(1) Subject to the following provisions of this section, this Act extends to England and Wales only.

NOTES
Commencement: 31 October 1984.
Sub-ss (2)-(11): outside the scope of this work.

122 Short title

This Act may be cited as the Police and Criminal Evidence Act 1984.

NOTE
Commencement: 31 October 1984.

COMPANIES ACT 1985

(C 6)

An Act to consolidate the greater part of the Companies Acts

[11 March 1985]

Part I
Formation and Registration of Companies; Juridical Status and Membership

Chapter I
Company Formation

Registration and its consequences

14 Effect of memorandum and articles

(1) Subject to the provisions of this Act, the memorandum and articles, when registered, bind the company and its members to the same extent as if they respectively had been signed and sealed by each member, and contained covenants on the part of each member to observe all the provisions of the memorandum and of the articles.

(2) Money payable by a member to the company under the memorandum or articles is a debt due from him to the company, and in England and Wales is of the nature of a specialty debt.

NOTES
Commencement: 1 July 1985.

Chapter III
A Company's Capacity; Formalities of Carrying on Business

[35 A company's capacity not limited by its memorandum

(1) The validity of an act done by a company shall not be called into question on the ground of lack of capacity by reason of anything in the company's memorandum.

(2) A member of a company may bring proceedings to restrain the doing of an act which but for subsection (1) would be beyond the company's capacity; but no such proceedings shall lie in respect of an act to be done in fulfilment of a legal obligation arising from a previous act of the company.

(3) It remains the duty of the directors to observe any limitations on their powers flowing from the company's memorandum; and action by the directors which but for subsection (1) would be beyond the company's capacity may only be ratified by the company by special resolution.

A resolution ratifying such action shall not affect any liability incurred by the directors or any other person; relief from any such liability must be agreed to separately by special resolution.

(4) The operation of this section is restricted by section 30B(1) of the Charities Act 1960 and section 112(3) of the Companies Act 1989 in relation to companies which are charities; and section 322A below (invalidity of certain transactions to which directors or their associates are parties) has effect notwithstanding this section.]

[272]

NOTES

Commencement: 4 February 1991.

Substituted with savings by the Companies Act 1989, s 108(1): for savings see SI 1990 / 2569, art 7(1).

[35A Power of directors to bind the company

(1) In favour of a person dealing with a company in good faith, the power of the board of directors to bind the company, or authorise others to do so, shall be deemed to be free of any limitation under the company's constitution.

(2) For this purpose—
  (a) a person "deals with" a company if he is a party to any transaction or other act to which the company is a party;
  (b) a person shall not be regarded as acting in bad faith by reason only of his knowing that an act is beyond the powers of the directors under the company's constitution; and
  (c) a person shall be presumed to have acted in good faith unless the contrary is proved.

(3) The references above to limitations on the directors' powers under the company's constitution include limitations deriving—
  (a) from a resolution of the company in general meeting or a meeting of any class of shareholders, or
  (b) from any agreement between the members of the company or of any class of shareholders.

(4) Subsection (1) does not affect any right of a member of the company to bring proceedings to restrain the doing of an act which is beyond the powers of the directors; but no such proceedings shall lie in respect of an act to be done in fulfilment of a legal obligation arising from a previous act of the company.

(5) Nor does that subsection affect any liability incurred by the directors, or any other person, by reason of the directors' exceeding their powers.

(6) The operation of this section is restricted by section 30B(1) of the Charities Act 1960 and section 112(3) of the Companies Act 1989 in relation to companies which are charities; and section 322A below (invalidity of certain transactions to which directors or their associates are parties) has effect notwithstanding this section.]

[273]

NOTES

Commencement: 4 February 1991.

Substituted with savings, together with new ss 35, 35B, for s 35 as originally enacted, by the Companies Act 1989, s 108: for savings see SI 1990/2569, art 7(2).

[35B No duty to enquire as to capacity of company or authority of directors

A party to a transaction with a company is not bound to enquire as to whether it is permitted by the company's memorandum or as to any limitation on the powers of the board of directors to bind the company or authorise others to do so.]

[274]

NOTES
Commencement: 4 February 1991.
Substituted, together with new ss 35, 35A, for s 35 as originally enacted, by the Companies Act 1989, s 108.

[36 Company contracts: England and Wales

Under the law of England and Wales a contract may be made—
- (a) by a company, by writing under its common seal, or
- (b) on behalf of a company, by any person acting under its authority, express or implied;

and any formalities required by law in the case of a contract made by an individual also apply, unless a contrary intention appears, to a contract made by or on behalf of a company.]

[275]

NOTES
Commencement: 31 July 1990.
Substituted by the Companies Act 1989, s 130(1).

[36A Execution of documents: England and Wales

(1) Under the law of England and Wales the following provisions have effect with respect to the execution of documents by a company.

(2) A document is executed by a company by the affixing of its common seal.

(3) A company need not have a common seal, however, and the following subsections apply whether it does or not.

(4) A document signed by a director and the secretary of a company, or by two directors of a company, and expressed (in whatever form of words) to be executed by the company has the same effect as if executed under the common seal of the company.

(5) A document executed by a company which makes it clear on its face that it is intended by the person or persons making it to be a deed has effect, upon delivery, as a deed; and it shall be presumed, unless a contrary intention is proved, to be delivered upon its being so executed.

(6) In favour of a purchaser a document shall be deemed to have been duly executed by a company if it purports to be signed by a director and the secretary of the company, or by two directors of the company, and, where it makes it clear on its face that

it is intended by the person or persons making it to be a deed, to have been delivered upon its being executed.

A "purchaser" means a purchaser in good faith for valuable consideration and includes a lessee, mortgagee or other person who for valuable consideration acquires an interest in property.]

[276]

NOTES
Commencement: 31 July 1990.
Added by the Companies Act 1989, s 130(2).

[36C Pre-incorporation contracts, deeds and obligations

(1) A contract which purports to be made by or on behalf of a company at a time when the company has not been formed has effect, subject to any agreement to the contrary, as one made with the person purporting to act for the company or as agent for it, and he is personally liable on the contract accordingly.

(2) Subsection (1) applies—
    (a) to the making of a deed under the law of England and Wales, and
    (b) ...,
as it applies to the making of a contract.]

[277]

NOTES
Commencement: 31 July 1990.
Added by the Companies Act 1989, s 130(4).
Sub-s (2)(b): applies to Scotland only.

LANDLORD AND TENANT ACT 1985

(C 70)

An Act to consolidate certain provisions of the law of landlord and tenant formerly found in the Housing Acts, together with the Landlord and Tenant Act 1962, with amendments to give effect to recommendations of the Law Commission.

[30 October 1985]

IMPLIED TERMS AS TO FITNESS FOR HUMAN HABITATION

8 Implied terms as to fitness for human habitation

(1) In a contract to which this section applies for the letting of a house for human habitation there is implied, notwithstanding any stipulation to the contrary—

(a) a condition that the house is fit for human habitation at the commencement of the tenancy, and
(b) an undertaking that the house will be kept by the landlord fit for human habitation during the tenancy.

(2) The landlord, or a person authorised by him in writing, may at reasonable times of the day, on giving 24 hours' notice in writing, to the tenant or occupier, enter premises to which this section applies for the purpose of viewing their state and condition.

(3)-(5)...

(6) In this section "house" includes—
(a) a part of a house, and
(b) any yard, garden, outhouses and appurtenances belonging to the house or usually enjoyed with it.

NOTES
Commencement: 1 April 1986.
Sub-ss (3)-(5): outside the scope of this work.

10 Fitness for human habitation

In determining for the purposes of this Act whether a house is unfit for human habitation, regard shall be had to its condition in respect of the following matters—
repair,
stability,
freedom from damp,
internal arrangement,
natural lighting,
ventilation,
water supply,
drainage and sanitary conveniences,
facilities for preparation and cooking of food and for the disposal of waste water;

and the house shall be regarded as unfit for human habitation if, and only if, it is so far defective in one or more of those matters that it is not reasonably suitable for occupation in that condition.

NOTES
Commencement: 1 April 1986.

Final Provisions

40 Short title, commencement and extent

(1) This Act may be cited as the Landlord and Tenant Act 1985.

(2) This Act comes into force on 1st April 1986.

(3) This Act extends to England and Wales.

NOTE
Commencement: 1 April 1986.

LATENT DAMAGE ACT 1986

(C 37)

An Act to amend the law about limitation of actions in relation to actions for damages for negligence not involving personal injuries; and to provide for a person taking an interest in property to have, in certain circumstances, a cause of action in respect of negligent damage to the property occurring before he takes that interest

[18 July 1986]

ACCRUAL OF CAUSE OF ACTION TO SUCCESSIVE OWNERS IN RESPECT OF LATENT DAMAGE TO PROPERTY

3 Accrual of cause of action to successive owners in respect of latent damage to property

(1) Subject to the following provisions of this section, where—
   (a) a cause of action ("the original cause of action") has accrued to any person in respect of any negligence to which damage to any property in which he has an interest is attributable (in whole or in part); and
   (b) another person acquires an interest in that property after the date on which the original cause of action accrued but before the material facts about the damage have become known to any person who, at the time when he first has knowledge of those facts, has any interest in the property;

a fresh cause of action in respect of that negligence shall accrue to that other person on the date on which he acquires his interest in the property.

(2) A cause of action accruing to any person by virtue of subsection (1) above—
   (a) shall be treated as if based on breach of a duty of care at common law owed to the person to whom it accrues; and
   (b) shall be treated for the purposes of section 14A of the 1980 Act (special time limit for negligence actions where facts relevant to cause of action are not known at date of accrual) as having accrued on the date on which the original cause of action accrued.

(3) Section 28 of the 1980 Act (extension of limitation period in case of disability) shall not apply in relation to any such cause of action.

(4) Subsection (1) above shall not apply in any case where the person acquiring an interest in the damaged property is either—
   (a) a person in whom the original cause of action vests by operation of law; or
   (b) a person in whom the interest in that property vests by virtue of any order made by a court under section 538 of the Companies Act 1985 (vesting of company property in liquidator).

(5) For the purposes of subsection (1)(b) above, the material facts about the dam-

age are such facts about the damage as would lead a reasonable person who has an interest in the damaged property at the time when those facts become known to him to consider it sufficiently serious to justify his instituting proceedings for damages against a defendant who did not dispute liability and was able to satisfy a judgment.

(6) For the purposes of this section a person's knowledge includes knowledge which he might reasonably have been expected to acquire—
  (a) from facts observable or ascertainable by him; or
  (b) from facts ascertainable by him with the help of appropriate expert advice which it is reasonable for him to seek;

but a person shall not be taken by virtue of this subsection to have knowledge of a fact ascertainable by him only with the help of expert advice so long as he has taken all reasonable steps to obtain (and, where appropriate, to act on) that advice.

(7) This section shall bind the Crown, but as regards the Crown's liability in tort shall not bind the Crown further than the Crown is made liable in tort by the Crown Proceedings Act 1947.

NOTES
Commencement: 18 September 1986.
The 1980 Act: Limitation Act 1980.

SUPPLEMENTARY

5 Citation, interpretation, commencement and extent

(1) This Act may be cited as the Latent Damage Act 1986.

(2) In this Act—
  "the 1980 Act" has the meaning given by section 1; and
  "action" includes any proceeding in a court of law, an arbitration and any new claim within the meaning of section 35 of the 1980 Act (new claims in pending actions).

(3) This Act shall come into force at the end of the period of two months beginning with the date on which it is passed.

(4) This Act extends to England and Wales only.

NOTES
Commencement: 18 September 1986.

FINANCIAL SERVICES ACT 1986

(C 60)

An Act to regulate the carrying on of investment business; to make related to provision with respect to insurance business and business carried on by friendly societies; to make new provision with respect to the official listing of securities, offers of unlisted securities, takeover offers and insider dealing; to make provision as to the disclosure of information obtained under enactments relating to fair trading, banking, companies and insurance; to make provision for securing reciprocity with other countries in respect of facilities for the provision of financial services; and for connected purposes

[7 November 1986]

PART V
OFFERS OF UNLISTED SECURITIES

162 Form and content of prospectus

(1) A prospectus shall contain such information and comply with such other requirements as may be prescribed by rules made by the Secretary of State for the purposes of this section.

(2) Rules under this section may make provision whereby compliance with any requirements imposed by or under the law of a country or territory outside the United Kingdom is treated as compliance with any requirements of the rules.

(3) If it appears to the Secretary of State that an approved exchange has rules in respect of prospectuses relating to securities dealt in on the exchange, and practices in exercising any powers conferred by the rules, which provide investors with protection at least equivalent to that provided by rules under this section he may direct that any such prospectus shall be subject to the rules of the exchange instead of the rules made under this section.

[283]

NOTES

Commencement: 29 April 1988 (so far as necessary to enable the Secretary of State to make rules under this section and so far as necessary for the purposes of s 169); to be appointed (remaining purposes).

Functions of the Secretary of State transferred to the Treasury, by the Transfer of Functions (Financial Services) Order 1992, SI 1992/1315, art 2(1)(b).

This Act extends to Northern Ireland.

163 General duty of disclosure in prospectus

(1) In addition to the information required to be included in a prospectus by virtue of rules applying to it by virtue of section 162 above a prospectus shall contain all such information as investors and their professional advisers would reasonably require, and reasonably expect to find there, for the purpose of making an informed assessment of—

    (a) the assets and liabilities, financial position, profits and losses, and prospects of the issuer of the securities; and

    (b) the rights attaching to those securities.

(2) The information to be included by virtue of this section shall be such information as is mentioned in subsection (1) above which is within the knowledge of any person responsible for the prospectus or which it would be reasonable for him to obtain by making enquiries.

(3) In determining what information is required to be included in a prospectus by virtue of this section regard shall be had—

    (a) to the nature of the securities and of the issuer of the securities;

    (b) to the nature of the persons likely to consider their acquisition;

(c) to the fact that certain matters may reasonably be expected to be within the knowledge of professional advisers of any kind which those persons may reasonably be expected to consult; and

(d) to any information available to investors or their professional advisers by virtue of any enactment or by virtue of requirements imposed by a recognised investment exchange for the purpose of complying with paragraph 2(2)(b) of Schedule 4 to this Act.

[284]

NOTES
Commencement: To be appointed.
This Act extends to Northern Ireland.

166 Compensation for false or misleading prospectus

(1) Subject to section 167 below, the person or persons responsible for a prospectus or supplementary prospectus shall be liable to pay compensation to any person who has acquired the securities to which the prospectus relates and suffered loss in respect of them as a result of any untrue or misleading statement in the prospectus of the omission from it of any matter required to be included by section 163 or 164 above.

(2) Where rules applicable to a prospectus by virtue of section 162 above require it to include information as to any particular matter on the basis that the prospectus must include a statement either as to that matter or, if such is the case, that there is no such matter, the omission from the prospectus of the information shall be treated for the purposes of subsection (1) above as a statement that there is no such matter.

(3) Subject to section 167 below, a person who fails to comply with section 164 above shall be liable to pay compensation to any person who has acquired any of the securities in question and suffered loss in respect of them as a result of the failure.

(4) This section does not affect any liability which any person may incur apart from this section.

(5) References in this section to the acquisition by any person of securities include references to his contracting to acquire them or an interest in them.

[285]

NOTES
Commencement: To be appointed.
This Act extends to Northern Ireland.

167 Exemption from liability to pay compensation

(1) A person shall not incur any liability under section 166(1) above for any loss in respect of securities caused by any such statement or omission as is there mentioned if he satisfies the court that at the time when the prospectus or supplementary prospectus was delivered for registration he reasonably believed, having made such enquiries (if any) as were reasonable, that the statement was true and not misleading or that the matter whose omission caused the loss was properly omitted and—

(a) that he continued in that belief until the time when the securities were acquired; or

(b) that they were acquired before it was reasonably practicable to bring a correction to the attention of persons likely to acquire the securities in question; or

(c) that before the securities were acquired he had taken all such steps as it was reasonable for him to have taken to secure that a correction was forthwith brought to the attention of those persons; or

(d) that the securities were acquired after such a lapse of time that he ought in the circumstances to be reasonably excused;

but paragraph (d) above does not apply where the securities are dealt in on an approved exchange unless he satisfies the court that he continued in that belief until after the commencement of dealings in the securities on that exchange.

(2) A person shall not incur any liability under section 166(1) above for any loss in respect of securities caused by a statement purporting to be made by or on the authority of another person as an expert which is, and is stated to be, included in the prospectus or supplementary prospectus with that other person's consent if he satisfies the court that at the time when the prospectus or supplementary prospectus was delivered for registration be believed on reasonable grounds that the other person was competent to make or authorise the statement and had consented to its inclusion in the form and context in which it was included and—

(a) that he continued in that belief until the time when the securities were acquired; or

(b) that they were acquired before it was reasonably practicable to bring the fact that the expert was not competent or had not consented to the attention of persons likely to acquire the securities in question; or

(c) that before the securities were acquired he had taken all such steps as it was reasonable for him to have taken to secure that that fact was forthwith brought to the attention of those persons; or

(d) that the securities were acquired after such a lapse of time that he ought in the circumstances to be reasonably excused;

but paragraph (d) above does not apply where the securities are dealt in on an approved exchange unless he satisfies the court that he continued in that belief until after the commencement of dealings in the securities on that exchange.

(3) Without prejudice to subsections (1) and (2) above, a person shall not incur any liability under section 166(1) above for any loss in respect of any securities caused by any such statement or omission as is there mentioned if he satisfies the court—

(a) that before the securities were acquired a correction or, where the statement was such as it mentioned in subsection (2) above the fact that the expert was not competent or had not consented had been published in a manner calculated to bring it to the attention of persons likely to acquire the securities in question; or

(b) that he took all such steps as it was reasonable for him to take to secure such publication and reasonably believed that it had taken place before the securities were acquired.

(4) A person shall not incur any liability under section 166(1) above for any loss resulting from a statement made by an official person or contained in a public official document which is included in the prospectus or supplementary prospectus if he satisfies the court that the statement is accurately and fairly reproduced.

(5) A person shall not incur any liability under section 166(1) or (3) above if he satisfies the court that the person suffering the loss acquired the securities in question with knowledge that the statement was false or misleading, of the omitted matter or of the change or new matter, as the case may be.

(6) A person shall not incur any liability under section 166(3) above if he satisfies the court that he reasonably believed that the change or new matter in question was not such as to call for a supplementary prospectus.

(7) In this section "expert" includes any engineer, valuer, accountant or other person whose profession, qualifications or experience give authority to a statement made by him; and references to the acquisition of securities include references to contracting to acquire them or an interest in them.

[286]

NOTES
Commencement: To be appointed.
This Act extends to Northern Ireland.

Part X
Miscellaneous and Supplementary

212 Short title, consequential amendments and repeals

(1) This Act may be cited as the Financial Services Act 1986.

(2) The enactments and instruments mentioned in Schedule 16 to this Act shall have effect with the amendments there specified, being amendments consequential on the provisions of this Act.

(3) The enactments mentioned in Part I of Schedule 17 to this Act and the instruments mentioned in Part II of that Schedule are hereby repealed or revoked to the extent specified in the third column of those Parts.

[287]

NOTES
Commencement: 1 May 1989 (certain purposes); 1 October 1989 (certain purposes); to be appointed (remaining purposes).
This Act extends to Northern Ireland.

MINORS' CONTRACTS ACT 1987

(C 13)

An Act to amend the law relating to minors' contracts

[9 April 1987]

2 Guarantees

Where—
    (a) a guarantee is given in respect of an obligation of a party to a contract made after the commencement of this Act, and
    (b) the obligation is unenforceable against him (or he repudiates the contract) because he was a minor when the contract was made,

the guarantee shall not for that reason alone be unenforceable against the guarantor.

[288]

3 Restitution

(1) Where—
 (a) a person ("the plaintiff") has after the commencement of this Act entered into a contract with another ("the defendant"), and
 (b) the contract is unenforceable against the defendant (or he repudiates it) because he was a minor when the contract was made,

the court may, if it is just and equitable to do so, require the defendant to transfer to the plaintiff any property acquired by the defendant under the contract, or any property representing it.

(2) Nothing in this section shall be taken to prejudice any other remedy available to the plaintiff.

NOTE
Commencement: 9 June 1987.

5 Short title, commencement and extent

(1) This Act may be cited as the Minors' Contracts Act 1987.

(2) This Act shall come into force at the end of the period of two months beginning with the date on which it is passed.

(3) This Act extends to England and Wales only.

NOTE
Commencement: 9 June 1987.

CONSUMER PROTECTION ACT 1987

(C 43)

An Act to make provision with respect to the liability of persons for damage caused by defective products; to consolidate with amendments the Consumer Safety Act 1978 and the Consumer Safety (Amendment) Act 1986; to make provision with respect to the giving of price indications; to amend Part I of the Health and Safety at Work etc. Act 1974 and sections 31 and 80 of the Explosives Act 1875; to repeal the Trade Descriptions Act 1972 and the Fabrics (Misdescription) Act 1913; and for connected purposes

[15 May 1987]

Part I
Product Liability

1 Purpose and construction of Part I

(1) This Part shall have effect for the purpose of making such provision as is necessary in order to comply with the product liability Directive and shall be construed accordingly.

(2) In this Part, except in so far as the context otherwise requires—

"agricultural produce" means any produce of the soil, of stock-farming or of fisheries;

"dependant" and "relative" have the same meanings as they have in, respectively, the Fatal Accidents Act 1976 and the Damages (Scotland) Act 1976;

"producer", in relation to a product, means—
   (a) the person who manufactured it;
   (b) in the case of a substance which has not been manufactured but has been won or abstracted, the person who won or abstracted it;
   (c) in the case of a product which has not been manufactured, won or abstracted but essential characteristics of which are attributable to an industrial or other process having been carried out (for example, in relation to agricultural produce), the person who carried out that process;

"product" means any goods or electricity and (subject to subsection (3) below) includes a product which is comprised in another product, whether by virtue of being a component part or raw material or otherwise; and

"the product liability Directive" means the Directive of the Council of the European Communities, dated 25th July 1985, (No. 85/374/EEC) on the approximation of the laws, regulations and administrative provisions of the member States concerning liability for defective products.

(3) For the purposes of this Part a person who supplies any product in which products are comprised, whether by virtue of being component parts or raw materials or otherwise, shall not be treated by reason only of his supply of that product as supplying any of the products so comprised.

[291]

NOTE
Commencement: 1 March 1988.

2 Liability for defective products

(1) Subject to the following provisions of this Part, where any damage is caused wholly or partly by a defect in a product, every person to whom subsection (2) below applies shall be liable for the damage.

(2) This subsection applies to—
   (a) the producer of the product;
   (b) any person who, by putting his name on the product or using a trade mark or other distinguishing mark in relation to the product, has held himself out to be the producer of the product;
   (c) any person who has imported the product into a member State from a place outside the member States in order, in the course of any business of his, to supply it to another.

(3) Subject as aforesaid, where any damage is caused wholly or partly by a defect in a product, any person who supplied the product (whether to the person who suffered the damage, to the producer of any product in which the product in question is comprised or to any other person) shall be liable for the damage if—
   (a) the person who suffered the damage requests the supplier to identify one or more of the persons (whether still in existence or not) to whom subsection (2) above applies in relation to the product;

(b) that request is made within a reasonable period after the damage occurs and at a time when it is not reasonably practicable for the person making the request to identify all those persons; and

(c) the supplier fails, within a reasonable period after receiving the request, either to comply with the request or to identify the person who supplied the product to him.

(4) Neither subsection (2) nor subsection (3) above shall apply to a person in respect of any defect in any game or agricultural produce if the only supply of the game or produce by that person to another was at a time when it had not undergone an industrial process.

(5) Where two or more persons are liable by virtue of this Part for the such damage, their liability shall be joint and several.

(6) This section shall be without prejudice to any liability arising otherwise than by virtue of this Part.

[292]

NOTE
Commencement: 1 March 1988.

3 Meaning of "defect"

(1) Subject to the following provisions of this section, there is a defect in a product for the purposes of this Part if the safety of the product is not such as persons generally are entitled to expect; and for those purposes "safety", in relation to a product, shall include safety with respect to products comprised in that product and safety in the context of risks of damage to property, as well as in the context of risks of death or personal injury.

(2) In determining for the purposes of subsection (1) above what persons generally are entitled to expect in relation to a product all the circumstances shall be taken into account, including—

(a) the manner in which, and purposes for which, the product has been marketed, its get-up, the use of any mark in relation to the product and any instructions for, or warnings with respect to, doing or refraining from doing anything with or in relation to the product;

(b) what might reasonably be expected to be done with or in relation to the product; and

(c) the time when the product was supplied by its producer to another;

and nothing in this section shall require a defect to be inferred from the fact alone that the safety of a product which is supplied after that time is greater than the safety of the product in question.

[293]

NOTE
Commencement: 1 March 1988.

4 Defences

(1) In any civil proceedings by virtue of this Part against any person ("the person proceeded against") in respect of a defect in a product it shall be a defence for him to show—

(a) that the defect is attributable to compliance with any requirement imposed by or under any enactment or with any Community obligation; or
(b) that the person proceeded against did not at any time supply the product to another, or
(c) that the following conditions are satisfied, that is to say—
   (i) that the only supply of the product to another by the person proceeded against was otherwise than in the course of a business of that person's; and
   (ii) that section 2(2) above does not apply to that person or applies to him by virtue only of things done otherwise than with a view to profit; or
(d) that the defect did not exist in the product at the relevant time; or
(e) that the state of scientific and technical knowledge at the relevant time was not such that a producer of products of the same description as the product in question might be expected to have discovered the defect if it had existed in his products while they were under his control; or
(f) that the defect—
   (i) constituted a defect in a product ("the subsequent product") in which the product in question had been comprised; and
   (ii) was wholly attributable to the design of the subsequent product or to compliance by the producer of the product in question with instructions given by the producer of the subsequent product.

(2) In this section "the relevant time", in relation to electricity, means the time at which it was generated, being a time before it was transmitted or distributed, and in relation to any other product, means—
   (a) if the person proceeded against is a person to whom subsection (2) of section 2 above applies in relation to the product, the time when he supplied the product to another;
   (b) if that subsection does not apply to that person in relation to the product, the time when the product was last supplied by a person to whom that subsection does apply in relation to the product.

[294]

NOTE
Commencement: 1 March 1988.

5 Damage giving rise to liability

(1) Subject to the following provisions of this section, in this Part "damage" means death or personal injury or any loss of or damage to any property (including land).

(2) A person shall not be liable under section 2 above in respect of any defect in a product for the loss of or any damage to the product itself or for the loss of or any damage to the whole or any part of any product which has been supplied with the product in question comprised in it.

(3) A person shall not be liable under section 2 above for any loss of or damage to any property which, at the time it is lost or damaged, is not—
   (a) of a description of property ordinarily intended for private use, occupation or consumption; and
   (b) intended by the person suffering the loss or damage mainly for his own private use, occupation or consumption.

(4) No damages shall be awarded to any person by virtue of this Part in respect of

any loss of or damage to any property if the amount which would fall to be so awarded to that person, apart from this subsection and any liability for interest, does not exceed £275.

(5) In determining for the purposes of this Part who has suffered any loss of or damage to property and when any such loss or damage occurred, the loss or damage shall be regarded as having occurred at the earliest time at which a person with an interest in the property had knowledge of the material facts about the loss or damage.

(6) For the purposes of subsections (5) above the material facts about any loss of or damage to any property are such facts about the loss or damage as would lead a reasonable person with an interest in the property to consider the loss or damage sufficiently serious to justify his instituting proceedings for damages against a defendant who did not dispute liability and was able to satisfy a judgment.

(7) For the purposes of subsection (5) above a person's knowledge includes knowledge which he might reasonably have been expected to acquire—
    (a) from facts observable or ascertainable by him; or
    (b) from facts ascertainable by him with the help of appropriate expert advice which it is reasonable for him to seek;

but a person shall not be taken by virtue of this subsection to have knowledge of a fact ascertainable by him only with the help of expert advice unless he has failed to take all reasonable steps to obtain (and, where appropriate, to act on) that advice.

(8) Subsections (5) to (7) above shall not extend to Scotland.

[295]

NOTE
Commencement: 1 March 1988.

6 Application of certain enactments etc

(1) Any damage for which a person is liable under section 2 above shall be deemed to have been caused—
    (a) for the purposes of the Fatal Accidents Act 1976, by that person's wrongful act, neglect or default;
    (b) for the purposes of section 3 of the Law Reform (Miscellaneous Provisions) (Scotland) Act 1940 (contribution among joint wrongdoers), by that person's wrongful act or negligent act or omission;
    (c) for the purposes of section 1 of the Damages (Scotland) Act 1976 (rights of relatives of a deceased), by that person's act or omission; and
    (d) for the purposes of Part II of the Administration of Justice Act 1982 (damages for personal injuries, etc. - Scotland), by an act or omission giving rise to liability in that person to pay damages.

(2) Where—
    (a) a person's death is caused wholly or partly by a defect in a product, or a person dies after suffering damage which has been so caused;
    (b) a request such as mentioned in paragraph (a) of subsection (3) of section 2 above is made to a supplier of the product by that person's personal representatives or, in the case of a person whose death is caused wholly or partly by the defect, by any dependant or relative of that person; and
    (c) the conditions specified in paragraphs (b) and (c) of that subsection are satisfied in relation to that request,

this Part shall have effect for the purposes of the Law Reform (Miscellaneous Provisions) Act 1934, the Fatal Accidents Act 1976 and the Damages (Scotland) Act 1976 as if liability of the supplier to that person under that subsection did not depend on that person having requested the supplier to identify certain persons or on the said conditions having been satisfied in relation to a request made by that person.

(3) Section 1 of the Congenital Disabilities (Civil Liability) Act 1976 shall have effect for the purposes of this Part as if—
   (a) a person were answerable to a child in respect of an occurrence caused wholly or partly by a defect in a product if he is or has been liable under section 2 above in respect of any effect of the occurrence on a parent of the child, or would be so liable if the occurrence caused a parent of the child to suffer damage;
   (b) the provisions of this Part relating to liability under section 2 above applied in relation to liability by virtue of paragraph (a) above under the said section 1; and
   (c) subsection (6) of the said section 1 (exclusion of liability) were omitted.

(4) Where any damage is caused partly by a defect in a product and partly by the fault of the person suffering the damage, the Law Reform (Contributory Negligence) Act 1945 and section 5 of the Fatal Accidents Act 1976 (contributory negligence) shall have effect as if the defect were the fault of every person liable by virtue of this Part for the damage caused by the defect.

(5) In subsection (4) above "fault" has the same meaning as in the said Act of 1945.

(6) Schedule 1 to this Act shall have effect for the purpose of amending the Limitation Act 1980 and the Prescription and Limitation (Scotland) Act 1973 in their application in relation to the bringing of actions by virtue of this Part.

(7) It is hereby declared that liability by virtue of this Part is to be treated as liability in tort for the purposes of any enactment conferring jurisdiction on any court with respect to any matter.

(8) Nothing in this Part shall prejudice the operation of section 12 of the Nuclear Installations Act 1965 (rights to compensation for certain breaches of duties confined to rights under that Act).

[296]

NOTE
Commencement: 1 March 1988.

7 Prohibition on exclusions from liability

The liability of a person by virtue of this Part to a person who has suffered damage caused wholly or partly by a defect in a product, or to a dependant or relative of such a person, shall not be limited or excluded by any contract term, by any notice or by any other provision.

[297]

NOTE
Commencement: 1 March 1988.

8 Power to modify Part I

(1) Her Majesty may by Order in Council make such modifications of this Part and of any other enactment (including an enactment contained in the following Parts of this Act, or in an Act passed after this Act) as appear to Her Majesty in Council to be necessary or expedient in consequence of any modification of the product liability Directive which is made at any time after the passing of this Act.

(2) An Order in Council under subsection (1) above shall not be submitted to Her Majesty in Council unless a draft of the Order has been laid before, and approved by a resolution of, each House of Parliament.

[298]

NOTE
Commencement: 1 March 1988.

9 Application of Part I to Crown

(1) Subject to subsection (2) below, this Part shall bind the Crown.

(2) The Crown shall not, as regards the Crown's liability by virtue of this Part, be bound by this Part further than the Crown is made liable in tort or in reparation under the Crown Proceedings Act 1947, as that Act has effect from time to time.

[299]

NOTE
Commencement: 1 March 1988.

Part II
Consumer Safety

10 The general safety requirement

(1) A person shall be guilty of an offence if he—
   (a) supplies any consumer goods which fail to comply with the general safety requirement;
   (b) offers or agrees to supply any such goods; or
   (c) exposes or possesses any such goods for supply.

(2) For the purposes of this section consumer goods fail to comply with the general safety requirement if they are not reasonably safe having regard to all the circumstances, including—
   (a) the manner in which, and purposes for which, the goods are being or would be marketed, the get-up of the goods, the use of any mark in relation to the goods and any instructions or warnings which are given or would be given with respect to the keeping, use or consumption of the goods;
   (b) any standards of safety published by any person either for goods of a description which applies to the goods in question or for matters relating to goods of that description; and
   (c) the existence of any means by which it would have been reasonable (taking into account the cost, likelihood and extent of any improvement) for the goods to have been made safer.

(3) For the purposes of this section consumer goods shall not be regarded as failing to comply with the general safety requirement in respect of—

(a) anything which is shown to be attributable to compliance with any requirement imposed by or under any enactment or with any Community obligation;

(b) any failure to do more in relation to any matter than is required by—
  (i) any safety regulations imposing requirements with respect to that matter;
  (ii) any standards of safety approved for the purposes of this subsection by or under any such regulations and imposing requirements with respect to that matter;
  (iii) any provision of any enactment or subordinate legislation imposing such requirements with respect to that matter as are designated for the purposes of this subsection by any such regulations.

(4) In any proceedings against any person for an offence under this section in respect of any goods it shall be a defence for that person to show—
  (a) that he reasonably believed that the goods would not be used or consumed in the United Kingdom; or
  (b) that the following conditions are satisfied, that is to say—
    (i) that he supplied the goods, offered or agreed to supply them or, as the case may be, exposed or possessed them for supply in the course of carrying on a retail business; and
    (ii) that, at the time he supplied the goods or offered or agreed to supply them or exposed or possessed them for supply, he neither knew nor had reasonable grounds for believing that the goods failed to comply with the general safety requirement; or
  (c) that the terms on which he supplied the goods or agreed or offered to supply them or, in the case of goods which he exposed or possessed for supply, the terms on which he intended to supply them—
    (i) indicated that the goods were not supplied or to be supplied as new goods; and
    (ii) provided for, or contemplated, the acquisition of an interest in the goods by the persons supplied or to be supplied.

(5) For the purposes of subsection (4)(b) above goods are supplied in the course of carrying on a retail business if—
  (a) whether or not they are themselves acquired for a person's private use or consumption, they are supplied in the course of carrying on a business of making a supply of consumer goods available to persons who generally acquire them for private use or consumption; and
  (b) the descriptions of goods the supply of which is made available in the course of that business do not, to a significant extent, include manufactured or imported goods which have not previously been supplied in the United Kingdom.

(6) A person guilty of an offence under this section shall be liable on summary conviction to imprisonment for a term not exceeding six months or to a fine not exceeding level 5 on the standard scale or to both.

(7) In this section "consumer goods" means any goods which are ordinarily intended for private use or consumption, not being—
  (a) growing crops or things comprised in land by virtue of being attached to it;
  (b) water, food, feeding stuff or fertiliser;
  (c) gas which is, is to be or has been supplied by a person authorised to supply it by or under section 6, 7 or 8 of the Gas Act 1986 (authorisation of supply

of gas through pipes);
- (d) aircraft (other than hang-gliders) or motor vehicles;
- (e) controlled drugs or licensed medicinal products;
- (f) tobacco.

[300]

NOTE
Commencement: 1 October 1987.

11 Safety regulations

(1) The Secretary of State may by regulations under this section ("safety regulations") make such provision as he considers appropriate for the purposes of section 10(3) above and for the purpose of securing—
- (a) that goods to which this section applies are safe;
- (b) that goods to which this section applies which are unsafe, or would be unsafe in the hands of persons of a particular description, are not made available to persons generally or, as the case may be, to persons of that description; and
- (c) that appropriate information is, and inappropriate information is not, provided in relation to goods to which this section applies.

(2) Without prejudice to the generality of subsection (1) above, safety regulations may contain provision—
- (a) with respect to the composition or contents, design, construction, finish or packing of goods to which this section applies, with respect to standards for such goods and with respect to other matters relating to such goods;
- (b) with respect to the giving, refusal, alteration or cancellation of approvals of such goods, of descriptions of such goods or of standards for such goods;
- (c) with respect to the conditions that may be attached to any approval given under the regulations;
- (d) for requiring such fees as may be determined by or under the regulations to be paid on the giving or alteration of any approval under the regulations and on the making of an application for such an approval or alteration;
- (e) with respect to appeals against refusals, alterations and cancellations of approvals given under the regulations and against the conditions contained in such approvals;
- (f) for requiring goods to which this section applies to be approved under the regulations or to conform to the requirements of the regulations or to descriptions or standards specified in or approved by or under the regulations;
- (g) with respect to the testing or inspection of goods to which this section applies (including provision for determining the standards to be applied in carrying out any test or inspection);
- (h) with respect to the ways of dealing with goods of which some or all do not satisfy a test required by or under the regulations or a standard connected with a procedure so required;
- (i) for requiring a mark, warning or instruction or any other information relating to goods to be put on or to accompany the goods or to be used or provided in some other manner in relation to the goods, and for securing that inappropriate information is not given in relation to goods either by means of misleading marks or otherwise;
- (j) for prohibiting persons from supplying, or from offering to supply, agreeing to supply, exposing for supply or possessing for supply, goods to which this section applies and component parts and raw materials for such goods;

(k) for requiring information to be given to any such person as may be determined by or under the regulations for the purpose of enabling that person to exercise any function conferred on him by the regulations.

(3) Without prejudice as aforesaid, safety regulations may contain provision—
   (a) for requiring persons on whom functions are conferred by or under section 27 below to have regard, in exercising their functions so far as relating to any provision of safety regulations, to matters specified in a direction issued by the Secretary of State with respect to that provision;
   (b) for securing that a person shall not be guilty of an offence under section 12 below unless it is shown that the goods in question do not conform to a particular standard;
   (c) for securing that proceedings for such an offence are not brought in England and Wales except by or with the consent of the Secretary of State or the Director of Public Prosecutions;
   (d) for securing that proceedings for such an offence are not brought in Northern Ireland except by or with the consent of the Secretary of State or the Director of Public Prosecutions for Northern Ireland;
   (e) for enabling a magistrates' court in England and Wales or Northern Ireland to try an information or, in Northern Ireland, a complaint in respect of such an offence if the information was laid or the complaint made within twelve months from the time when the offence was committed;
   (f) for enabling summary proceedings for such an offence to be brought in Scotland at any time within twelve months from the time when the offence was committed; and
   (g) for determining the persons by whom, and the manner in which, anything required to be done by or under the regulations is to be done.

(4) Safety regulations shall not provide for any contravention of the regulations to be an offence.

(5) Where the Secretary of State proposes to make safety regulations it shall be his duty before he makes them—
   (a) to consult such organisations as appear to him to be representative of interests substantially affected by the proposal;
   (b) to consult such other persons as he considers appropriate; and
   (c) in the case of proposed regulations relating to goods suitable for use at work, to consult the Health and Safety Commission in relation to the application of the proposed regulations to Great Britain;

but the preceding provisions of this subsection shall not to apply in the case of regulations which provide for the regulations to cease to have effect at the end of a period of not more than twelve months beginning with the day on which they come into force and which contain a statement that it appears to the Secretary of State that the need to protect the public requires that the regulations should be made without delay.

(6) The power to make safety regulations shall be exercisable by statutory instrument subject to annulment in pursuance of a resolution of either House of Parliament and shall include power—
   (a) to make different provision for different cases; and
   (b) to make such supplemental, consequential and transitional provision as the Secretary of State considers appropriate.

(7) This section applies to any goods other than—
   (a) growing crops and things comprised in land by virtue of being attached to it;

(b) water, food, feeding stuff and fertiliser;
(c) gas which is, is to be or has been supplied by a person authorised to supply it by or under section 6, 7 or 8 of the Gas Act 1986 (authorisation of supply of gas through pipes);
(d) controlled drugs and licensed medicinal products.

[301]

NOTE
Commencement: 1 October 1987.

12 Offences against the safety regulations

(1) Where safety regulations prohibit a person from supplying or offering or agreeing to supply any goods or from exposing or possessing any goods for supply, that person shall be guilty of an offence if he contravenes the prohibition.

(2) Where safety regulations require a person who makes or processes any goods in the course of carrying on a business—
(a) to carry out a particular test or use a particular procedure in connection with the making or processing of the goods with a view to ascertaining whether the goods satisfy any requirements of such regulations; or
(b) to deal or not to deal in a particular way with a quantity of the goods of which the whole or part does not satisfy such a test or does not satisfy standards connected with such a procedure,

that person shall be guilty of an offence if he does not comply with the requirement.

(3) If a person contravenes a provision of safety regulations which prohibits or requires the provision, by means of a mark or otherwise, of information of a particular kind in relation to goods, he shall be guilty of an offence.

(4) Where safety regulations require any person to give information to another for the purpose of enabling that other to exercise any function, that person shall be guilty of an offence if—
(a) he fails without reasonable cause to comply with the requirement; or
(b) in giving the information which is required of him—
(i) he makes any statement which he knows is false in a material particular; or
(ii) he recklessly makes any statement which is false in a material particular.

(5) A person guilty of an offence under this section shall be liable on summary conviction to imprisonment for a term not exceeding six months or to a fine not exceeding level 5 on the standard scale or to both.

[302]

NOTE
Commencement: 1 October 1987.

13 Prohibition notices and notices to warn

(1) The Secretary of State may—
(a) serve on any person a notice ("a prohibition notice") prohibiting that person, except with the consent of the Secretary of State, from supplying, or from offering to supply, agreeing to supply, exposing for supply or possess-

ing for supply, any relevant goods which the Secretary of State considers are unsafe and which are described in the notice;

(b) serve on any person a notice ("a notice to warn") requiring that person at his own expense to publish, in a form and manner and on occasions specified in the notice, a warning about any relevant goods which the Secretary of State considers are unsafe, which that person supplies or has supplied and which are described in the notice.

(2) Schedule 2 to this Act shall have effect with respect to prohibition notices and notices to warn; and the Secretary of State may by regulations make provision specifying the manner in which information is to be given to any person under that Schedule.

(3) A consent given by the Secretary of State for the purposes of a prohibition notice may impose such conditions on the doing of anything for which the consent is required as the Secretary of State considers appropriate.

(4) A person who contravenes a prohibition notice or a notice to warn shall be guilty of an offence and liable on summary conviction to imprisonment for a term not exceeding six months or to a fine not exceeding level 5 on the standard scale or to both.

(5) The power to make regulations under subsection (2) above shall be exercisable by statutory instrument subject to annulment in pursuance of a resolution of either House of Parliament and shall include power—
   (a) to make different provision for different cases; and
   (b) to make such supplemental, consequential and transitional provision as the Secretary of State considers appropriate.

(6) In this section "relevant goods" means—
   (a) in relation to a prohibition notice, any goods to which section 11 above applies; and
   (b) in relation to a notice to warn, any goods to which that section applies or any growing crops or things comprised in land by virtue of being attached to it.

[303]

NOTE
Commencement: 1 October 1987.

14 Suspension notices

(1) Where an enforcement authority has reasonable grounds for suspecting that any safety provision has been contravened in relation to any goods, the authority may serve a notice ("a suspension notice") prohibiting the person on whom it is served, for such period ending not more than six months after the date of the notice as is specified therein, from doing any of the following things without the consent of the authority, that is to say, supplying the goods, offering to supply them, agreeing to supply them, agreeing to supply them or exposing them for supply.

(2) A suspension notice served by an enforcement authority in respect of any goods shall—
   (a) describe the goods in a manner sufficient to identify them;
   (b) set out the grounds on which the authority suspects that a safety provision has been contravened in relation to the goods; and
   (c) state that, and the manner in which, the person on whom the notice is served may appeal against the notice under section 15 below.

(3) A suspension notice served by an enforcement authority for the purpose of prohibiting a person for any period from doing the things mentioned in subsection (1) above in relation to any goods may also require that person to keep the authority informed of the whereabouts throughout that period of any of those goods in which he has an interest.

(4) Where a suspension notice has been served on any person in respect of any goods, no further such notice shall be served on that person in respect of the same goods unless—
- (a) proceedings against that person for an offence in respect of a contravention in relation to the goods of a safety provision (not being an offence under this section); or
- (b) proceedings for the forfeiture of the goods under section 16 or 17 below,

are pending at the end of the period suspended in the first-mentioned notice.

(5) A consent given by an enforcement authority for the purposes of subsection (1) above may impose such conditions on the doing of anything for which the consent is required as the authority considers appropriate.

(6) Any person who contravenes a suspension notice shall be guilty of an offence and liable on summary conviction to imprisonment for a term not exceeding six months or to a fine not exceeding level 5 on the standard scale or to both.

(7) Where an enforcement authority serves a suspension notice in respect of any goods, the authority shall be liable to pay compensation to any person having an interest in the goods in respect of any loss or damage caused by reason of the service of the notice if—
- (a) there has been no contravention in relation to the goods of any safety provision; and
- (b) the exercise of the power is not attributable to any neglect or default by that person.

(8) Any disputed question as to the right to or the amount of any compensation payable under this section shall be determined by arbitration or, in Scotland, by a single arbiter appointed, failing agreement between the parties, by the sheriff.

[304]

NOTES
Commencement: 1 October 1987.

15 Appeals against suspension notices

(1) Any person having an interest in any goods in respect of which a suspension notice is for the time being in force may apply for an order setting aside the notice.

(2) An application under this section may be made—
- (a) to any magistrates' court in which proceedings have been brought in England and Wales or Northern Ireland—
  - (i) for an offence in respect of a contravention in relation to the goods of any safety provision; or
  - (ii) for the forfeiture of the goods under section 16 below;
- (b) where no such proceedings have been so brought, by way of complaint to a magistrates' court; or
- (c) in Scotland, by summary application to the sheriff.

(3) On an application under this section to a magistrates' court in England and Wales or Northern Ireland the court shall make an order setting aside the suspension notice

only if the court is satisfied that there has been no contravention in relation to the goods of any safety provision.

(4) On an application under this section to the sheriff he shall make an order setting aside the suspension notice only if he is satisfied that at the date of making the order—
   (a) proceedings for any offence in respect of a contravention in relation to the goods of any safety provision; or
   (b) proceedings for the forfeiture of the goods under section 17 below,

have not been brought or, having been brought, have been concluded.

(5) Any person aggrieved by an order made under this section by a magistrates' court in England and Wales or Northern Ireland, or by a decision of such a court not to make such an order, may appeal against that order or decision—
   (a) in England and Wales, to the Crown Court;
   (b) in Northern Ireland, to the county court;

and an order so made may contain such provision as appears to the court to be appropriate for delaying the coming into force of the order pending the making and determination of any appeal (including any application under section 111 of the Magistrates' Courts Act 1980 or Article 146 of the Magistrates' Courts (Northern Ireland) Order 1981 (statement of case)).

[305]

NOTES
Commencement: 1 October 1987.

16 Forfeiture: England and Wales and Northern Ireland

(1) An enforcement authority in England and Wales or Northern Ireland may apply under this section for an order for the forfeiture of any goods on the grounds that there has been a contravention in relation to the goods of a safety provision.

(2) An application under this section may be made—
   (a) where proceedings have been brought in a magistrates' court for an offence in respect of a contravention in relation to some or all of the goods of any safety provision, to that court;
   (b) where an application with respect to some or all of the goods has been made to a magistrates' court under section 15 above or section 33 below, to that court; and
   (c) where no application for the forfeiture of the goods has been made under paragraph (a) or (b) above, by way of complaint to a magistrates' court.

(3) On an application under this section the court shall make an order for the forfeiture of any goods only if it is satisfied that there has been a contravention in relation to the goods of a safety provision.

(4) For the avoidance of doubt it is declared that a court may infer for the purposes of this section that there has been a contravention in relation to any goods of a safety provision if it is satisfied that any such provision has been contravened in relation to goods which are representative of those goods (whether by reason of being of the same design or part of the same consignment or batch or otherwise).

(5) Any person aggrieved by an order made under this section by a magistrates' court, or by a decision of such a court not to make such an order, may appeal against that order or decision—
   (a) in England and Wales, to the Crown Court;

(b) in Northern Ireland, to the county court;

and an order so made may contain such provision as appears to the court to be appropriate for delaying the coming into force of the order pending the making and determination of any appeal (including any application under section 111 of the Magistrates' Courts Act 1980 or Article 146 of the Magistrates' Courts (Northern Ireland) Order 1981 (statement of case)).

(6) Subject to subsection (7) below, where any goods are forfeited under this section they shall be destroyed in accordance with such directions as the court may give.

(7) On making an order under this section a magistrates' court may, if it considers it appropriate to do so, direct that the goods to which the order relates shall (instead of being destroyed) be released, to such person as the court may specify, on condition that that person—
- (a) does not supply those goods to any person otherwise than as mentioned in section 46(7)(a) or (b) below; and
- (b) complies with any order to pay costs or expenses (including any order under section 35 below) which has been made against that person in the proceedings for the order for forfeiture.

[306]

NOTE
Commencement: 1 October 1987.

18 Power to obtain information

(1) If the Secretary of State considers that, for the purpose of deciding whether—
- (a) to make, vary or revoke any safety regulations; or
- (b) to serve, vary or revoke a prohibition notice; or
- (c) to serve or revoke a notice to warn,

he requires information which another person is likely to be able to furnish, the Secretary of State may serve on the other person a notice under this section.

(2) A notice served on any person under this section may require that person—
- (a) to furnish to the Secretary of State, within a period specified in the notice, such information as is so specified;
- (b) to produce such records as are specified in the notice at a time and place so specified and to permit a person appointed by the Secretary of State for the purpose to take copies of the records at that time and place.

(3) A person shall be guilty of an offence if he—
- (a) fails, without reasonable cause, to comply with a notice served on him under this section; or
- (b) in purporting to comply with a requirement which by virtue of paragraph (a) of subsection (2) above is contained in such a notice—
  - (i) furnishes information which he knows is false in a material particular; or
  - (ii) recklessly furnishes information which is false in a material particular.

(4) A person guilty of an offence under subsection (3) above shall—
- (a) in the case of an offence under paragraph (a) of that subsection, be liable on summary conviction to a fine not exceeding level 5 on the standard scale; and

(b) in the case of an offence under paragraph (b) of that subsection be liable—
  (i) on conviction on indictment, to a fine;
  (ii) on summary conviction, to a fine not exceeding the statutory maximum.

[307]

NOTE
Commencement: 1 October 1987.

19 Interpretation of Part II

(1) In this Part—

"controlled drug" means a controlled drug within the meaning of the Misuse of Drugs Act 1971;

"feeding stuff" and "fertiliser" have the same meanings as in Part IV of the Agriculture Act 1970;

"food" does not include anything containing tobacco but, subject to that, has the same meaning as in the [Food Safety Act 1990] or, in relation to Northern Ireland, the same meaning as in the Food and Drugs Act (Northern Ireland) 1958;

"licensed medicinal product" means—
  (a) any medicinal product within the meaning of the Medicines Act 1968 in respect of which a product licence within the meaning of that Act is for the time being in force; or
  (b) any other article or substance in respect of which any such licence is for the time being in force in pursuance of an order under section 104 or 105 of that Act (application of Act to other articles and substances);

"safe", in relation to any goods, means such that there is no risk, or no risk apart from one reduced to a minimum, that any of the following will (whether immediately or after a definite or indefinite period) cause the death of, or any personal injury to, any person whatsoever, that is to say—
  (a) the goods;
  (b) the keeping, use or consumption of the goods;
  (c) the assembly of any of the goods which are, or are to be, supplied unassembled;
  (d) any emission or leakage from the goods or, as a result of the keeping, use or consumption of the goods, from anything else; or
  (e) reliance on the accuracy of any measurement, calculation or other reading made by or by means of the goods,
and "safer" and "unsafe" shall be construed accordingly;

"tobacco" includes any tobacco product within the meaning of the Tobacco Products Duty Act 1979 and any article or substance containing tobacco and intended for oral or nasal use.

(2) In the definition of "safe" in subsection (1) above, references to the keeping, use or consumption of any goods are references to—
  (a) the keeping, use or consumption of the goods by the persons by whom, and in all or any of the ways or circumstances in which, they might reasonably be expected to be kept, used or consumed; and
  (b) the keeping, use or consumption of the goods either alone or in conjunction with other goods in conjunction with which they might reasonably be expected to be kept, used or consumed.

[308]

NOTES

Commencement: 1 October 1987.

Sub-s (1): in definition "food" words in square brackets substituted by the Food Safety Act 1990, s 59(1), Sch 3, para 37.

PART III
MISLEADING PRICE INDICATIONS

20 Offence of giving misleading indication

(1) Subject to the following provisions of this Part, a person shall be guilty of an offence if, in the course of any business of his, he gives (by any means whatever) to any consumers an indication which is misleading as to the price at which any goods, services, accommodation or facilities are available (whether generally or from particular persons).

(2) Subject as aforesaid, a person shall be guilty of an offence if—
   (a) in the course of any business of his, he has given an indication to any consumer which, after it was given, has become misleading as mentioned in subsection (1) above; and
   (b) some or all of those consumers might reasonably be expected to rely on the indication at a time after it has become misleading; and
   (c) he fails to take all such steps as are reasonable to prevent those consumers from relying on the indication.

(3) For the purposes of this section it shall be immaterial—
   (a) whether the person who gives or gave the indication is or was acting on his own behalf or on behalf of another;
   (b) whether or not that person is the person, or included among the persons, from whom the goods, services, accommodation or facilities are available; and
   (c) whether the indication is or has become misleading in relation to all the consumers to whom it is or was given or only in relation to some of them.

(4) A person guilty of an offence under subsection (1) or (2) above shall be liable—
   (a) on conviction on indictment, to a fine;
   (b) on summary conviction, to a fine not exceeding the statutory maximum.

(5) No prosecution for an offence under subsection (1) or (2) above shall be brought after whichever is the earlier of the following, that is to say—
   (a) the end of the period of three years beginning with the day on which the offence was committed; and
   (b) the end of the period of one year beginning with the day on which the person bringing the prosecution discovered that the offence had been committed.

(6) In this Part—
   "consumer"—
      (a) in relation to any goods, means any person who might wish to be supplied with the goods for his own private use or consumption;
      (b) in relation to any services or facilities, means any person who might wish to be provided with the services or facilities otherwise than for the purposes of any business of his; and
      (c) in relation to any accommodation, means any person who might wish to occupy the accommodation otherwise than for the purposes of any business of his;

"price", in relation to any goods, services, accommodation or facilities, means—
  (a) the aggregate of the sums required to be paid by a consumer for or otherwise in respect of the supply of the goods or the provision of the services, accommodation or facilities; or
  (b) except in section 21 below, any method which will be or has been applied for the purpose of determining that aggregate.

[309]

NOTE
Commencement: 1 March 1989.

21 Meaning of "misleading"

(1) For the purposes of section 20 above an indication given to any consumers is misleading as to a price if what is conveyed by the indication, or what those consumers might reasonably be expected to infer from the indication or any omission from it, includes any of the following, that is to say—
  (a) that the price is less than in fact it is;
  (b) that the applicability of the price does not depend on facts or circumstances on which its applicability does in fact depend;
  (c) that the price covers matters in respect of which an additional charge is in fact made;
  (d) that a person who in fact has no such expectation—
    (i) expects the price to be increased or reduced (whether or not at a particular time or by a particular amount); or
    (ii) expects the price, or the price as increased or reduced, to be maintained (whether or not for a particular period); or
  (e) that the facts or circumstances by reference to which the consumers might reasonably be expected to judge the validity of any relevant comparison made or implied by the indication are not what in fact they are.

(2) For the purposes of section 20 above, an indication given to any consumers is misleading as to a method of determining a price if what is conveyed by the indication, or what those consumers might reasonably be expected to infer from the indication or any omission from it, includes any of the following, that is to say—
  (a) that the method is not what in fact it is;
  (b) that the applicability of the method does not depend on facts or circumstances on which its applicability does in fact depend;
  (c) that the method takes into account matters in respect of which an additional charge will in fact be made;
  (d) that a person who in fact has no such expectation—
    (i) expects the method to be altered (whether or not at a particular time or in a particular respect); or
    (ii) expects the method, or that method as altered, to remain unaltered (whether or not for a particular period); or
  (e) that the facts or circumstances by reference to which the consumers might reasonably be expected to judge the validity of any relevant comparison made or implied by the indication are not what in fact they are.

(3) For the purposes of subsections (1)(e) and (2)(e) above a comparison is a relevant comparison in relation to a price or method of determining a price if it is made between that price or that method, or any price which has been or may be determined by that method, and—
  (a) any price or value which is stated or implied to be, to have been or to be likely to be attributed or attributable to the goods, services, accommoda-

tion or facilities in question or to any other goods, services, accommodation or facilities; or

(b) any method, or other method, which is stated or implied to be, to have been or to be likely to be applied or applicable for the determination of the price or value of the goods, services, accommodation or facilities in question or of the price or value of any other goods, services, accommodation or facilities.

[310]

NOTE
Commencement: 1 March 1989.

22 Application to provision of services and facilities

(1) Subject to the following provisions of this section, references in this Part to services or facilities are references to any services or facilities whatever including, in particular—

(a) the provision of credit or of banking or insurance services and the provision of facilities incidental to the provision of such services;
(b) the purchase or sale of foreign currency;
(c) the supply of electricity;
(d) the provision of a place, other than on a highway, for the parking of a motor vehicle;
(e) the making of arrangements for a person to put or keep a caravan on any land other than arrangements by virtue of which that person may occupy the caravan as his only or main residence.

(2) References in this Part to services shall not include references to services provided to an employer under a contract of employment.

(3) References in this Part to services or facilities shall not include references to services or facilities which are provided by an authorised person or appointed representative in the course of the carrying on of an investment business.

(4) In relation to a service consisting in the purchase or sale of foreign currency, references in this Part to the method by which the price of the service is determined shall include references to the rate of exchange.

(5) In this section—
"appointed representative", "authorised person" and "investment business" have the same meanings as in the Financial Services Act 1986;
"caravan" has the same meaning as in the Caravan Sites and Control of Development Act 1960;
"contract of employment" and "employer" have the same meanings as in the Employment Protection (Consolidation) Act 1978;
"credit" has the same meaning as in the Consumer Credit Act 1974.

[311]

NOTES
Commencement: 1 March 1989.

23 Application to provision of accommodation etc

(1) Subject to subsection (2) below, references in this Part to accommodation or facilities being available shall not include references to accommodation or facilities

being available to be provided by means of the creation or disposal of an interest in land except where—
   (a) the person who is to create or dispose of the interest will do so in the course of any business of his; and
   (b) the interest to be created or disposed of is a relevant interest in a new dwelling and is to be created or disposed of for the purpose of enabling that dwelling to be occupied as a residence, or one of the residences, of the person acquiring the interest.

(2) Subsection (1) above shall not prevent the application of any provision of this Part in relation to—
   (a) the supply of any goods as part of the same transaction as any creation or disposal of an interest in land; or
   (b) the provision of any services or facilities for the purposes of, or in connection with, any transaction for the creation or disposal of such an interest.

(3) In this section—
"new dwelling" means any building or part of a building in Great Britain which—
   (a) has been constructed or adapted to be occupied as a residence; and
   (b) has not previously been so occupied or has been so occupied only with other premises or as more than one residence,

and includes any yard, garden, out-houses or appurtenances which belong to that building or part or are to be enjoyed with it;
"relevant interest"—
   (a) in relation to a new dwelling in England and Wales, means the freehold estate in the dwelling or a leasehold interest in the dwelling for a term of years absolute of more than twenty-one years, not being a term of which twenty-one years or less remains unexpired;
   (b) in relation to a new dwelling in Scotland, means the dominium utile of the land comprising the dwelling, or a leasehold interest in the dwelling where twenty-one years or more remains unexpired.

[312]

NOTE
Commencement: 1 March 1989.

24 Defences

(1) In any proceedings against a person for an offence under subsection (1) or (2) of section 20 above in respect of any indication it shall be a defence for that person to show that his acts or omissions were authorised for the purposes of this subsection by regulations made under section 26 below.

(2) In proceedings against a person for an offence under subsection (1) or (2) of section 20 above in respect of an indication published in a book, newspaper, magazine [or film or in a programme included in a programme service (within the meaning of the Broadcasting Act 1990),] it shall be a defence for that person to show that the indication was not contained in an advertisement.

(3) In proceedings against a person for an offence under subsection (1) or (2) of section 20 above in respect of an indication published in an advertisement it shall be a defence for that person to show that—
   (a) he is a person who carries on a business of publishing or arranging for the publication of advertisements;

(b) he received the advertisement for publication in the ordinary course of that business; and
(c) at the time of publication he did not know and had no grounds for suspecting that the publication would involve the commission of the offence.

(4) In any proceedings against a person for an offence under subsection (1) of section 20 above in respect of any indication, it shall be a defence for that person to show that—
   (a) the indication did not relate to the availability from him of any goods, services, accommodation or facilities;
   (b) a price had been recommended to every person from whom the goods, services, accommodation or facilities were indicated as being available;
   (c) the indication related to that price and was misleading as to that price only by reason of a failure by any person to follow the recommendation; and
   (d) it was reasonable for the person who gave the indication to assume that the recommendation was for the most part being followed.

(5) The provisions of this section are without prejudice to the provisions of section 39 below.

(6) In this section—
   "advertisement" includes a catalogue, a circular and a price list;
   ...

[313]

NOTES

Commencement: 1 March 1989.

Sub-s (2): words in square brackets substituted by the Broadcasting Act 1990, s 203(1), Sch 20, para 48.

Sub-s (6): definition omitted repealed by the Broadcasting Act 1990, s 203(1), (3), Sch 20, para 48, Sch 21.

25 Code of practice

(1) The Secretary of State may, after consulting the Director General of Fair Trading and such other persons as the Secretary of State considers it appropriate to consult, by order approve any code of practice issued (whether by the Secretary of State or another person) for the purpose of—
   (a) giving practical guidance with respect to any of the requirements of section 20 above; and
   (b) promoting what appear to the Secretary of State to be desirable practices as to the circumstances and manner in which any person gives an indication as to the price at which any goods, services, accommodation or facilities are available or indicates any other matter in respect of which any such indication may be misleading.

(2) A contravention of a code of practice approved under this section shall not of itself give rise to any criminal or civil liability, but in any proceedings against any person for an offence under section 20(1) or (2) above—
   (a) any contravention by that person of such a code may be relied on in relation to any matter for the purpose of establishing that that person committed the offence or of negativing any defence; and
   (b) compliance by that person with such a code may be relied on in relation to any matter for the purpose of showing that the commission of the offence by that person has not been established or that that person has a defence.

(3) Where the Secretary of State approves a code of practice under this section he may, after such consultation as is mentioned in subsection (1) above, at any time by order—
   (a) approve any modification of the code; or
   (b) withdraw his approval;

and references in subsection (2) above to a code of practice approved under this section shall be construed accordingly.

(4) The power to make an order under this section shall be exercisable by statutory instrument subject to annulment in pursuance of a resolution of either House of Parliament.

[314]

NOTE
Commencement: 1 March 1989.

26 Power to make regulations

(1) The Secretary of State may, after consulting the Director General of Fair Trading and such other persons as the Secretary of State considers it appropriate to consult, by regulations make provision—
   (a) for the purpose of regulating the circumstances and manner in which any person—
      (i) gives any indication as to the price at which any goods, services, accommodation or facilities will be or are available or have been supplied or provided; or
      (ii) indicates any other matter in respect of which any such indication may be misleading;
   (b) for the purpose of facilitating the enforcement of the provisions of section 20 above or of any regulations made under this section.

(2) The Secretary of State shall not make regulations by virtue of subsection (1)(a) above except in relation to—
   (a) indications given by persons in the course of business; and
   (b) such indications given otherwise than in the course of business as—
      (i) are given by or on behalf of persons by whom accommodation is provided to others by means of leases or licences; and
      (ii) relate to goods, services or facilities supplied or provided to those others in connection with the provision of the accommodation.

(3) Without prejudice to the generality of subsection (1) above, regulations under this section may—
   (a) prohibit an indication as to a price from referring to such matters as may be prescribed by the regulations;
   (b) require an indication as to a price or other matter to be accompanied or supplemented by such explanation or such additional information as may be prescribed by the regulations;
   (c) require information or explanations with respect to a price or other matter to be given to an officer of an enforcement authority and to authorise such an officer to require such information or explanations to be given;
   (d) require any information or explanation provided for the purposes of any regulations made by virtue of paragraph (b) or (c) above to be accurate;
   (e) prohibit the inclusion in indications as to a price or other matter of statements that the indications are not to be relied upon;

(f) provide that expressions used in any indication as to a price or other matter shall be construed in a particular way for the purposes of this Part;
(g) provide that a contravention of any provision of the regulations shall constitute a criminal offence punishable—
   (i) on conviction on indictment, by a fine;
   (ii) on summary conviction, by a fine not exceeding the statutory maximum;
(h) apply any provision of this Act which relates to a criminal offence to an offence created by virtue of paragraph (g) above.

(4) The power to make regulations under this section shall be exercisable by statutory instrument subject to annulment in pursuance of a resolution of either House of Parliament and shall include power—
   (a) to make different provision for different cases; and
   (b) to make such supplemental, consequential and transitional provision as the Secretary of State considers appropriate.

(5) In this section "lease" includes a sub-lease and an agreement for a lease and a statutory tenancy (within the meaning of the Landlord and Tenant Act 1985 or the Rent (Scotland) Act 1984).

[315]

NOTE
Commencement: 1 March 1989.

Part IV
Enforcement of Parts II and III

27 Enforcement

(1) Subject to the following provisions of this section—
   (a) it shall be the duty of every weights and measures authority in Great Britain to enforce within their area the safety provisions and the provisions made by or under Part III of this Act; and
   (b) it shall be the duty of every district council in Northern Ireland to enforce within their area the safety provisions.

(2) The Secretary of State may by regulations—
   (a) wholly or partly transfer any duty imposed by subsection (1) above on a weights and measures authority or a district council in Northern Ireland to such other person who has agreed to the transfer as is specified in the regulations;
   (b) relieve such an authority or council of any such duty so far as it is exercisable in relation to such goods as may be described in the regulations.

(3) The power to make regulations under subsection (2) above shall be exercisable by statutory instrument subject to annulment in pursuance of a resolution of either House of Parliament and shall include power—
   (a) to make different provision for different cases; and
   (b) to make such supplemental, consequential and transitional provision as the Secretary of State considers appropriate.

(4) Nothing in this section shall authorise any weights and measures authority, or

any person on whom functions are conferred by regulations under subsection (2) above, to bring proceedings in Scotland for an offence.

NOTE
Commencement: 1 October 1987 (for purposes of or in relation to Pt II); 1 March 1989 (remaining purposes).

28 Test purchases

(1) An enforcement authority shall have power, for the purpose of ascertaining whether any safety provision or any provision made by or under Part III of this Act has been contravened in relation to any goods, services, accommodation or facilities—
   (a) to make, or to authorise an officer of the authority to make, any purchase of any goods; or
   (b) to secure, or to authorise an officer of the authority to secure, the provision of any services, accommodation or facilities.

(2) Where—
   (a) any goods purchased under this section by or on behalf of an enforcement authority are submitted to a test; and
   (b) the test leads to—
      (i) the bringing of proceedings for an offence in respect of a contravention in relation to the goods of any safety provision or of any provision made by or under Part III of this Act or for the forfeiture of the goods under section 16 or 17 above; or
      (ii) the serving of a suspension notice in respect of any goods; and
   (c) the authority is requested to do so and it is practicable for the authority to comply with the request,

the authority shall allow the person from whom the goods were purchased or any person who is a party to the proceedings or has an interest in any goods to which the notice relates to have the goods tested.

(3) The Secretary of State may by regulations provide that any test of goods purchased under this section by or on behalf of an enforcement authority shall—
   (a) be carried out at the expense of the authority in a manner and by a person prescribed by or determined under the regulations; or
   (b) be carried out either as mentioned in paragraph (a) above or by the authority in a manner prescribed by the regulations.

(4) The power to make regulations under subsection (3) above shall be exercisable by statutory instrument subject to annulment in pursuance of a resolution of either House of Parliament and shall include power—
   (a) to make different provision for different cases; and
   (b) to make such supplemental, consequential and transitional provision as the Secretary of State considers appropriate.

(5) Nothing in this section shall authorise the acquisition by or on behalf of an enforcement authority of any interest in land.

NOTES
Commencement: 1 October 1987 (for purposes of or in relation to Pt II); 1 March 1989 (remaining purposes).

29 Powers of search etc

(1) Subject to the following provisions of this Part, a duly authorised officer of an enforcement authority may at any reasonable hour and on production, if required, of his credentials exercise any of the powers conferred by the following provisions of this section.

(2) The officer may, for the purpose of ascertaining whether there has been any contravention of any safety provision or of any provision made by or under Part III of this Act, inspect any goods and enter any premises other than premises occupied only as a person's residence.

(3) The officer may, for the purpose of ascertaining whether there has been any contravention of any safety provision, examine any procedure (including any arrangements for carrying out a test) connected with the production of any goods.

(4) If the officer has reasonable grounds for suspecting that any goods are manufactured or imported goods which have not been supplied in the United Kingdom since they were manufactured or imported he may—
  (a) for the purpose of ascertaining whether there has been any contravention of any safety provision in relation to the goods, require any person carrying on a business, or employed in connection with a business, to produce any records relating to the business;
  (b) for the purpose of ascertaining (by testing or otherwise) whether there has been any such contravention, seize and detain the goods;
  (c) take copies of, or of any entry in, any records produced by virtue of paragraph (a) above.

(5) If the officer has reasonable grounds for suspecting that there has been a contravention in relation to any goods of any safety provision or of any provision made by or under Part III of this Act, he may—
  (a) for the purpose of ascertaining whether there has been any such contravention, require any person carrying on a business, or employed in connection with a business, to produce any records relating to the business;
  (b) for the purpose of ascertaining (by testing or otherwise) whether there has been any such contravention, seize and detain the goods;
  (c) take copies of, or of any entry in, any records produced by virtue of paragraph (a) above.

(6) The officer may seize and detain—
  (a) any goods or records which he has reasonable grounds for believing may be required as evidence in proceedings for an offence in respect of a contravention of any safety provision or of any provision made by or under Part III of this Act;
  (b) any goods which he has reasonable grounds for suspecting may be liable to be forfeited under section 16 or 17 above.

(7) If and to the extent that it is reasonably necessary to do so to prevent a contravention of any safety provision or of any provision made by or under Part III of this Act, the officer may, for the purpose of exercising his power under subsection (4), (5) or (6) above to seize any goods or records—
  (a) require any person having authority to do so to open any container or to open any vending machine; and
  (b) himself open or break open any such container or machine where a requirement made under paragraph (a) above in relation to the container or machine has not been complied with.

NOTES

Commencement: 1 October 1987 (for purposes of or in relation to Pt II); 1 March 1989 (remaining purposes).

30 Provisions supplemental to s 29

(1) An officer seizing any goods or records under section 29 above shall inform the following persons that the goods or records have been so seized, that is to say—
   (a) the person from whom they are seized; and
   (b) in the case of imported goods seized on any premises under the control of the Commissioners of Customs and Excise, the importer of those goods (within the meaning of the Customs and Excise Management Act 1979).

(2) If a justice of the peace—
   (a) is satisfied by any written information on oath that there are reasonable grounds for believing either—
      (i) that any goods or records which any officer has power to inspect under section 29 above are on any premises and that their inspection is likely to disclose evidence that there has been a contravention of any safety provision or of any provision made by or under Part III of this Act; or
      (ii) that such a contravention has taken place, is taking place or is about to take place on any premises; and
   (b) is also satisfied by any such information either—
      (i) that admission to the premises has been or is likely to be refused and that notice of intention to apply for a warrant under this subsection has been given to the occupier; or
      (ii) that an application for admission, or the giving of such a notice, would defeat the object of the entry or that the premises are unoccupied or that the occupier is temporarily absent and it might defeat the object of the entry to await his return,

the justice may by warrant under his hand, which shall continue in force for a period of one month, authorise any officer of an enforcement authority to enter the premises, if need be by force.

(3) An officer entering any premises by virtue of section 29 above or a warrant under subsection (2) above may take with him such other persons and such equipment as may appear to him necessary.

(4) On leaving any premises which a person is authorised to enter by a warrant under subsection (2) above, that person shall, if the premises are unoccupied or the occupier is temporarily absent, leave the premises as effectively secured against trespassers as he found them.

(5) If any person who is not an officer of an enforcement authority purports to act as such under section 29 above or this section he shall be guilty of an offence and liable on summary conviction to a fine not exceeding level 5 on the standard scale.

(6) Where any goods seized by an officer under section 29 above are submitted to a test, the officer shall inform the persons mentioned in subsection (1) above of the result of the test and, if—
   (a) proceedings are brought for an offence in respect of a contravention in relation to the goods of any safety provision or of any provision made by or under Part III of this Act or for the forfeiture of the goods under section 16 or 17 above, or a suspension notice is served in respect of any goods; and

(b) the officer is requested to do so and it is practicable to comply with the request,

the officer shall allow any person who is a party to the proceedings or, as the case may be, has an interest in the goods to which the notice relates to have the goods tested.

(7) The Secretary of State may by regulations provide that any test of goods seized under section 29 above by an officer of an enforcement authority shall—
- (a) be carried out at the expense of the authority in a manner and by a person prescribed by or determined under the regulations; or
- (b) be carried out either as mentioned in paragraph (a) above or by the authority in a manner prescribed by the regulations.

(8) The power to make regulations under subsection (7) above shall be exercisable by statutory instrument subject to annulment in pursuance of a resolution of either House of Parliament and shall include power—
- (a) to make different provision for different cases; and
- (b) to make such supplemental, consequential and transitional provision as the Secretary of State considers appropriate.

(9) In the application of this section to Scotland, the reference in subsection (2) above to a justice of the peace shall include a reference to a sheriff and the references to written information on oath shall be construed as references to evidence on oath.

(10) In the application of this section to Northern Ireland, the references in subsection (2) above to any information on oath shall be construed as references to any complaint on oath.

NOTES

Commencement: 1 October 1987 (for purposes of or in relation to Pt II); 1 March 1989 (remaining purposes).

31 Power of customs officer to detain goods

(1) A customs officer may, for the purpose of facilitating the exercise by an enforcement authority or officer of such an authority of any functions conferred on the authority or officer by or under Part II of this Act, or by or under this Part in its application for the purposes of the safety provisions, seize any imported goods and detain them for not more than two working days.

(2) Anything seized and detained under this section shall be dealt with during the period of its detention in such manner as the Commissioners of Customs and Excise may direct.

(3) In subsection (1) above the reference to two working days is a reference to a period of forty-eight hours calculated from the time when the goods in question are seized but disregarding so much of any period as falls on a Saturday or Sunday or on Christmas Day, Good Friday or a day which is a bank holiday under the Banking and Financial Dealings Act 1971 in the part of the United Kingdom where the goods are seized.

(4) In this section and section 32 below "customs officer" means any officer within the meaning of the Customs and Excise Management Act 1979.

NOTES

Commencement: 1 October 1987 (for purposes of or in relation to Pt II); 1 March 1989 (remaining purposes).

32 Obstruction of authorised officer

(1) Any person who—
  (a) intentionally obstructs any officer of an enforcement authority who is acting in pursuance of any provision of this Part or any customs officer who is so acting; or
  (b) intentionally fails to comply with any requirement made of him by any officer of an enforcement authority under any provision of this Part; or
  (c) without reasonable cause fails to give any officer of an enforcement authority who is so acting any other assistance or information which the officer may reasonably require of him for the purposes of the exercise of the officer's functions under any provision of this Part,

shall be guilty of an offence and liable on summary conviction to a fine not exceeding level 5 on the standard scale.

(2) A person shall be guilty of an offence if, in giving any information which is required of him by virtue of subsection (1)(c) above—
  (a) he makes any statement which he knows is false in a material particular; or
  (b) he recklessly makes a statement which is false in a material particular.

(3) A person guilty of an offence under subsection (2) above shall be liable—
  (a) on conviction on indictment, to a fine;
  (b) on summary conviction, to a fine not exceeding the statutory maximum.

[321]

NOTES

Commencement: 1 October 1987 (for purposes of or in relation to Pt II); 1 March 1989 (remaining purposes).

33 Appeals against detention of goods

(1) Any person having an interest in any goods which are for the time being detained under any provision of this Part by an enforcement authority or by an officer of such an authority may apply for an order requiring the goods to be released to him or to another person.

(2) An application under this section may be made—
  (a) to any magistrates' court in which proceedings have been brought in England and Wales or Northern Ireland—
    (i) for an offence in respect of a contravention in relation to the goods of any safety provision or of any provision made by or under Part III of this Act; or
    (ii) for the forfeiture of the goods under section 16 above;
  (b) where no such proceedings have been so brought, by way of complaint to a magistrates' court; or
  (c) ...

(3) On an application under this section to a magistrates' court or to the sheriff, an order requiring goods to be released shall be made only if the court or sheriff is satisfied—

(a) that proceedings—
   (i) for an offence in respect of a contravention in relation to the goods of any safety provision or of any provision made by or under Part III of this Act; or
   (ii) for the forfeiture of the goods under section 16 or 17 above,
   have not been brought or, having been brought, have been concluded without the goods being forfeited; and
(b) where no such proceedings have been brought, that more than six months have elapsed since the goods were seized.

(4) Any person aggrieved by an order made under this section by a magistrates' court in England and Wales or Northern Ireland, or by a decision of such a court not to make such an order, may appeal against that order or decision—
   (a) in England and Wales, to the Crown Court;
   (b) in Northern Ireland, to the county court;

and an order so made may contain such provision as appears to the court to be appropriate for delaying the coming into force of the order pending the making and determination of any appeal (including any application under section 111 of the Magistrates' Courts Act 1980 or Article 146 of the Magistrates' Courts (Northern Ireland) Order 1981 (statement of case)).

[322]

NOTES
Commencement: 1 October 1987 (for purposes of or in relation to Pt II); 1 March 1989 (remaining purposes).
Sub-s (2): para (c) applies to Scotland only.

34 Compensation for seizure and detention

(1) Where an officer of an enforcement authority exercises any power under section 29 above to seize and detain goods, the enforcement authority shall be liable to pay compensation to any person having an interest in the goods in respect of any loss or damage caused by reason of the exercise of the power if—
   (a) there has been no contravention in relation to the goods of any safety provision or of any provision made by or under Part III of this Act; and
   (b) the exercise of the power is not attributable to any neglect or default by that person.

(2) Any disputed question as to the right to or the amount of any compensation payable under this section shall be determined by arbitration or, in Scotland, by a single arbiter appointed, failing agreement between the parties, by the sheriff.

[323]

NOTES
Commencement: 1 October 1987 (for purposes of or in relation to Pt II); 1 March 1989 (remaining purposes).

35 Recovery of expenses of enforcement

(1) This section shall apply where a court—
   (a) convicts a person of an offence in respect of a contravention in relation to any goods of any safety provision or of any provision made by or under Part III of this Act; or

(b) makes an order under section 16 or 17 above for the forfeiture of any goods.

(2) The court may (in addition to any other order it may make as to costs or expenses) order the person convicted or, as the case may be, any person having an interest in the goods to reimburse an enforcement authority for any expenditure which has been or may be incurred by that authority—
   (a) in connection with any seizure or detention of the goods by or on behalf of the authority; or
   (b) in connection with any compliance by the authority with directions given by the court for the purposes of any order for the forfeiture of the goods.

NOTES

Commencement: 1 October 1987 (for purposes of or in relation to Pt II); 1 March 1989 (remaining purposes).

PART V
MISCELLANEOUS AND SUPPLEMENTAL

36 Amendments of Part I of the Health and Safety at Work etc Act 1974

Part I of the Health and Safety at Work etc. Act 1974 (which includes provision with respect to the safety of certain articles and substances) shall have effect with the amendments specified in Schedule 3 to this Act; and, accordingly, the general purposes of that Part of that Act shall include the purpose of protecting persons from the risks protection from which would not be afforded by virtue of that Part but for those amendments.

NOTE

Commencement: 1 March 1988.

37 Power of Commissioners of Customs and Excise to disclose information

(1) If they think it appropriate to do so for the purpose of facilitating the exercise by any person to whom subsection (2) below applies of any functions conferred on that person by or under Part II of this Act, or by or under Part IV of this Act in its application for the purposes of the safety provisions, the Commissioners of Customs and Excise may authorise the disclosure to that person of any information obtained for the purposes of the exercise by the Commissioners of their functions in relation to imported goods.

(2) This subsection applies to an enforcement authority and to any officer of an enforcement authority.

(3) A disclosure of information made to any person under subsection (1) above shall be made in such manner as may be directed by the Commissioners of Customs and Excise and may be made through such persons acting on behalf of that person as may be so directed.

(4) Information may be disclosed to a person under subsection (1) above whether or not the disclosure of the information has been requested by or on behalf of that person.

NOTES

Commencement: 1 October 1987 (for purposes of or in relation to Pt II); 1 March 1989 (remaining purposes).

38 Restrictions on disclosure of information

(1) Subject to the following provisions of this section, a person shall be guilty of an offence if he discloses any information—
- (a) which was obtained by him in consequence of its being given to any person in compliance with any requirement imposed by safety regulations or regulations under section 26 above;
- (b) which consists in a secret manufacturing process or a trade secret and was obtained by him in consequence of the inclusion of the information—
  - (i) in written or oral representations made for the purposes of Part I or II of Schedule 2 to this Act; or
  - (ii) in a statement of a witness in connection with any such oral representations;
- (c) which was obtained by him in consequence of the exercise by the Secretary of State of the power conferred by section 18 above;
- (d) which was obtained by him in consequence of the exercise by any person of any power conferred by Part IV of this Act; or
- (e) which was disclosed to or through him under section 37 above.

(2) Subsection (1) above shall not apply to a disclosure of information if the information is publicised information or the disclosure is made—
- (a) for the purpose of facilitating the exercise of a relevant person's functions under this Act or any enactment or subordinate legislation mentioned in subsection (3) below;
- (b) for the purposes of compliance with a Community obligation; or
- (c) in connection with the investigation of any criminal offence or for the purposes of any civil or criminal proceedings.

(3) The enactments and subordinate legislation referred to in subsection (2)(a) above are—
- (a) the Trade Descriptions Act 1968;
- (b) Parts II and III and section 125 of the Fair Trading Act 1973;
- (c) the relevant statutory provisions within the meaning of Part I of the Health and Safety at Work etc. Act 1974 or within the meaning of the Health and Safety at Work (Northern Ireland) Order 1978;
- (d) the Consumer Credit Act 1974;
- (e) the Restrictive Trade Practices Act 1976;
- (f) the Resale Prices Act 1976;
- (g) the Estate Agents Act 1979;
- (h) the Competition Act 1980;
- (i) the Telecommunications Act 1984;
- (j) the Airports Act 1986;
- (k) the Gas Act 1986;
- (l) any subordinate legislation made (whether before or after the passing of this Act) for the purpose of securing compliance with the Directive of the Council of the European Communities, dated 10th September 1984 (No. 84/450/EEC) on the approximation of the laws, regulations and administrative provisions of the member States concerning misleading advertising;
- [(m) the Electricity Act 1989;]
- [(n) the Electricity (Northern Ireland) Order 1992.]

(4) In subsection (2)(a) above the reference to a person's functions shall include a reference to any function of making, amending or revoking any regulations or order.

(5) A person guilty of an offence under this section shall be liable—
   (a) on summary conviction, to a fine not exceeding the statutory maximum;
   (b) on conviction on indictment, to imprisonment for a term not exceeding two years or to a fine or to both.

(6) In this section—
   "publicised information" means any information which has been disclosed in any civil or criminal proceedings or is or has been required to be contained in a warning published in pursuance of a notice to warn; and
   "relevant person" means any of the following, that is to say—
   (a) a Minister of the Crown, Government department or Northern Ireland department;
   (b) the Monopolies and Mergers Commission, the Director General of Fair Trading, the Director General of Telecommunications or the Director General of Gas Supply [or the Director General of Electricity Supply] [or the Director General of Electricity Supply for Northern Ireland];
   (c) the Civil Aviation Authority;
   (d) any weights and measures authority, any district council in Northern Ireland or any person on whom functions are conferred by regulations under section 27(2) above;
   (e) any person who is an enforcing authority for the purposes of Part I of the Health and Safety at Work etc. Act 1974 or for the purposes of Part II of the Health and Safety at Work (Northern Ireland) Order 1978.

[327]

NOTES
Commencement: 1 October 1987 (for purposes of or in relation to Pt II); 1 March 1989 (remaining purposes).
Sub-ss (3): para (m) added by the Electricity Act 1989, s 112(1), Sch 16, para 36; para (n) added by the Electricity (Northern Ireland) Order 1992, SI 1992 No 231, art 95(1), Sch 12, para 31(a).
Sub-s (6): in sub-para (b) first words in square brackets added by the Electricity Act 1989, s 112(1), Sch 16, para 36; final words in square brackets added by the Electricity (Northern Ireland) Order 1992, SI 1992 No 231, art 95(1), Sch 12, para 31(b).

39 Defence of due diligence

(1) Subject to the following provisions of this section, in proceedings against any person for an offence to which this section applies it shall be a defence for that person to show that he took all reasonable steps and exercised all due diligence to avoid committing the offence.

(2) Where in any proceedings against any person for such an offence the defence provided by subsection (1) above involves an allegation that the commission of the offence was due—
   (a) to the act or default of another; or
   (b) to reliance on information given by another,
that person shall not, without the leave of the court, be entitled to rely on the defence unless, not less than seven clear days before the hearing of the proceedings, he has served a notice under subsection (3) below on the person bringing the proceedings.

(3) A notice under this subsection shall give such information identifying or assisting in the identification of the person who committed the act or default or gave the

information as is in the possession of the person serving the notice at the time he serves it.

(4) It is hereby declared that a person shall not be entitled to rely on the defence provided by subsection (1) above by reason of his reliance on information supplied by another, unless he shows that it was reasonable in all the circumstances for him to have relied on the information, having regard in particular—
- (a) to the steps which he took, and those which might reasonably have been taken, for the purpose of verifying the information; and
- (b) to whether he had any reason to disbelieve the information.

(5) This section shall apply to an offence under section 10, 12(1), (2) or (3), 13(4), 14(6) or 20(1) above.

[328]

NOTE

Commencement: 1 October 1987 (for purposes of or in relation to Pt II); 1 March 1989 (remaining purposes).

40 Liability of persons other than principal offender

(1) Where the commission by any person of an offence to which section 39 above applies is due to an act or default committed by some other person in the course of any business of his, the other person shall be guilty of the offence and may be proceeded against and punished by virtue of this subsection whether or not proceedings are taken against the first-mentioned person.

(2) Where a body corporate is guilty of an offence under this Act (including where it is so guilty by virtue of subsection (1) above) in respect of any act or default which is shown to have been committed with the consent or connivance of, or to be attributable to any neglect on the part of, any director, manager, secretary or other similar officer of the body corporate or any person who was purporting to act in any such capacity he, as well as the body corporate, shall be guilty of that offence and shall be liable to be proceeded against and punished accordingly.

(3) Where the affairs of a body corporate are managed by its members, subsection (2) above shall apply in relation to the acts and defaults of a member in connection with his functions of management as if he were a director of the body corporate.

[329]

NOTE

Commencement: 1 October 1987 (for purposes of or in relation to Pt II); 1 March 1989 (remaining purposes).

41 Civil proceedings

(1) An obligation imposed by safety regulations shall be a duty owed to any person who may be affected by a contravention of the obligation and, subject to any provision to the contrary in the regulations and to the defences and other incidents applying to actions for breach of statutory duty, a contravention of any such obligation shall be actionable accordingly.

(2) This Act shall not be construed as conferring any other right of action in civil proceedings, apart from the right conferred by virtue of Part I of this Act, in respect of any loss or damage suffered in consequence of a contravention of a safety provision or of a provision made by or under Part III of this Act.

(3) Subject to any provision to the contrary in the agreement itself, an agreement shall not be void or unenforceable by reason only of a contravention of a safety provision or of a provision made by or under Part III of this Act.

(4) Liability by virtue of subsection (1) above shall not be limited or excluded by any contract term, by any notice or (subject to the power contained in subsection (1) above to limit or exclude it in safety regulations) by any other provision.

(5) Nothing in subsection (1) above shall prejudice the operation of section 12 of the Nuclear Installations Act 1965 (rights to compensation for certain breaches of duties confined to rights under that Act).

(6) In this section "damage" includes personal injury and death.

[330]

NOTES
Commencement: 1 March 1989 (certain purposes); 1 March 1988 (sub-ss (2), (6), (certain purposes); 1 October 1987 (remaining purposes).

42 Reports etc

(1) It shall be the duty of the Secretary of State at least once in every five years to lay before each House of Parliament a report on the exercise during the period to which the report relates of the functions which under Part II of this Act, or under Part IV of this Act in its application for the purposes of the safety provisions, are exercisable by the Secretary of State, weights and measures authorities, district councils in Northern Ireland and persons on whom functions are conferred by regulations made under section 27(2) above.

(2) The Secretary of State may from time to time prepare and lay before each House of Parliament such other reports on the exercise of those functions as he considers appropriate.

(3) Every weights and measures authority, every district council in Northern Ireland and every person on whom functions are conferred by regulations under subsection (2) of section 27 above shall, whenever the Secretary of State so directs, make a report to the Secretary of State on the exercise of the functions exercisable by that authority or council under that section or by that person by virtue of any such regulations.

(4) A report under subsection (3) above shall be in such form and shall contain such particulars as are specified in the direction of the Secretary of State.

(5) The first report under subsection (1) above shall be laid before each House of Parliament not more than five years after the laying of the last report under section 8(2) of the Consumer Safety Act 1978.

[331]

NOTE
Commencement: 1 October 1987 (for purposes of or in relation to Pt II); 1 March 1989 (remaining purposes).

43 Financial provisions

(1) There shall be paid out of money provided by Parliament—
    (a) any expenses incurred or compensation payable by a Minister of the Crown

or Government department in consequence of any provision of this Act; and

(b) any increase attributable to this Act in the sums payable out of money so provided under any other Act.

(2) Any sums received by a Minister of the Crown or Government department by virtue of this Act shall be paid into the Consolidated Fund.

NOTE

Commencement: 1 October 1987 (for purposes of or in relation to Pt II); 1 March 1989 (remaining purposes).

44 Service of documents etc

(1) Any document required or authorised by virtue of this Act to be served on a person may be so served—
- (a) by delivering it to him or by leaving it at his proper address or by sending it by post to him at that address; or
- (b) if the person is a body corporate, by serving it in accordance with paragraph (a) above on the secretary or clerk of that body; or
- (c) if the person is a partnership, by serving it in accordance with that paragraph on a partner or on a person having control or management of the partnership business.

(2) For the purposes of subsection (1) above, and for the purposes of section 7 of the Interpretation Act 1978 (which relates to the service of documents by post) in its application to that subsection, the proper address of any person on whom a document is to be served by virtue of this Act shall be his last known address except that—
- (a) in the case of service on a body corporate or its secretary or clerk, it shall be the address of the registered or principal office of the body corporate;
- (b) in the case of service on a partnership or a partner or a person having the control or management of a partnership business, it shall be the principal office of the partnership;

and for the purposes of this subsection the principal office of a company registered outside the United Kingdom or of a partnership carrying on business outside the United Kingdom is its principal office within the United Kingdom.

(3) The Secretary of State may by regulations make provision for the manner in which any information is to be given to any person under any provision of Part IV of this Act.

(4) Without prejudice to the generality of subsection (3) above regulations made by the Secretary of State may prescribe the person, or manner of determining the person, who is to be treated for the purposes of section 28(2) or 30 above as the person from whom any goods were purchased or seized where the goods were purchased or seized from a vending machine.

(5) The power to make regulations under subsection (3) or (4) above shall be exercisable by statutory instrument subject to annulment in pursuance of a resolution of either House of Parliament and shall include power—
- (a) to make different provision for different cases; and
- (b) to make such supplemental, consequential and transitional provision as the Secretary of State considers appropriate.

NOTES
Commencement: 1 October 1987 (for purposes of or in relation to Pt II); 1 March 1989 (remaining purposes).

45 Interpretation

(1) In this Act, except in so far as the context otherwise requires—
"aircraft" includes gliders, balloons and hovercraft;
"business" includes a trade or profession and the activities of a professional or trade association or of a local authority or other public authority;
"conditional sale agreement", "credit-sale agreement" and "hire-purchase agreement" have the same meanings as in the Consumer Credit Act 1974 but as if in the definitions in that Act "goods" had the same meaning as in this Act;
"contravention" includes a failure to comply and cognate expressions shall be construed accordingly;
"enforcement authority" means the Secretary of State, any other Minister of the Crown in charge of a Government department, any such department and any authority, council or other person on whom functions under this Act are conferred by or under section 27 above;
"gas" has the same meaning as in Part I of the Gas Act 1986;
"goods" includes substances, growing crops and things comprised in land by virtue of being attached to it and any ship, aircraft or vehicle;
"information" includes accounts, estimates and returns;
"magistrates' court", in relation to Northern Ireland, means a court of summary jurisdiction;
"mark" and "trade mark" have the same meanings as in the Trade Marks Act 1938;
"modifications" includes additions, alterations and omissions, and cognate expressions shall be construed accordingly;
"motor vehicle" has the same meaning as in [the Road Traffic Act 1988];
"notice" means a notice in writing;
"notice to warn" means a notice under section 13(1)(b) above;
"officer", in relation to an enforcement authority, means a person authorised in writing to assist the authority in carrying out its functions under or for the purposes of the enforcement of any of the safety provisions or of any of the provisions made by or under Part III of this Act;
"personal injury" includes any disease and any other impairment of a person's physical or mental condition;
"premises" includes any place and any ship, aircraft or vehicle;
"prohibition notice" means a notice under section 13(1)(a) above;
"records" includes any books or documents and any records in non-documentary form;
"safety provision" means the general safety requirement in section 10 above or any provision of safety regulations, a prohibition notice or a suspension notice;
"safety regulations" means regulations under section 11 above;
"ship" includes any boat and any other description of vessel used in navigation;
"subordinate legislation" has the same meaning as in the Interpretation Act 1978;
"substance" means any natural or artificial substance, whether in solid, liquid or gaseous form or in the form of a vapour, and includes substances that are comprised in or mixed with other goods;
"supply" and cognate expressions shall be construed in accordance with section 46 below;

"suspension notice" means a notice under section 14 above.

(2) Except in so far as the context otherwise requires, references in this Act to a contravention of a safety provision shall, in relation to any goods, include references to anything which would constitute such a contravention if the goods were supplied to any person.

(3) References in this Act to any goods in relation to which any safety provision has been or may have been contravened shall include references to any goods which it is not reasonably practicable to separate from any such goods.

(4) Section 68(2) of the Trade Marks Act 1938 (construction of references to use of a mark) shall apply for the purposes of this Act as it applies for the purposes of that Act.

(5) ...

[334]

NOTES

Commencement: 1 October 1987 (so far as has effect for the purposes of or in relation to Pt II); 1 March 1988 (so far as has effect for the purposes of or in relation to Pt I); 1 March 1989 (otherwise).

Sub-s (1): in definition "motor vehicle", words in square brackets substituted by the Road Traffic (Consequential Provisions) Act 1988, s 4, Sch 3, para 35.

Sub-s (5): applies to Scotland only.

46 Meaning of "supply"

(1) Subject to the following provisions of this section, references in this Act to supplying goods shall be construed as references to doing any of the following, whether as principal or agent, that is to say—
- (a) selling, hiring out or lending the goods;
- (b) entering into a hire-purchase agreement to furnish the goods;
- (c) the performance of any contract for work and materials to furnish the goods;
- (d) providing the goods in exchange for any consideration (including trading stamps) other than money;
- (e) providing the goods in or in connection with the performance of any statutory function; or
- (f) giving the goods as a prize or otherwise making a gift of the goods;

and, in relation to gas or water, those references shall be construed as including references to providing the service by which the gas or water is made available for use.

(2) For the purposes of any reference in this Act to supplying goods, where a person ("the ostensible supplier") supplies goods to another person ("the customer") under a hire-purchase agreement, conditional sale agreement or credit-sale agreement or under an agreement for the hiring of goods (other than a hire-purchase agreement) and the ostensible supplier—
- (a) carries on the business of financing the provision of goods for others by means of such agreements; and
- (b) in the course of that business acquired his interest in the goods supplied to the customer as a means of financing the provision of them for the customer by a further person ("the effective supplier"),

the effective supplier and not the ostensible supplier shall be treated as supplying the goods to the customer.

(3) Subject to subsection (4) below, the performance of any contract by the erection of any building or structure on any land or by the carrying out of any other building

works shall be treated for the purposes of this Act as a supply of goods in so far as, but only in so far as, it involves the provision of any goods to any person by means of their incorporation into the building, structure or works.

(4) Except for the purposes of, and in relation to, notices to warn or any provision made by or under Part III of this Act, references in this Act to supplying goods shall not include references to supplying goods comprised in land where the supply is effected by the creation or disposal of an interest in the land.

(5) Except in Part I of this Act references in this Act to a person's supplying goods shall be confined to references to that person's supplying goods in the course of a business of his, but for the purposes of this subsection it shall be immaterial whether the business is a business of dealing in the goods.

(6) For the purposes of subsection (5) above goods shall not be treated as supplied in the course of a business if they are supplied, in pursuance of an obligation arising under or in connection with the insurance of the goods, to the person with whom they were insured.

(7) Except for the purposes of, and in relation to, prohibition notices or suspension notices, references in Parts II to IV of this Act to supplying goods shall not include—
   (a) references to supplying goods where the person supplied carries on a business of buying goods of the same description as those goods and repairing or reconditioning them;
   (b) references to supplying goods by a sale of articles as scrap (that is to say, for the value of materials included in the articles rather than for the value of the articles themselves).

(8) Where any goods have at any time been supplied by being hired out or lent to any person, neither a continuation or renewal of the hire or loan (whether on the same or different terms) nor any transaction for the transfer after that time of any interest in the goods to the person to whom they were hired or lent shall be treated for the purposes of this Act as a further supply of the goods to that person.

(9) A ship, aircraft or motor vehicle shall not be treated for the purposes of this Act as supplied to any person by reason only that services consisting in the carriage of goods or passengers in that ship, aircraft or vehicle, or in its use for any other purpose, are provided to that person in pursuance of an agreement relating to the use of the ship, aircraft or vehicle for a particular period or for particular voyages, flights or journeys.

[335]

NOTE
Commencement: 1 October 1987 (so far as has effect for the purposes of or in relation to Pt II); 1 March 1988 (so far as has effect for the purposes of or in relation to Pt I); 1 March 1989 (otherwise).

50 Short title, commencement and transitional provision

(1) This Act may be cited as the Consumer Protection Act 1987.

(2) This Act shall come into force on such day as the Secretary of State may by order made by statutory instrument appoint, and different days may be so appointed for different provisions or for different purposes.

(3) The Secretary of State shall not make an order under subsection (2) above bringing into force the repeal of the Trade Descriptions Act 1972, a repeal of any provision of that Act or a repeal of that Act or of any provision of it for any purposes, unless a draft of the order has been laid before, and approved by a resolution of, each House of Parliament.

(4) An order under subsection (2) above bringing a provision into force may contain such transitional provision in connection with the coming into force of that provision as the Secretary of State considers appropriate.

(5) Without prejudice to the generality of the power conferred by subsection (4) above, the Secretary of State may by order provide for any regulations made under the Consumer Protection Act 1961 or the Consumer Protection Act (Northern Ireland) 1965 to have effect as if made under section 11 above and for any such regulations to have effect with such modifications as he considers appropriate for that purpose.

(6) The power of the Secretary of State by order to make such provision as is mentioned in subsection (5) above, shall, in so far as it is not exercised by an order under subsection (2) above, be exercisable by statutory instrument subject to annulment in pursuance of a resolution of either House of Parliament.

(7) Nothing in this Act or in any order under subsection (2) above shall make any person liable by virtue of Part I of this Act for any damage caused wholly or partly by a defect in a product which was supplied to any person by its producer before the coming into force of Part I of this Act.

(8) Expressions used in subsection (7) above and in Part I of this Act have the same meanings in that subsection as in that Part.

[336]

NOTE
Commencement: 1 October 1987.

SCHEDULE 2
PROHIBITION NOTICES AND NOTICES TO WARN

Section 13

PART I
PROHIBITION NOTICES

1 A prohibition notice in respect of any goods shall—
    (a) state that the Secretary of State considers that the goods are unsafe;
    (b) set out the reasons why the Secretary of State considers that the goods are unsafe;
    (c) specify the day on which the notice is to come into force; and
    (d) state that the trader may at any time make representations in writing to the Secretary of State for the purpose of establishing that the goods are safe.

2—(1) If representations in writing about a prohibition notice are made by the trader to the Secretary of State, it shall be the duty of the Secretary of State to consider whether to revoke the notice and—
    (a) if he decides to revoke it, to do so;
    (b) in any other case, to appoint a person to consider those representations, any further representations made (whether in writing or orally) by the trader about the notice and the statements of any witnesses examined under this Part of this Schedule.

(2) Where the Secretary of State has appointed a person to consider representations about a prohibition notice, he shall serve a notification on the trader which—
    (a) states that the trader may make oral representations to the appointed person for the purpose of establishing that the goods to which the notice relates are safe; and
    (b) specifies the place and time at which the oral representations may be made.

(3) The time specified in a notification served under sub-paragraph (2) above shall not be before the end of the period of twenty-one days beginning with the day on which the notification is served, unless the trader otherwise agrees.

(4) A person on whom a notification has been served under sub-paragraph (2) above or his representative may, at the place and time specified in the notification—
  (a) make oral representations to the appointed person for the purpose of establishing that the goods in question are safe; and
  (b) call and examine witnesses in connection with the representations.

3—(1) Where representations in writing about a prohibition notice are made by the trader to the Secretary of State at any time after a person has been appointed to consider representations about that notice, then, whether or not the appointed person has made a report to the Secretary of State, the following provisions of this paragraph shall apply instead of paragraph 2 above.

(2) The Secretary of State shall, before the end of the period of one month beginning with the day on which he receives the representations, serve a notification on the trader which states—
  (a) that the Secretary of State has decided to revoke the notice, has decided to vary it or, as the case may be, has decided neither to revoke nor to vary it; or
  (b) that, a person having been appointed to consider representations about the notice, the trader may, at a place and time specified in the notification, make oral representations to the appointed person for the purpose of establishing that the goods to which the notice relates are safe.

(3) The time specified in a notification served for the purposes of sub-paragraph (2)(b) above shall not be before the end of the period of twenty-one days beginning with the day on which the notification is served, unless the trader otherwise agrees or the time is the time already specified for the purposes of paragraph 2(2)(b) above.

(4) A person on whom a notification has been served for the purposes of sub-paragraph (2)(b) above or his representative may, at the place and time specified in the notification—
  (a) make oral representations to the appointed person for the purpose of establishing that the goods in question are safe; and
  (b) call and examine witnesses in connection with the representations.

4—(1) Where a person is appointed to consider representations about a prohibition notice, it shall be his duty to consider—
  (a) any written representations made by the trader about the notice, other than those in respect of which a notification is served under paragraph 3(2)(a) above;
  (b) any oral representations made under paragraph 2(4) or 3(4) above; and
  (c) any statements made by witnesses in connection with the oral representations,

and, after considering any matters under this paragraph, to make a report (including recommendations) to the Secretary of State about the matters considered by him and the notice.

(2) It shall be the duty of the Secretary of State to consider any report made to him under sub-paragraph (1) above and, after considering the report, to inform the trader of his decision with respect to the prohibition notice to which the report relates.

5—(1) The Secretary of State may revoke or vary a prohibition notice by serving on the trader a notification stating that the notice is revoked or, as the case may be, is varied as specified in the notification.

(2) The Secretary of State shall not vary a prohibition notice so as to make the effect of the notice more restrictive for the trader.

(3) Without prejudice to the power conferred by section 13(2) of this Act, the service of a notification under sub-paragraph (1) above shall be sufficient to satisfy the requirement of paragraph 4(2) above that the trader shall be informed of the Secretary of State's decision.

NOTE
Commencement: 1 October 1987.

Part II
Notices to warn

6—(1) If the Secretary of State proposes to serve a notice to warn on any person in respect of any goods, the Secretary of State, before he serves the notice, shall serve on that person a notification which—
  (a) contains a draft of the proposed notice;
  (b) states that the Secretary of State proposes to serve a notice in the form of the draft on that person;
  (c) states that the Secretary of State considers that the goods described in the draft are unsafe;
  (d) sets out the reasons why the Secretary of State considers that those goods are unsafe; and
  (e) states that that person may make representations to the Secretary of State for the purpose of establishing that the goods are safe if, before the end of the period of fourteen days beginning with the day on which the notification is served, he informs the Secretary of State—
    (i) of his intention to make representations; and
    (ii) whether the representations will be made only in writing or both in writing and orally.

(2) Where the Secretary of State has served a notification containing a draft of a proposed notice to warn on any person, he shall not serve a notice to warn on that person in respect of the goods to which the proposed notice relates unless—
  (a) the period of fourteen days beginning with the day on which the notification was served expires without the Secretary of State being informed as mentioned in sub-paragraph (1)(e) above;
  (b) the period of twenty-eight days beginning with that day expires without any written representations being made by that person to the Secretary of State about the proposed notice; or
  (c) the Secretary of State has considered a report about the proposed notice by a person appointed under paragraph 7(1) below.

7—(1) Where a person on whom a notification containing a draft of a proposed notice to warn has been served—
  (a) informs the Secretary of State as mentioned in paragraph 6(1)(e) above before the end of the period of fourteen days beginning with the day on which the notification was served; and
  (b) makes written representations to the Secretary of State about the proposed notice before the end of the period of twenty-eight days beginning with that day,

the Secretary of State shall appoint a person to consider those representations, any further representations made by that person about the draft notice and the statements of any witnesses examined under this Part of this Schedule.

(2) Where—
  (a) the Secretary of State has appointed a person to consider representations about a proposed notice to warn; and
  (b) the person whose representations are to be considered has informed the Secretary of State for the purposes of paragraph 6(1)(e) above that the representations he intends to make will include oral representations,

the Secretary of State shall inform the person intending to make the representations of the place and time at which oral representations may be made to the appointed person.

(3) Where a person on whom a notification containing a draft of a proposed notice to warn has been served is informed of a time for the purposes of sub-paragraph (2) above, that time shall not be—
   (a) before the end of the period of twenty-eight days beginning with the day on which the notification was served; or
   (b) before the end of the period of seven days beginning with the day on which that person is informed of the time.

(4) A person who has been informed of a place and time for the purposes of sub-paragraph (2) above or his representative may, at that place and time—
   (a) make oral representations to the appointed person for the purpose of establishing that the goods to which the proposed notice relates are safe; and
   (b) call and examine witnesses in connection with the representations.

8—(1) Where a person is appointed to consider representations about a proposed notice to warn, it shall be his duty to consider—
   (a) any written representations made by the person on whom it is proposed to serve the notice; and
   (b) in a case where a place and time has been appointed under paragraph 7(2) above for oral representations to be made by that person or his representative, any representations so made and any statements made by witnesses in connection with those representations,

and, after considering those matters, to make a report (including recommendations) to the Secretary of State about the matters considered by him and the proposal to serve the notice.

(2) It shall be the duty of the Secretary of State to consider any report made to him under sub-paragraph (1) above and, after considering the report, to inform the person on whom it was proposed that a notice to warn should be served of his decision with respect to the proposal.

(3) If at any time after serving a notification on a person under paragraph 6 above the Secretary of State decides not to serve on that person either the proposed notice to warn or that notice with modifications, the Secretary of State shall inform that person of the decision; and nothing done for the purposes of any of the preceding provisions of this Part of this Schedule before that person was so informed shall—
   (a) entitle the Secretary of State subsequently to serve the proposed notice or that notice with modifications; or
   (b) require the Secretary of State, or any person appointed to consider representations about the proposed notice, subsequently to do anything in respect of, or in consequence of, any such representations.

(4) Where a notification containing a draft of a proposed notice to warn is served on a person in respect of any goods, a notice to warn served on him in consequence of a decision made under sub-paragraph (2) above shall either be in the form of the draft or shall be less onerous than the draft.

9 The Secretary of State may revoke a notice to warn by serving on the person on whom the notice was served a notification stating that the notice is revoked.

NOTE
Commencement: 1 October 1987.

Part III
General

10 (1) Where in a notification served on any person under this Schedule the Secretary of State has appointed a time for the making of oral representations or the examination of wit-

nesses, he may, by giving that person such notification as the Secretary of State considers appropriate, change that time to a later time or appoint further times at which further representations may be made or the examination of witnesses may be continued; and paragraphs 2(4), 3(4) and 7(4) above shall have effect accordingly.

(2) For the purposes of this Schedule the Secretary of State may appoint a person (instead of the appointed person) to consider any representations or statements, if the person originally appointed, or last appointed under this sub-paragraph, to consider those representations or statements has died or appears to the Secretary of State to be otherwise unable to act.

11 In this Schedule—
"the appointed person" in relation to a prohibition notice or a proposal to serve a notice to warn, means the person for the time being appointed under this Schedule to consider representations about the notice or, as the case may be, about the proposed notice;
"notification" means a notification in writing;
"trader", in relation to a prohibition notice, means the person on whom the notice is or was served.

[339]

NOTE
Commencement: 1 October 1987.

CRIMINAL JUSTICE ACT 1988
(C 33)

An Act to make fresh provision for extradition; to amend the rules of evidence in criminal proceedings; to provide for the reference to the Attorney General of certain questions relating to sentencing to the Court of Appeal; to amend the law with regard to the jurisdiction and powers of criminal courts, the collection, enforcement and remission of fines imposed by coroners, juries, supervision orders, the detention of children and young persons, probation and the probation service, criminal appeals, anonymity in cases of rape and similar cases, orders under sections 4 and 11 of the Contempt of Court Act 1981 relating to trials on indictment, orders restricting the access of the public to the whole or any part of a trial on indictment or to any proceedings ancillary to such a trial and orders restricting the publication of any report of the whole or any part of a trial on indictment or any such ancillary proceedings, the alteration of names of petty sessions areas, officers of inner London magistrates' courts and the costs and expenses of prosecution witnesses and certain other persons; to make fresh provision for the payment of compensation by the Criminal Injuries Compensation Board; to make provision for the payment of compensation for a miscarriage of justice which has resulted in a wrongful conviction; to create an offence of torture and an offence of having an article with a blade or point in a public place; to create further offences relating to weapons; to create a summary offence of possession of an indecent photograph of a child; to amend the Police and Criminal Evidence Act 1984 in relation to searches, computer data about fingerprints and bail for persons in customs detention; to make provision in relation to the taking of body samples by the police in Northern Ireland; to amend the Bail Act 1976; to give a justice of the peace power to authorise entry and search of premises for offensive weapons; to provide for the enforcement of the Video Recordings Act 1984 by officers of a weights and measures authority and in Northern Ireland by officers of the Department of Economic Development; to extend to the purchase of easements and other rights over land the power to purchase land conferred on the Secretary of State by section 36 of the Prisons Act 1952; and for connected purposes

[29 July 1988]

Part VII
COMPENSATION BY COURT AND CRIMINAL INJURIES COMPENSATION BOARD

The Criminal Injuries Compensation Scheme

108 The Criminal Injuries Compensation Board and the administration of the scheme

(1) The Criminal Injuries Compensation Board ("the Board") shall by that name be a body corporate.

(2) The Board shall administer the scheme for the payment of compensation for criminal injuries established by the following provisions of this Part of this Act (in this Act referred to as "the scheme") and shall be responsible for determining claims for compensation under the scheme and for paying compensation due under it.

(3) Schedule 6 to this Act shall have effect with respect to the Board and Schedule 7 shall have effect with respect to the scheme.

[339A]

NOTE
Commencement: Up to 1 August 1993 this section has not been brought into force.

109 Criminal injuries

(1) In this Part of this Act "criminal injury" means any personal injury caused by—
  (a) conduct constituting—
    (i) an offence which is specified in subsection (3) below; or
    (ii) an offence which is not so specified but which requires proof of intent to cause death or personal injury or recklessness as to whether death or personal injury is caused; or
  (b) any of the following activities—
    (i) the apprehension or attempted apprehension of an offender or suspected offender;
    (ii) the prevention or attempted prevention of the commission of an offence; or
    (iii) assisting a constable engaged in any of the activities mentioned in paragraph (i) or (ii) above;

and "personal injury includes any disease, any harm to a person's physical or mental condition and pregnancy.

(2) Harm to a person's mental condition is only a criminal injury if it is attributable—
  (a) to his having been put in fear of immediate physical injury to himself or another; or
  (b) to his being present when another sustained a criminal injury other than harm to his mental condition.

(3) The offences mentioned in subsection (1)(a)(i) above are—
  (a) rape;
  (b) assault;
  (c) an offence which falls to be charged as arson;
  (d) wilful fireraising;

(e) any offence under section 2 (causing explosion likely to endanger life or property) or 3 (attempt to cause explosion, or making or keeping explosive with intent to endanger life or property) of the Explosive Substances Act 1883;
(f) an offence under section 16 (possession of firearm with intent to injure), 17 (use of firearm to resist arrest), 18 (carrying firearm with criminal intent), 19 (carrying firearm in a public place) or 20 (trespassing with firearm) of the Firearms Act 1968;
(g) an offence under section 1 (riot), 2 (violent disorder) or 3 (affray) of the Public Order Act 1986;
(h) mobbing;
(j) kidnapping;
(k) false imprisonment;
(l) abduction;
(m) trespass on a railway; and
(n) any attempt to commit an offence mentioned in this subsection.

(4) For the purposes of this Part of this Act, a person's conduct shall be treated as constituting an offence notwithstanding that he may not be convicted of the offence by reason of age, insanity or diplomatic immunity.

[339B]

NOTE

Commencement: Up to 1 August 1993 this section has not been brought into force.

110 Qualifying injuries

(1) Compensation for a criminal injury shall only be payable under this Part of this Act if the injury is a qualifying injury.

(2) A criminal injury is only a qualifying injury if it is sustained—
(a) in Great Britain;
(b) within the limits of the territorial waters adjacent to the United Kingdom;
(c) on board a British ship, a British aircraft or a British hovercraft;
(d) on, under or above an installation in a designated area within the meaning of section 1(7) of the Continental Shelf Act 1964 or any waters within 500 metres of such an installation; or
(e) on, under or above any waters in respect of which an Order in Council made under section 23 of the Oil and Gas (Enterprise) Act 1982 provides that questions arising from acts or omissions on, under or above such waters are to be determined in accordance with the law of England and Wales or the law of Scotland.

(3) In subsection (2) above—
"British aircraft" means a British-controlled aircraft within the meaning of section 92 of the Civil Aviation Act 1982 (application of criminal law to aircraft), or one of Her Majesty's aircraft;
"British hovercraft" means a British-controlled hovercraft within the meaning of that section (as applied in relation to hovercraft by virtue of provision made under the Hovercraft Act 1968), or one of Her Majesty's hovercraft; and
"British ship" means—
(a) any vessel used in navigation which is owned wholly by persons of the following descriptions, namely—

(i) British citizens; and
(ii) bodies corporate incorporated under the law of some part of, and having their principal place of business in, the United Kingdom; or
(b) one of Her Majesty's ships.

(4) The references to Her Majesty's aircraft, hovercraft and ships in subsection (3) above are references to aircraft, hovercraft or ships which belong to, or are exclusively used in the service of, Her Majesty in right of the government of the United Kingdom.

(5) Where any injury which is a criminal injury by virtue of section 109(1)(a) above is sustained by a person not under the age of 18 years who, when he sustains the injury is living in the same household as the person or, if more than one, any of the persons, responsible for causing it, that injury is not a qualifying injury unless—
(a) the Board are satisfied in relation to the person responsible for causing the injury or, where more than one person is responsible for causing it, each of the persons responsible who was living in the same household as the person injured when the injury was sustained—
(i) that he has been prosecuted in connection with the injury; or
(ii) that there is sufficient reason why he has not been prosecuted; and
(b) the Board are satisfied—
(i) that the person injured has ceased to live, and does not intend to live again, in the same household as the person responsible for causing the injury or, where more than one person is responsible for causing it, any of the persons responsible who was living in the same household as the person injured when the injury was sustained; or
(ii) that the person injured has not ceased to live but that the reason why he has not so ceased to love but that the reason why he has not so ceased to live is that circumstances prevent him from doing so.

(6) Where a person accidentally sustains an injury which is a criminal injury only by virtue of section 109(1)(b) above, that injury is not a qualifying injury unless the Board are satisfied that the risk he was taking when he was injured was an exceptional risk which was justifiable in all the circumstances.

(7) Where any criminal injury is sustained in circumstances such that the compensation in respect of the injury is payable—
(a) under any policy of insurance maintained in pursuance of Part VI of the Road Traffic Act 1972 (compulsory insurance in relation to the use of a motor vehicle on a road); or
(b) under any arrangements for the compensation of victims of uninsured or unidentified drivers to which the Secretary of State is a party;

that injury is not a qualifying injury.

(8) Any reference in this section to a person who is responsible for causing an injury includes, where the injury is a criminal injury by virtue of an offence, a reference to any person who is a party to the commission of that offence.

[339C]

NOTES
Commencement: Up to 1 August 1993 this section has not been brought into force.
Road Traffic Act 1972, Pt VI: repealed by the Road Traffic (Consequential Provisions) Act 1988, s 3, Sch 1, Pt I, and replaced by the Road Traffic Act 1988, Pt VI.

111 Awards of compensation

(1) An award of compensation may be made—
   (a) to any person who satisfies the Board that he has sustained a qualifying injury;
   (b) to any person who satisfies the Board that he is a dependant of a person who died after sustaining a qualifying injury (whether or not he died as a result of it);

and in this subsection "satisfies" means satisfies on a balance of probabilities.

(2) The heads of compensation are those specified in subsections (3) to (6) below.

(3) An award may be made under subsection (1)(a) above—
   (a) for the injury; and
   (b) for any loss or damage to property of the claimant which occurred in the course of his sustaining the injury,

but compensation shall only be payable under paragraph (b) above if he relied on the property as a physical aid and for damage only if the damage impaired the utility of the property as a physical aid and shall only be for the cost of replacing it with other property of equal utility as a physical aid or carrying out repairs to restore its utility as a physical aid.

(4) If a person dies as a result of qualifying injury—
   (a) an award of compensation for funeral expenses may be made to any person other than a public authority but shall not exceed a reasonable amount;
   (b) where a claim falls to be determined in accordance with the rules of the law of England and Wales, an award of compensation for bereavement may be made to any person falling within section 1A(2) of the Fatal Accidents Act 1976;
   (c) where a claim falls to be determined in accordance with the rules of the law of Scotland, an award of compensation for loss of society may be made to any person who is a member of the deceased's immediate family within the meaning of section 10(2) of the Damages (Scotland) Act 1976; and
   (d) an award may be made to a dependant or the deceased (whether or not an award is made to him or to any other person under paragraph (a), (b) or (c) above) in respect of any loss of support suffered by the dependant.

(5) Subject to subsection (8) below, if a person who has sustained a qualifying injury dies otherwise than as a result of it, the Board may award compensation to a dependant of his in respect of any loss which he has suffered by reason—
   (a) of any reduction in earnings (not being prospective earnings) by the deceased; and
   (b) of any expenses and liabilities incurred by the deceased as a result of the injury.

(6) If—
   (a) a woman is awarded compensation for rape; and
   (b) she has given birth to a child conceived as a result of the rape; and
   (c) at the time of the award she intends to keep the child,

the Board shall award her the additional statutory sum in respect of each child so conceived that she then intends to keep.

(7) The Board may make an interim award, but without prejudice to their powers on a final determination.

(8) If a person who has sustained a qualifying injury dies otherwise as a result of it, the Board may not award compensation to a dependant of his if before he died he became entitled, otherwise than in an interim award, to a payment of compensation in respect of it.

(9) If—
   (a) a deceased person was entitled to a payment of compensation for an injury; and
   (b) a claim for compensation for the same injury is made by one of his dependants,

any compensation awarded to the dependant shall be reduced by the amount of the compensation to payment of which the deceased was entitled; and proportionate reductions shall be made on awards to two or more dependants.

(10) Where a person has been awarded compensation by the Board in respect of a qualifying injury sustained by him, he may be awarded further compensation in respect of the injury if the Board are satisfied—
   (a) that since the date of the previous award his medical condition has deteriorated as a result of having sustained the injury; and
   (b) that the extent to which his condition has so deteriorated is such that it would be unjust not to make an award of further compensation to him in respect of the injury.

(11) In this Part of this Act—
   "the additional statutory sum" means £5,000 or such other sum as may for the time being be specified by virtue of an order under subsection (12) below; and
   "dependant"—
      (a) where the appropriate law for the determination of a claim is the law of England and Wales, has the same meaning as in the Fatal Accidents Act 1976; and
      (b) ...

(12) The Secretary of State may by order made by statutory instrument substitute a different sum for the sum specified in subsection (11) above.

(13) A statutory instrument containing an order under subsection (12) above shall be subject to annulment in pursuance of a resolution of either House of Parliament.

[339D]

NOTES

Commencement: Up to 1 August 1993 this section has not been brought into force.
Sub-s (11): sub-para (b) applies to Scotland only.

---

115 Reimbursement and recovery

(1) Where—
   (a) a person has been convicted in England and Wales of an offence; and
   (b) the Board have made an award of compensation in respect of an injury which is a criminal injury by virtue of the offence,

proceedings may be brought by the Board in a county court for an order for the repayment by the offender to the Board of the whole of the award or such part of it as the court thinks fit.

(2) The Board shall only make an application for an order under subsection (1) above if they have reason to believe that the offender is able to pay the whole or a substantial part of the award.

(3) In considering whether to make an order under subsection (1) above, the court shall have regard to the financial position of the offender and to such other matters (not including the question whether he was properly convicted) as the court considers relevant.

(4) Where after an award of compensation under this Part of this Act has been made to a person he receives any payment which, had he received i before the making of the award, would, under any provision contained in Schedule 7 to this Act, have led to any reduction in the amount of compensation payable to him he shall be liable to repay to the Board a sum equal to the amount of that reduction.

(5) The Board may set-off any sum owed to them by any person by virtue of subsection (4) above against any compensation under this Part of this Act to which that person is or becomes entitled.

(6) Where by virtue of any order under section 35 of the Powers of Criminal Courts Act 1973 (compensation orders against convicted persons) compensation is required to be paid for any personal injury, loss or damage which the Board are satisfied has been the subject of compensation under this Part of this Act, they may by notice require the magistrates' court for the time being having functions in relation to the enforcement of that order to pay to them any amount recovered in pursuance of that order in respect of any personal injury, loss or damage.

[339E]

NOTE
Commencement: Up to 1 August 1993 this section has not been brought into force.

Part XII
General and Supplementary

171 Commencement

(1) Subject to the following provisions of this section, this Act shall come into force on such day as the Secretary of State may by order made by statutory instrument appoint and different days may be appointed in pursuance of this subsection for different provisions or different purposes of the same provision.

(2)-(7) ...

[339F]

NOTES
Commencement: 29 July 1988.
Sub-ss (2)-(7): not relevant to this work.

172 Extent

(1) Subject to the following provisions of this section, and to sections 19, 20 and 21 above, this Act extends to England and Wales only.

(2)-(12) ...

[339G]

NOTES
Commencement: 29 July 1988.
Sub-ss (2)- (12): not relevant to this work.

173 Citation

This Act may be cited as the Criminal Justice Act 1988.

[339H]

NOTE
Commencement: 29 July 1988.

ROAD TRAFFIC ACT 1988

(C 52)

An Act to consolidate certain enactments relating to road traffic with amendments to give effect to recommendations of the Law Commission and the Scottish Law Commission

[15 November 1988]

PART I

PRINCIPAL ROAD SAFETY PROVISIONS

Promotion of road safety

38 The Highway Code

(1) The Highway Code shall continue to have effect, subject however to revision in accordance with the following provisions of this section.

(2) Subject to the following provisions of this section, the Secretary of State may from time to time revise the Highway Code by revoking, varying, amending or adding to the provisions of the Code in such manner as he thinks fit.

(3) Where the Secretary of State proposes to revise the Highway Code by making any alterations in the provisions of the Code (other than alterations merely consequential on the passing, amendment or repeal of any statutory provision) he must lay the proposed alterations before both Houses of Parliament and must not make the proposed revision until after the end of a period of forty days beginning with the day on which the alterations were so laid.

(4) If within the period mentioned in subsection (3) above either House resolves that the proposed alterations be not made, the Secretary of State must not make the proposed revision (but without prejudice to the laying before Parliament of further proposals for alteration in accordance with that subsection).

(5) Before revising the Highway Code by making any alterations in its provisions which are required by subsection (3) above to be laid before Parliament, the Secretary of State must consult with such representative organisations as he thinks fit.

(6) The Secretary of State must cause the Highway Code to be printed and may cause copies of it to be sold to the public at such price as he may determine.

(7) A failure on the part of a person to observe a provision of the Highway Code shall not of itself render that person liable to criminal proceedings of any kind but any

such failure may in any proceedings (whether civil or criminal, and including proceedings for an offence under the Traffic Acts, the Public Passenger Vehicles Act 1981 or sections 18 to 23 of the Transport Act 1985) be relied upon by any party to the proceedings as tending to establish or negative any liability which is in question in those proceedings.

(8) In this section "the Highway Code" means the code comprising directions for the guidance of persons using roads issued under section 45 of the Road Traffic Act 1930, as from time to time revised under this section or under any previous enactment.

(9) For the purposes of subsection (3) above—
   (a) "statutory provision" means a provision contained in an Act or in subordinate legislation within the meaning of the Interpretation Act 1978 (and the reference to the passing or repeal of any such provision accordingly includes the making or revocation of any such provision),
   (b) where the proposed alterations are laid before each House of Parliament on different days, the later day shall be taken to be the day on which they were laid before both Houses, and
   (c) in reckoning any period of forty days, no account shall be taken of any time during which Parliament is dissolved or prorogued or during which both Houses are adjourned for more than four days.

[340]

NOTES
Commencement: 15 May 1989.
Traffic Acts: Road Traffic Regulation Act 1984, Road Traffic Offenders Act 1988, Road Traffic (Consequential Provisions) Act 1988 (so far as it reproduces the effect of provisions repealed by that Act), Road Traffic Act 1988.

PART VI
THIRD-PARTY LIABILITIES

Compulsory insurance or security against third-party risks

143 Users of motor vehicles to be insured or secured against third-party risks

(1) Subject to the provisions of this Part of this Act—
   (a) a person must not use a motor vehicle on a road unless there is in force in relation to the use of the vehicle by that person such a policy of insurance or such a security in respect of third party risks as complies with the requirements of this Part of this Act, and
   (b) a person must not cause or permit any other person to use a motor vehicle on a road unless there is in force in relation to the use of the vehicle by that other person such a policy of insurance or such a security in respect of third party risks as complies with the requirements of this Part of this Act.

(2) If a person acts in contravention of subsection (1) above he is guilty of an offence.

(3) A person charged with using a motor vehicle in contravention of this section shall not be convicted if he proves—
   (a) that the vehicle did not belong to him and was not in his possession under a contract of hiring or of loan,
   (b) that he was using the vehicle in the course of his employment, and

(c) that he neither knew nor had reason to believe that there was not in force in relation to the vehicle such a policy of insurance or security as is mentioned in subsection (1) above.

(4) This Part of this Act does not apply to invalid carriages.

[341]

NOTE
Commencement: 15 May 1989.

144 Exceptions from requirement of third party insurance or security

(1) Section 143 of this Act does not apply to a vehicle owned by a person who has deposited and keeps deposited with the Accountant General of the Supreme Court the sum of [£500,000], at a time when the vehicle is being driven under the owner's control.

[(1A) The Secretary of State may by order made by statutory instrument substitute a greater sum for the sum for the time being specified in subsection (1) above.

(1B) No order shall be made under subsection (1A) above unless a draft of it has been laid before and approved by resolution of each House of Parliament.]

(2) Section 143 does not apply—
    (a) to a vehicle owned—
        (i) by the council of a county or county district in England and Wales, the Common Council of the City of London, the council of a London borough, the Inner London Education Authority, or a joint authority (other than a police authority) established by Part IV of the Local Government Act 1985,
        (ii) by a regional, islands or district council in Scotland, or
        (iii) by a joint board or committee in England or Wales, or joint committee in Scotland, which is so constituted as to include among its members representatives of any such council,
    at a time when the vehicle is being driven under the owner's control,

(b) to a vehicle owned by a police authority or the Receiver for the Metropolitan Police district, at a time when it is being driven under the owner's control, or to a vehicle at a time when it is being driven for police purposes by or under the direction of a constable, or by a person employed by a police authority, or employed by the Receiver, or

(c) to a vehicle at a time when it is being driven on a journey to or from any place undertaken for salvage purposes pursuant to Part IX of the Merchant Shipping Act 1894,

(d) to the use of a vehicle for the purpose of its being provided in pursuance of a direction under section 166(2)(b) of the Army Act 1955 or under the corresponding provision of the Air Force Act 1955,

[(da) to a vehicle owned by a health service body, as defined in section 60(7) of the National Health Service and Community Care Act 1990, at a time when the vehicle is being driven under the owner's control,

(db) to an ambulance owned by a National Health Service trust established under Part I of the National Health Service and Community Care Act 1990 or the National Health Service (Scotland) Act 1978, at a time when a vehicle is being driven under the owner's control,]

(e) to a vehicle which is made available by the Secretary of State to any person, body or local authority in pursuance of section 23 or 26 of the National Health Service Act 1977 at a time when it is being used in accordance with the terms on which it is so made available,

(f) to a vehicle which is made available by the Secretary of State to any local authority, education authority or voluntary organisation in Scotland in pursuance of section 15 or 16 of the National Health Service (Scotland) Act 1978 at a time when it is being used in accordance with the terms on which it is so made available.

[342]

NOTES
Commencement: 1 July 1992 (sub-ss (1A), (1B)); 15 May 1989 (remainder).
Sub-s (1): sum in square brackets substituted by the Road Traffic Act 1991, s 20(2).
Sub-ss (1A), (1B): added by the Road Traffic Act 1991, s 20(3).
Sub-s (2): paras (da), (db) added by the National Health Service and Community Care Act 1990, s 60, Sch 8, Part I, para 4.

145 Requirements in respect of policies of insurance

(1) In order to comply with the requirements of this Part of this Act, a policy of insurance must satisfy the following conditions.

(2) The policy must be issued by an authorised insurer.

(3) Subject to subsection (4) below, the policy—
    (a) must insure such person, persons or classes of persons as may be specified in the policy in respect of any liability which may be incurred by him or them in respect of the death of or bodily injury to any person or damage to property caused by, or arising out of, the use of the vehicle on a road in Great Britain, and
    [(aa) must, in the case of a vehicle normally based in the territory of another member State, insure him or them in respect of any civil liability which may be incurred by him or them as a result of an event related to the use of the vehicle in Great Britain if,—
        (i) according to the law of that territory, he or they would be required to be insured in respect of a civil liability which would arise under that law as a result of that event if the place where the vehicle was used when the event occurred were in that territory, and
        (ii) the cover required by that law would be higher than that required by paragraph (a) above, and]
    (b) must [, in the case of a vehicle normally based in Great Britain,] insure him or them in respect of any liability which may be incurred by him or them in respect of the use of the vehicle and of any trailer, whether or not coupled, in the territory other than Great Britain and Gibraltar of each of the member States of the Communities according to—
        [(i) the law on compulsory insurance against civil liability in respect of the use of vehicles of the State in whose territory the event giving rise to the liability occurred; or
        (ii) if it would give higher cover, the law which would be applicable under this Part of this Act if the place where the vehicle was used when that event occurred were in Great Britain; and]
    (c) must also insure him or them in respect of any liability which may be incurred by him or them under the provisions of this Part of this Act relating to payment for emergency treatment.

(4) The policy shall not, by virtue of subsection (3)(a) above, be required—
- (a) to cover liability in respect of the death, arising out of and in the course of his employment, of a person in the employment of a person insured by the policy or of bodily injury sustained by such a person arising out of and in the course of his employment, or
- (b) to provide insurance of more than £250,000 in respect of all such liabilities as may be insured in respect of damage to property caused by, or arising out of, any one accident involving the vehicle, or
- (c) to cover liability in respect of damage to the vehicle, or
- (d) to cover liability in respect of damage to goods carried for hire or reward in or on the vehicle or in or on any trailer (whether or not coupled) drawn by the vehicle, or
- (e) to cover any liability of a person in respect of damage to property in his custody or under his control, or
- (f) to cover any contractual liability.

[(4A) In the case of a person—
- (a) carried in or upon a vehicle, or
- (b) entering or getting on to, or alighting from, a vehicle,

the provisions of paragraph (a) of subsection (4) above do not apply unless cover in respect of the liability referred to in that paragraph is in fact provided pursuant to a requirement of the Employers' Liability (Compulsory Insurance) Act 1969.]

(5) In this Part of this Act "authorised insurer" means a person or body of persons carrying on insurance business within Group 2 in Part II of Schedule 2 to the Insurance Companies Act 1982 and being a member of the Motor Insurers' Bureau (a company limited by guarantee and incorporated under the Companies Act 1929 on 14th June 1946).

(6) If any person or body of persons ceases to be a member of the Motor Insurers' Bureau, that person or body shall not by virtue of that cease to be treated as an authorised insurer for the purposes of this Part of this Act—
- (a) in relation to any policy issued by the insurer before ceasing to be such a member, or
- (b) in relation to any obligation (whether arising before or after the insurer ceased to be such a member) which the insurer may be called upon to meet under or in consequence of any such policy or under section 157 of this Act by virtue of making a payment in pursuance of such an obligation.

NOTES

Commencement: 31 December 1992 (sub-s (4A)); 15 May 1989 (remainder).

Sub-s (3): para (aa) added, in para (b) first words in square brackets added and second words in square brackets substituted, by SI 1992/3036, reg 2(1), (2).

Sub-s (4A): added by SI 1992/3036, reg 2(3).

146 Requirements in respect of securities

(1) In order to comply with the requirements of this Part of this Act, a security must satisfy the following conditions.

(2) The security must be given either by an authorised insurer or by some body of persons which carries on in the United Kingdom the business of giving securities of a like kind and has deposited and keeps deposited with the Accountant General of the Supreme Court the sum of £15,000 in respect of that business.

(3) Subject to subsection (4) below, the security must consist of an undertaking by the giver of the security to make good, subject to any conditions specified in it, any failure by the owner of the vehicle or such other persons or classes of persons as may be specified in the security duly to discharge any liability which may be incurred by him or them, being a liability required under section 145 of this Act to be covered by a policy of insurance.

(4) In the case of liabilities arising out of the use of a motor vehicle on a road in Great Britain the amount secured need not exceed—
- (a) in the case of an undertaking relating to the use of public service vehicles (within the meaning of the Public Passenger Vehicles Act 1981), £25,000,
- (b) in any other case, £5,000.

[344]

NOTE
Commencement: 15 May 1989.

147 Issue and surrender of certificates of insurance and of security

(1) A policy of insurance shall be of no effect for the purposes of this Part of this Act unless and until there is delivered by the insurer to the person by whom the policy is effected a certificate (in this Part of this Act referred to as a "certificate of insurance") in the prescribed form and containing such particulars of any conditions subject to which the policy is issued and of any other matters as may be prescribed.

(2) A security shall be of no effect for the purposes of this Part of this Act unless and until there is delivered by the person giving the security to the person to whom it is given a certificate (in this Part of this Act referred to as a "certificate of security") in the prescribed form and containing such particulars of any conditions subject to which the security is issued and of any other matters as may be prescribed.

(3) Different forms and different particulars may be prescribed for the purposes of subsection (1) or (2) above in relation to different cases or circumstances.

(4) Where a certificate has been delivered under this section and the policy or security to which it relates is cancelled by mutual consent or by virtue of any provision in the policy or security, the person to whom the certificate was delivered must, within seven days from the taking effect of the cancellation—
- (a) surrender the certificate to the person by whom the policy was issued or the security was given, or
- (b) if the certificate has been lost or destroyed, make a statutory declaration to that effect.

(5) A person who fails to comply with subsection (4) above is guilty of an offence.

[345]

NOTE
Commencement: 15 May 1989.

148 Avoidance of certain exceptions to policies or securities

(1) Where a certificate of insurance or certificate of security has been delivered under section 147 of this Act to the person by whom a policy has been effected or to whom a security has been given, so much of the policy or security as purports to restrict—
- (a) the insurance of the persons insured by the policy, or

(b) the operation of the security,

(as the case may be) by reference to any of the matters mentioned in subsection (2) below shall, as respects such liabilities as are required to be covered by a policy under section 145 of this Act, be of no effect.

(2) Those matters are—
   (a) the age or physical or mental condition of persons driving the vehicle,
   (b) the condition of the vehicle,
   (c) the number of persons that the vehicle carries,
   (d) the weight or physical characteristics of the goods that the vehicle carries,
   (e) the time at which or the areas within which the vehicle is used,
   (f) the horsepower or cylinder capacity or value of the vehicle,
   (g) the carrying on the vehicle of any particular apparatus, or
   (h) the carrying on the vehicle of any particular means of identification other than any means of identification required to be carried by or under the Vehicles (Excise) Act 1971.

(3) Nothing in subsection (1) above requires an insurer or the giver of a security to pay any sum in respect of the liability of any person otherwise than in or towards the discharge of that liability.

(4) Any sum paid by an insurer or the giver of a security in or towards the discharge of any liability of any person which is covered by the policy or security by virtue only of subsection (1) above is recoverable by the insurer or giver of the security from that person.

(5) A condition in a policy or security issued or given for the purposes of this Part of this Act providing—
   (a) that no liability shall arise under the policy or security, or
   (b) that any liability so arising shall cease,

in the event of some specified thing being done or omitted to be done after the happening of the event giving rise to a claim under the policy or security, shall be of no effect in connection with such liabilities as are required to be covered by a policy under section 145 of this Act.

(6) Nothing in subsection (5) above shall be taken to render void any provision in a policy or security requiring the person insured or secured to pay to the insurer or the giver of the security any sums which the latter may have become liable to pay under the policy or security and which have been applied to the satisfaction of the claims of third parties.

(7) Notwithstanding anything in any enactment, a person issuing a policy of insurance under section 145 of this Act shall be liable to indemnify the persons or classes of persons specified in the policy in respect of any liability which the policy purports to cover in the case of those persons or classes of persons.

[346]

NOTE
Commencement: 15 May 1989.

149 Avoidance of certain agreements as to liability towards passengers

(1) This section applies where a person uses a motor vehicle in circumstances such that under section 143 of this Act there is required to be in force in relation to his use

of it such a policy of insurance or such a security in respect of third-party risks as complies with the requirements of this Part of this Act.

(2) If any other person is carried in or upon the vehicle while the user is so using it, any antecedent agreement or understanding between them (whether intended to be legally binding or not) shall be of no effect so far as it purports or might be held—
   (a) to negative or restrict any such liability of the user in respect of persons carried in or upon the vehicle as is required by section 145 of this Act to be covered by a policy of insurance, or
   (b) to impose any conditions with respect to the enforcement of any such liability of the user.

(3) The fact that a person so carried has willingly accepted as his the risk of negligence on the part of the user shall not be treated as negativing any such liability of the user.

(4) For the purposes of this section—
   (a) references to a person being carried in or upon a vehicle include references to a person entering or getting on to, or alighting from, the vehicle, and
   (b) the reference to an antecedent agreement is to one made at any time before the liability arose.

[347]

NOTE
Commencement: 15 May 1989.

150 Insurance or security in respect of private use of vehicle to cover use under car-sharing arrangements

(1) To the extent that a policy or security issued or given for the purposes of this Part of this Act—
   (a) restricts the insurance of the persons insured by the policy or the operation of the security (as the case may be) to use of the vehicle for specified purposes (for example, social, domestic and pleasure purposes) of a non-commercial character, or
   (b) excludes from that insurance or the operation of the security (as the case may be)—
      (i) use of the vehicle for hire or reward, or
      (ii) business or commercial use of the vehicle, or
      (iii) use of the vehicle for specified purposes of a business or commercial character,

then, for the purposes of that policy or security so far as it relates to such liabilities as are required to be covered by a policy under section 145 of this Act, the use of a vehicle on a journey in the course of which one or more passengers are carried at separate fares shall, if the conditions specified in subsection (2) below are satisfied, be treated as falling within that restriction or as not falling within that exclusion (as the case may be).

(2) The conditions referred to in subsection (1) above are—
   (a) the vehicle is not adapted to carry more than eight passengers and is not a motor cycle,
   (b) the fare or aggregate of the fares paid in respect of the journey does not exceed the amount of the running costs of the vehicle for the journey (which

for the purposes of this paragraph shall be taken to include an appropriate amount in respect of depreciation and general wear), and
  (c) the arrangements for the payment of fares by the passenger or passengers carried at separate fares were made before the journey began.

(3) Subsections (1) and (2) above apply however the restrictions or exclusions described in subsection (1) are framed or worded.

(4) In subsections (1) and (2) above "fare" and "separate fares" have the same meaning as in section 1(4) of the Public Passenger Vehicles Act 1981.

[348]

NOTE
Commencement: 15 May 1989.

151 Duty of insurers or persons giving security to satisfy judgment against persons insured or secured against third-party risks

(1) This section applies where, after a certificate of insurance or certificate of security has been delivered under section 147 of this Act to the person by whom a policy has been effected or to whom a security has been given, a judgment to which this subsection applies is obtained.

(2) Subsection (1) above applies to judgments relating to a liability with respect to any matter where liability with respect to that matter is required to be covered by a policy of insurance under section 145 of this Act and either—
  (a) it is a liability covered by the terms of the policy or security to which the certificate relates, and the judgment is obtained against any person who is insured by the policy or whose liability is covered by the security, as the case may be, or
  (b) it is a liability, other than an excluded liability, which would be so covered if the policy insured all persons or, as the case may be, the security covered the liability of all persons, and the judgment is obtained against any person other than one who is insured by the policy or, as the case may be, whose liability is covered by the security.

(3) In deciding for the purposes of subsection (2) above whether a liability is or would be covered by the terms of a policy or security, so much of the policy or security as purports to restrict, as the case may be, the insurance of the persons insured by the policy or the operation of the security by reference to the holding by the driver of the vehicle of a licence authorising him to drive it shall be treated as of no effect.

(4) In subsection (2)(b) above "excluded liability" means a liability in respect of the death of, or bodily injury to, or damage to the property of any person who, at the time of the use which gave rise to the liability, was allowing himself to be carried in or upon the vehicle and knew or had reason to believe that the vehicle had been stolen or unlawfully taken, not being a person who—
  (a) did not know and had no reason to believe that the vehicle had been stolen or unlawfully taken until after the commencement of his journey, and
  (b) could not reasonably have been expected to have alighted from the vehicle.

In this subsection the reference to a person being carried in or upon a vehicle includes a reference to a person entering or getting on to, or alighting from, the vehicle.

(5) Notwithstanding that the insurer may be entitled to avoid or cancel, or may have avoided or cancelled, the policy or security, he must, subject to the provisions of this section, pay to the persons entitled to the benefit of the judgment—
    (a) as regards liability in respect of death or bodily injury, any sum payable under the judgment in respect of the liability, together with any sum which, by virtue of any enactment relating to interest on judgments, is payable in respect of interest on that sum,
    (b) as regards liability in respect of damage to property, any sum required to be paid under subsection (6) below, and
    (c) any amount payable in respect of costs.

(6) This subsection requires—
    (a) where the total of any amount paid, payable or likely to be payable under the policy or security in respect of damage to property caused by, or arising out of, the accident in question does not exceed £250,000, the payment of any sum payable under the judgment in respect of the liability, together with any sum which, by virtue of any enactment relating to interest on judgments, is payable in respect of interest on that sum,
    (b) where that total exceeds £250,000, the payment of either—
        (i) such proportion of any sum payable under the judgment in respect of the liability as £250,000 bears to that total, together with the same proportion of any sum which, by virtue of any enactment relating to interest on judgments, is payable in respect of interest on that sum, or
        (ii) the difference between the total of any amounts already paid under the policy or security in respect of such damage and £250,000, together with such proportion of any sum which, by virtue of any enactment relating to interest on judgments is payable in respect of interest on any sum payable under the judgment in respect of the liability as the difference bears to that sum,
    whichever is the less, unless not less than £250,000 has already been paid under the policy or security in respect of such damage (in which case nothing is payable).

(7) Where an insurer becomes liable under this section to pay an amount in respect of a liability of a person who is insured by a policy or whose liability is covered by a security, he is entitled to recover from that person—
    (a) that amount, in a case where he became liable to pay it by virtue only of subsection (3) above, or
    (b) in a case where that amount exceeds the amount for which he would, apart from the provisions of this section, be liable under the policy or security in respect of that liability, the excess.

(8) Where an insurer becomes liable under this section to pay an amount in respect of a liability of a person who is not insured by a policy or whose liability is not covered by a security, he is entitled to recover the amount from that person or from any person who—
    (a) is insured by the policy, or whose liability is covered by the security, by the terms of which the liability would be covered if the policy insured all persons or, as the case may be, the security covered the liability of all persons, and
    (b) caused or permitted the use of the vehicle which gave rise to the liability.

(9) In this section—
    (a) "insurer" includes a person giving a security,
    (b) ...

(c) "liability covered by the terms of the policy or security" means a liability which is covered by the policy or security or which would be so covered but for the fact that the insurer is entitled to avoid or cancel, or has avoided or cancelled, the policy or security.

(10) In the application of this section to Scotland, the words "by virtue of any enactment relating to interest on judgments" in subsections (5) and (6) (in each place where they appear) shall be omitted.

[349]

NOTES
Commencement: 15 May 1989.
Sub-s (9): para (b) repealed by the Road Traffic Act 1991, s 83, Sch 8.

152 Exceptions to section 151

(1) No sum is payable by an insurer under section 151 of this Act—
  (a) in respect of any judgment unless, before or within seven days after the commencement of the proceedings in which the judgment was given, the insurer had notice of the bringing of the proceedings, or
  (b) in respect of any judgment so long as execution on the judgment is stayed pending an appeal, or
  (c) in connection with any liability if, before the happening of the event which was the cause of the death or bodily injury or damage to property giving rise to the liability, the policy or security was cancelled by mutual consent or by virtue of any provision contained in it, and also—
    (i) before the happening of that event the certificate was surrendered to the insurer, or the person to whom the certificate was delivered made a statutory declaration stating that the certificate had been lost or destroyed, or
    (ii) after the happening of that event, but before the expiration of a period of fourteen days from the taking effect of the cancellation of the policy or security, the certificate was surrendered to the insurer, or the person to whom it was delivered made a statutory declaration stating that the certificate had been lost or destroyed, or
    (iii) either before or after the happening of that event, but within that period of fourteen days, the insurer has commenced proceedings under this Act in respect of the failure to surrender the certificate.

(2) Subject to subsection (3) below, no sum is payable by an insurer under section 151 of this Act if, in an action commenced before, or within three months after, the commencement of the proceedings in which the judgment was given, he has obtained a declaration—
  (a) that, apart from any provision contained in the policy or security, he is entitled to avoid it on the ground that it was obtained—
    (i) by the non-disclosure of a material fact, or
    (ii) by a representation of fact which was false in some material particular, or
  (b) if he has avoided the policy or security on that ground, that he was entitled so to do apart from any provision contained in it

[and, for the purposes of this section, "material" means of such a nature as to influence the judgment of a prudent insurer in determining whether he will take the risk and, if so, at what premium and on what conditions.]

(3) An insurer who has obtained such a declaration as is mentioned in subsection (2) above in an action does not by reason of that become entitled to the benefit of that subsection as respects any judgment obtained in proceedings commenced before the commencement of that action unless before, or within seven days after, the commencement of that action he has given notice of it to the person who is the plaintiff (or in Scotland pursuer) in those proceedings specifying the non-disclosure or false representation on which he proposes to rely.

(4) A person to whom notice of such an action is so given is entitled, if he thinks fit, to be made a party to it.

[350]

NOTES
Commencement: 15 May 1989.
Sub-s (2): words in square brackets added by the Road Traffic Act 1991, s 48, Sch 4, para 66.

153 Bankruptcy, etc, of insured or secured persons not to affect claims by third parties

(1) Where, after a certificate of insurance or certificate of security has been delivered under section 147 of this Act to the person by whom a policy has been effected or to whom a security has been given, any of the events mentioned in subsection (2) below happens, the happening of that event shall, notwithstanding anything in the Third Parties (Rights Against Insurers) Act 1930, not affect any such liability of that person as is required to be covered by a policy of insurance under section 145 of this Act.

(2) In the case of the person by whom the policy was effected or to whom the security was given, the events referred to in subsection (1) above are—
  (a) that he becomes bankrupt or makes a composition or arrangement with his creditors or that his estate is sequestrated or he grants a trust deed for his creditors,
  (b) that he dies and—
    (i) his estate falls to be administered in accordance with an order under section 421 of the Insolvency Act 1986,
    (ii) an award of sequestration of his estate is made, or
    (iii) a judicial factor is appointed to administer his estate under section 11A of the Judicial Factors (Scotland) Act 1889,
  (c) that if that person is a company—
    (i) a winding-up order or an administration order is made with respect to the company,
    (ii) a resolution for a voluntary winding-up is passed with respect to the company,
    (iii) a receiver or manager of the company's business or undertaking is duly appointed, or
    (iv) possession is taken, by or on behalf of the holders of any debentures secured by a floating charge, of any property comprised in or subject to the charge.

(3) Nothing in subsection (1) above affects any rights conferred by the Third Parties (Rights Against Insurers) Act 1930 on the person to whom the liability was incurred, being rights so conferred against the person by whom the policy was issued or the security was given.

[351]

NOTE
Commencement: 15 May 1989.

PART VII
MISCELLANEOUS AND GENERAL

Supplementary

197 Short title, commencement and extent

(1) This Act may be cited as the Road Traffic Act 1988.

(2) This Act shall come into force, subject to the transitory provisions in Schedule 5 to the Road Traffic (Consequential Provisions) Act 1988, at the end of the period of six months beginning with the day on which it is passed.

(3) This Act, except section 80 and except as provided by section 184, does not extend to Northern Ireland.

NOTE
Commencement: 15 May 1989.

LAW OF PROPERTY (MISCELLANEOUS PROVISIONS) ACT 1989
(C 34)

An Act to make new provision with respect to deeds and their execution and contracts for the sale or other disposition of interests in land; and to abolish the rule of law known as the rule in Bain v. Fothergill

[27 July 1989]

2 Contracts for sale etc of land to be made by signed writing

(1) A contract for the sale or other disposition of an interest in land can only be made in writing and only by incorporating all the terms which the parties have expressly agreed in one document or, where contracts are exchanged, in each.

(2) The terms may be incorporated in a document either by being set out in it or by reference to some other document.

(3) The document incorporating the terms or, where contracts are exchanged, one of the documents incorporating them (but not necessarily the same one) must be signed by or on behalf of each party to the contract.

(4) Where a contract for the sale or other disposition of an interest in land satisfies the conditions of this section by reason only of the rectification of one or more documents in pursuance of an order of a court, the contract shall come into being, or be deemed to have come into being, at such time as may be specified in the order.

(5) This section does not apply in relation to—
   (a) a contract to grant such a lease as is mentioned in section 54(2) of the Law Property Act 1925 (short leases);
   (b) a contract made in the course of a public auction; or
   (c) a contract regulated under the Financial Services Act 1986;

and nothing in this section affects the creation or operation of resulting, implied or constructive trusts.

(6) In this section—
"disposition" has the same meaning as in the Law of Property Act 1925;
"interest in land" means any estate, interest or charge in or over land or in or over the proceeds of sale of land.

(7) Nothing in this section shall apply in relation to contracts made before this section comes into force.

(8) ...

NOTES
Commencement: 27 September 1989.
Sub-s (8): repeals the Law of Property Act 1925, s 40.

5 Commencement

(1) The provisions of this Act to which this subsection applies shall come into force on such day as the Lord Chancellor may by order made by statutory instrument appoint.

(2) The provisions to which subsection (1) above applies are—
   (a) section 1 above; and
   (b) section 4 above, except so far as it relates to section 40 of the Law of Property Act 1925.

(3) The provisions of this Act to which this subsection applies shall come into force at the end of the period of two months beginning with the day on which this Act is passed.

(4) The provisions of this Act to which subsection (3) above applies are—
   (a) sections 2 and 3 above; and
   (b) section 4 above, so far as it relates to section 40 of the Law of Property Act 1925.

NOTE
Commencement: 27 July 1989.

6 Citation

(1) This Act may be cited as the Law of Property (Miscellaneous Provisions) Act 1989.

(2) This Act extends to England and Wales only.

NOTE
Commencement: 27 July 1989.

BROADCASTING ACT 1990
(C 42)

An Act to make new provision with respect to the provision and regulation of independent television and sound programme services and of other services provided on television or radio frequencies; to make provision with respect to the provision and regulation of local delivery services; to amend in other respects the law relating to broadcasting and the provision of television and sound programme services and to make provision with respect to the supply and use of information about programmes; to make provision with respect to the transfer of the property, rights and liabilities of the Independent Broadcasting Authority and the Cable Authority and the dissolution of those bodies; to make new provision relating to the Broadcasting Complaints Commission; to provide for the establishment and functions of a Broadcasting Standards Council; to amend the Wireless Telegraphy Acts 1949 to 1967 and the Marine, &c., Broadcasting (Offences) Act 1967; to revoke a class licence granted under the Telecommunications Act 1984 to run broadcast relay systems; and for connected purposes

[1 November 1990]

PART VII
PROHIBITION ON INCLUSION OF OBSCENE AND OTHER MATERIAL IN PROGRAMME SERVICES

Defamation

166 Defamatory material

(1) For the purposes of the law of libel and slander (including the law of criminal libel so far as it relates to the publication of defamatory matter) the publication of words in the course of any programme included in a programme service shall be treated as publication in permanent form.

(2) Subsection (1) above shall apply for the purposes of section 3 of each of the Defamation Acts (slander of title etc.) as it applies for the purposes of the law of libel and slander.

(3) Section 7 of each of those Acts (qualified privilege of newspapers) shall apply in relation to—
   (a) reports or matters included in a programme service, and
   (b) any inclusion in such a service of any such report or matter,

as it applies in relation to reports and matters published in a newspaper and to publication in a newspaper; and subsection (2) of that section shall have effect, in relation to any such inclusion, as if for the words "in the newspaper in which" there were substituted the words "in the programme service in which".

(4) In this section "the Defamation Acts" means the Defamation Act 1952 and the Defamation Act (Northern Ireland) 1955.

(5) Subsections (1) and (2) above do not extend to Scotland.

[356]

NOTE
Commencement: 1 January 1991.

PART X
MISCELLANEOUS AND GENERAL

General

204 Short title, commencement and extent

(1) This Act may be cited as the Broadcasting Act 1990.

(2) This Act shall come into force on such day as the Secretary of State may by order appoint; and different days may be so appointed for different provisions or for different purposes.

(3) Subject to subsections (4) and (5), this Act extends to the whole of the United Kingdom.

(4) In Part VII—
     (a) section 162 and Schedule 15 extend to England and Wales only;
     (b) section 163 extends to Scotland only;
     (c) section 164 extends to England and Wales and Scotland; and
     (d) section 165 extends to Northern Ireland only.

(5) The amendments and repeals in Schedules 20 and 21 have the same extent as the enactments to which they refer.

(6) Her Majesty may by Order in Council direct that any of the provisions of this Act shall extend to the Isle of Man or any of the Channel Islands with such modifications, if any, as appear to Her Majesty to be appropriate.

[357]

NOTE
Commencement: 1 December 1990.

ACCESS TO NEIGHBOURING LAND ACT 1992

(C 23)

An Act to enable persons who desire to carry out works to any land which are reasonably necessary for the preservation of that land to obtain access to neighbouring land in order to do so; and for purposes connected therewith

[16 March 1992]

1 Access orders

(1) A person—
     (a) who, for the purpose of carrying out works to any land (the "dominant land"), desires to enter upon any adjoining or adjacent land (the "servient land"), and
     (b) who needs, but does not have, the consent of some other person to that entry,

may make an application to the court for an order under this section ("an access order") against that other person.

(2) On an application under this section, the court shall make an access order if, and only if, it is satisfied—
     (a) that the works are reasonably necessary for the preservation of the whole or any part of the dominant land; and
     (b) that they cannot be carried out, or would be substantially more difficult to carry out, without entry upon the servient land;

but this subsection is subject to subsection (3) below.

(3) The court shall not make an access order in any case where it is satisfied that, were it to make such an order—

(a) the respondent or any other person would suffer interference with, or disturbance of, his use or enjoyment of the servient land, or
(b) the respondent, or any other person (whether of full age or capacity or not) in occupation of the whole or any part of the servient land, would suffer hardship,

to such a degree by reason of the entry (notwithstanding any requirement of this Act or any term or condition that may be imposed under it) that it would be unreasonable to make the order.

(4) Where the court is satisfied on an application under this section that it is reasonably necessary to carry out any basic preservation works to the dominant land, those works shall be taken for the purposes of this Act to be reasonably necessary for the preservation of the land; and in this subsection "basic preservation works" means any of the following, that is to say—
(a) the maintenance, repair or renewal of any part of a building or other structure comprised in, or situate on, the dominant land;
(b) the clearance, repair or renewal of any drain, sewer, pipe or cable so comprised or situate;
(c) the treatment, cutting back, felling, removal or replacement of any hedge, tree, shrub or other growing thing which is so comprised and which is, or is in danger of becoming, damaged, diseased, dangerous, insecurely rooted or dead;
(d) the filling in, or clearance, of any ditch so comprised;

but this subsection is without prejudice to the generality of the works which may, apart from it, be regarded by the court as reasonably necessary for the preservation of any land.

(5) If the court considers it fair and reasonable in all the circumstances of the case, works may be regarded for the purposes of this Act as being reasonably necessary for the preservation of any land (or, for the purposes of subsection (4) above, as being basic preservation works which it is reasonably necessary to carry out to any land) notwithstanding that the works incidentally involve—
(a) the making of some alteration, adjustment or improvement to the land, or
(b) the demolition of the whole or any part of a building or structure comprised in or situate upon the land.

(6) Where any works are reasonably necessary for the preservation of the whole or any part of the dominant land, the doing to the dominant land of anything which is requisite for, incidental to, or consequential on, the carrying out of those works shall be treated for the purposes of this Act as the carrying out of works which are reasonably necessary for the preservation of that land; and references in this Act to works, or to the carrying out of works, shall be construed accordingly.

(7) Without prejudice to the generality of subsection (6) above, if it is reasonably necessary for a person to inspect the dominant land—
(a) for the purpose of ascertaining whether any works may be reasonably necessary for the preservation of the whole or any part of that land,
(b) for the purpose of making any map or plan, or ascertaining the course of any drain, sewer, pipe or cable, in preparation for, or otherwise in connection with, the carrying out of works which are so reasonably necessary, or
(c) otherwise in connection with the carrying out of any such works,

the making of such an inspection shall be taken for the purposes of this Act to be the carrying out to the dominant land of works which are reasonably necessary for the preservation of that land; and references in this Act to works, or to the carrying out of works, shall be construed accordingly.

[358]

NOTES

Commencement: 31 January 1993

3 Effect of access order

(1) An access order requires the respondent, so far as he has power to do so, to permit the applicant or any of his associates to do anything which the applicant or associate is authorised or required to do under or by virtue of the order or this section.

(2) Except as otherwise provided by or under this Act, an access order authorises the applicant or any of his associates, without the consent of the respondent,—
  (a) to enter upon the servient land for the purpose of carrying out the specified works;
  (b) to bring on to that land, leave there during the period permitted by the order and, before the end of that period, remove, such materials, plant and equipment as are reasonably necessary for the carrying out of those works; and
  (c) to bring on to that land any waste arising from the carrying out of those works, if it is reasonably necessary to do so in the course of removing it from the dominant land;

but nothing in this Act or in any access order shall authorise the applicant or any of his associates to leave anything in, on or over the servient land (otherwise than in discharge of their duty to make good that land) after their entry for the purpose of carrying out works to the dominant land ceases to be authorised under or by virtue of the order.

(3) An access order requires the applicant—
  (a) to secure that any waste arising from the carrying out of the specified works is removed from the servient land forthwith;
  (b) to secure that, before the entry ceases to be authorised under or by virtue of the order, the servient land is, so far as reasonably practicable, made good; and
  (c) to indemnify the respondent against any damage which may be caused to the servient land or any goods by the applicant or any of his associates which would not have been so caused had the order not been made;

but this subsection is subject to subsections (4) and (5) below.

(4) In making an access order, the court may vary or exclude, in whole or in part,—
  (a) any authorisation that would otherwise be conferred by subsection (2)(b) or (c) above; or
  (b) any requirement that would otherwise be imposed by subsection (3) above.

(5) Without prejudice to the generality of subsection (4) above, if the court is satisfied that it is reasonably necessary for any such waste as may arise from the carrying out of the specified works to be left on the servient land for some period before removal, the access order may, in place of subsection (3)(a) above, include provision—
  (a) authorising the waste to be left on that land for such period as may be permitted by the order; and
  (b) requiring the applicant to secure that the waste is removed before the end of that period.

(6) Where the applicant or any of his associates is authorised or required under or by virtue of an access order or this section to enter, or do any other thing, upon the servient land, he shall not (as respects that access order) be taken to be a trespasser from the beginning on account of his, or any other person's, subsequent conduct.

(7) For the purposes of this section, the applicant's "associates" are such number of persons (whether or not servants or agents of his) whom he may reasonably authorise under this subsection to exercise the power of entry conferred by the access order as may be reasonably necessary for carrying out the specified works.

NOTES
Commencement: 31 January 1993.

9 Short title, commencement and extent

(1) This Act may be cited as the Access to Neighbouring Land Act 1992.

(2) This Act shall come into force on such day as the Lord Chancellor may by order made by statutory instrument appoint.

(3) This Act extends to England and Wales only.

PROVISION AND USE OF WORK EQUIPMENT REGULATIONS 1992

(SI 1992/2932)

Made: 17 November 1992.

Authority: The Health and Safety at Work etc Act 1974, ss 15(1), (2), (3)(a), (5)(b), (9), 82(3)(a), Sch 3, paras 1(1)-(3), 13(1), 14.

1 Citation and commencement

(1) These Regulations may be cited as the Provision and Use of Work Equipment Regulations 1992.

(2) Subject to paragraph (3), these Regulations shall come into force on 1st January 1993.

(3) Regulations 11 to 24 and 27 and Schedule 2 in so far as they apply to work equipment first provided for use in the premises or undertaking before 1st January 1993 shall come into force on 1st January 1997.

2 Interpretation

(1) In these Regulations, unless the context otherwise requires—
"use" in relation to work equipment means any activity involving work equipment and includes starting, stopping, programming, setting, transporting, repairing, modifying, maintaining, servicing and cleaning, and related expressions shall be construed accordingly;
"work equipment" means any machinery, appliance, apparatus or tool and any assembly of components which, in order to achieve a common end, are arranged and controlled so that they function as a whole.

(2) Any reference in these Regulations to—
(a) a numbered regulation or Schedule is a reference to the regulation or Schedule in these Regulations so numbered; and
(b) a numbered paragraph is a reference to the paragraph so numbered in the regulation in which the reference appears.

3 Disapplication of these Regulations

These Regulations shall not apply to or in relation to the master or crew of a seagoing ship or to the employer of such persons, in respect of the normal ship-board activities of a ship's crew under the direction of the master.

(Reg 4 is not relevant to this work.)

5 Suitability of work equipment

(1) Every employer shall ensure that work equipment is so constructed or adapted as to be suitable for the purpose for which it is used or provided.

(2) In selecting work equipment, every employer shall have regard to the working conditions and to the risks to the health and safety of persons which exist in the premises or undertaking in which that work equipment is to be used and any additional risk posed by the use of that work equipment.

(3) Every employer shall ensure that work equipment is used only for operations for which, and under conditions for which, it is suitable.

(4) In this regulation "suitable" means suitable in any respect which it is reasonably foreseeable will affect the health or safety of any person.

6 Maintenance

(1) Every employer shall ensure that work equipment is maintained in an efficient state, in efficient working order and in good repair.

(2) Every employer shall ensure that where any machinery has a maintenance log, the log is kept up to date.

7 Specific risks

(1) Where the use of work equipment is likely to involve a specific risk to health or safety, every employer shall ensure that—
(a) the use of that work equipment is restricted to those persons given the task of using it; and
(b) repairs, modifications, maintenance or servicing of that work equipment is restricted to those persons who have been specifically designated to perform operations of that description (whether or not also authorised to perform other operations).

(2) The employer shall ensure that the persons designated for the purposes of sub-paragraph (b) of paragraph (1) have received adequate training related to any operations in respect of which they have been so designated.

8 Information and instructions

(1) Every employer shall ensure that all persons who use work equipment have available to them adequate health and safety information and, where appropriate, written instructions pertaining to the use of the work equipment.

(2) Every employer shall ensure that any of his employees who supervises or manages the use of work equipment has available to him adequate health and safety information and, where appropriate, written instructions pertaining to the use of the work equipment.

(3) Without prejudice to the generality of paragraphs (1) or (2), the information and instructions required by either of those paragraphs shall include information and, where appropriate, written instructions on—
  (a) the conditions in which and the methods by which the work equipment may be used;
  (b) foreseeable abnormal situations and the action to be taken if such a situation were to occur; and
  (c) any conclusions to be drawn from experience in using the work equipment.

(4) Information and instructions required by this regulation shall be readily comprehensible to those concerned.

9 Training

(1) Every employer shall ensure that all persons who use work equipment have received adequate training for purposes of health and safety, including training in the methods which may be adopted when using the work equipment, any risks which such use may entail and precautions to be taken.

(2) Every employer shall ensure that any of his employees who supervises or manages the use of work equipment has received adequate training for purposes of health and safety, including training in the methods which may be adopted when using the work equipment, any risks which such use may entail and precautions to be taken.

10 Conformity with Community requirements

(1) Every employer shall ensure that any item of work equipment provided for use in the premises or undertaking of the employer complies with any enactment (whether in an Act or instrument) which implements in Great Britain any of the relevant Community directives listed in Schedule 1 which is applicable to that item of work equipment.

(2) Where it is shown that an item of work equipment complies with an enactment (whether in an Act or instrument) to which it is subject by virtue of paragraph (1), the requirements of regulations 11 to 24 shall apply in respect of that item of work equipment only to the extent that the relevant Community directive implemented by that enactment is not applicable to that item of work equipment.

(3) This regulation applies to items of work equipment provided for use in the premises or undertaking of the employer for the first time after 31st December 1992.

11 Dangerous parts of machinery

(1) Every employer shall ensure that measures are taken in accordance with paragraph (2) which are effective—
- (a) to prevent access to any dangerous part of machinery or to any rotating stock-bar; or
- (b) to stop the movement of any dangerous part of machinery or rotating stock-bar before any part of a person enters a danger zone.

(2) The measures required by paragraph (1) shall consist of—
- (a) the provision of fixed guards enclosing every dangerous part or rotating stock-bar where and to the extent that it is practicable to do so, but where or to the extent that it is not, then
- (b) the provision of other guards or protection devices where and to the extent that it is practicable to do so, but where or to the extent that it is not, then
- (c) the provision of jigs, holders, push-sticks or similar protection appliances used in conjunction with the machinery where and to the extent that it is practicable to do so, but where or to the extent that it is not, then
- (d) the provision of information, instruction, training and supervision.

(3) All guards and protection devices provided under sub-paragraphs (a) or (b) of paragraph (2) shall—
- (a) be suitable for the purpose for which they are provided;
- (b) be of good construction, sound material and adequate strength;
- (c) be maintained in an efficient state, in efficient working order and in good repair;
- (d) not give rise to any increased risk to health or safety;
- (e) not be easily bypassed or disabled;
- (f) be situated at sufficient distance from the danger zone;
- (g) not unduly restrict the view of the operating cycle of the machinery, where such a view is necessary;
- (h) be so constructed or adapted that they allow operations necessary to fit or replace parts and for maintenance work, restricting access so that it is allowed only to the area where the work is to be carried out and, if possible, without having to dismantle the guard or protection device.

(4) All protection appliances provided under sub-paragraph (c) of paragraph (2) shall comply with sub-paragraphs (a) to (d) and (g) of paragraph (3).

(5) In this regulation—
"danger zone" means any zone in or around machinery in which a person is exposed to a risk to health or safety from contact with a dangerous part of machinery or a rotating stock-bar;
"stock-bar" means any part of a stock-bar which projects beyond the head-stock of a lathe.

12 Protection against specified hazards

(1) Every employer shall take measures to ensure that the exposure of a person using work equipment to any risk to his health or safety from any hazard specified in paragraph (3) is either prevented, or, where that is not reasonably practicable, adequately controlled.

(2) The measures required by paragraph (1) shall—
   (a) be measures other than the provision of personal protective equipment or of information, instruction, training and supervision, so far as is reasonably practicable; and
   (b) include, where appropriate, measures to minimise the effects of the hazard as well as to reduce the likelihood of the hazard occurring.

(3) The hazards referred to in paragraph (1) are—
   (a) any article or substance falling or being ejected from work equipment;
   (b) rupture or disintegration of parts of work equipment;
   (c) work equipment catching fire or overheating;
   (d) the unintended or premature discharge of any article or of any gas, dust, liquid, vapour or other substance which, in each case, is produced, used or stored in the work equipment;
   (e) the unintended or premature explosion of the work equipment or any article or substance produced, used or stored in it.

(4) For the purposes of this regulation "adequate" means adequate having regard only to the nature of the hazard and the nature and degree of exposure to the risk, and "adequately" shall be construed accordingly.

(5) This regulation shall not apply where any of the following Regulations apply in respect of any risk to a person's health or safety for which such Regulations require measures to be taken to prevent or control such risk, namely—
   (a) the Control of Lead at Work Regulations 1980;
   (b) the Ionising Radiations Regulations 1985;
   (c) the Control of Asbestos at Work Regulations 1987;
   (d) the Control of Substances Hazardous to Health Regulations 1988;
   (e) the Noise at Work Regulations 1989;
   (f) the Construction (Head Protection) Regulations 1989.

[371]

13 High or very low temperature

Every employer shall ensure that work equipment, parts of work equipment and any article or substance produced, used or stored in work equipment which, in each case, is at a high or very low temperature shall have protection where appropriate so as to prevent injury to any person by burn, scald or sear.

[372]

14 Controls for starting or making a significant change in operating conditions

(1) Every employer shall ensure that, where appropriate, work equipment is provided with one or more controls for the purposes of—
   (a) starting the work equipment (including re-starting after a stoppage for any reason); or
   (b) controlling any change in the speed, pressure or other operating conditions of the work equipment where such conditions after the change result in risk to health and safety which is greater than or of a different nature from such risks before the change.

(2) Subject to paragraph (3), every employer shall ensure that where a control is required by paragraph (1), it shall not be possible to perform any operation mentioned

in sub-paragraph (a) or (b) of that paragraph except by a deliberate action on such control.

(3) Paragraph (1) shall not apply to re-starting or changing operating conditions as a result of the normal operating cycle of an automatic device.

[373]

15 Stop controls

(1) Every employer shall ensure that, where appropriate, work equipment is provided with one or more readily accessible controls the operation of which will bring the work equipment to a safe condition in a safe manner.

(2) Any control required by paragraph (1) shall bring the work equipment to a complete stop where necessary for reasons of health and safety.

(3) Any control required by paragraph (1) shall, if necessary for reasons of health and safety, switch off all sources of energy after stopping the functioning of the work equipment.

(4) Any control required by paragraph (1) shall operate in priority to any control which starts or changes the operating conditions of the work equipment.

[374]

16 Emergency stop controls

(1) Every employer shall ensure that, where appropriate, work equipment is provided with one or more readily accessible emergency stop controls unless it is not necessary by reason of the nature of the hazards and the time taken for the work equipment to come to a complete stop as a result of the action of any control provided by virtue of regulation 15(1).

(2) Any control required by paragraph (1) shall operate in priority to any control required by regulation 15(1).

[375]

17 Controls

(1) Every employer shall ensure that all controls for work equipment shall be clearly visible and identifiable, including by appropriate marking where necessary.

(2) Except where necessary, the employer shall ensure that no control for work equipment is in a position where any person operating the control is exposed to a risk to his health or safety.

(3) Every employer shall ensure where appropriate—
    (a) that, so far as is reasonably practicable, the operator of any control is able to ensure from the position of that control that no person is in a place where he would be exposed to any risk to his health or safety as a result of the operation of that control, but where or to the extent that it is not reasonably practicable;
    (b) that, so far as is reasonably practicable, systems of work are effective to ensure that, when work equipment is about to start, no person is in a place where he would be exposed to a risk to his health or safety as a result of the work equipment starting, but where neither of these is reasonably practicable;
    (c) that an audible, visible or other suitable warning is given by virtue of regulation 24 whenever work equipment is about to start.

(4) Every employer shall take appropriate measures to ensure that any person who is in a place where he would be exposed to a risk to his health or safety as a result of the starting or stopping of work equipment has sufficient time and suitable means to avoid that risk.

[376]

18 Control systems

(1) Every employer shall ensure, so far as is reasonably practicable, that all control systems of work equipment are safe.

(2) Without prejudice to the generality of paragraph (1), a control system shall not be safe unless—
  (a) its operation does not create any increased risk to health or safety;
  (b) it ensures, so far as is reasonably practicable, that any fault in or damage to any part of the control system or the loss of supply of any source of energy used by the work equipment cannot result in additional or increased risk to health or safety;
  (c) it does not impede the operation of any control required by regulation 15 or 16.

[377]

19 Isolation from sources of energy

(1) Every employer shall ensure that where appropriate work equipment is provided with suitable means to isolate it from all its sources of energy.

(2) Without prejudice to the generality of paragraph (1), the means mentioned in that paragraph shall not be suitable unless they are clearly identifiable and readily accessible.

(3) Every employer shall take appropriate measures to ensure that re-connection of any energy source to work equipment does not expose any person using the work equipment to any risk to his health or safety.

[378]

20 Stability

Every employer shall ensure that work equipment or any part of work equipment is stabilised by clamping or otherwise where necessary for purposes of health or safety.

[379]

21 Lighting

Every employer shall ensure that suitable and sufficient lighting, which takes account of the operations to be carried out, is provided at any place where a person uses work equipment.

[380]

22 Maintenance operations

Every employer shall take appropriate measures to ensure that work equipment is so constructed or adapted that, so far as is reasonably practicable, maintenance operations which involve a risk to health or safety can be carried out while the work equipment is shut down or, in other cases—
  (a) maintenance operations can be carried out without exposing the person carrying them out to a risk to his health or safety; or

(b) appropriate measures can be taken for the protection of any person carrying out maintenance operations which involve a risk to his health or safety.

[381]

23 Markings

Every employer shall ensure that work equipment is marked in a clearly visible manner with any marking appropriate for reasons of health and safety.

[382]

24 Warnings

(1) Every employer shall ensure that work equipment incorporates any warnings or warning devices which are appropriate for reasons of health and safety.

(2) Without prejudice to the generality of paragraph (1), warnings given by warning devices on work equipment shall not be appropriate unless they are unambiguous, easily perceived and easily understood.

[383]

(Regs 25-27 and Schs 1 and 2 are not relevant to this work.)

INDEX

References are to paragraph number

A

ABDUCTION
criminal injuries and, 339B

ACCESS
to neighbouring land
access orders, 358
effect of, 359
waste disposal, 359

ACCIDENT
fatal
right of action for wrongful act causing death, 122, 123
assessment of damages, 125
persons entitled to bring action, 124
time limit for actions, 208
fire, 2

ACCOMMODATION
provision of, 312
acts of omission, 312
defences to, 313

ACKNOWLEDGMENT AND PART PAYMENT
effect of on persons other than maker or recipient, 217
formal provisions, 216
time limits, extension or exclusion of, 215

ACQUIESCENCE
relief refused on grounds of, 221

ACTION, RIGHTS OF
accrual, 222
land, to recover, 144

ACTIONS
concurrent, 139
interpretation of, 193, 222
specialty, on, time limit for, 203
tort, founded on, 196-9

ADVERTISEMENT
interpretation of, 313
misleading indications and, 313

AGRICULTURAL PRODUCE
interpretation of, 291

AIRCRAFT
interpretation of, 334
supply of goods and, 335

AMBULANCES
motor insurance, exceptions from requirements of, 342

AMENDS
defamation, unintentional and, 40
libel actions, payment into court by way of, 7

ANIMALS
dangerous, damage done by, 92-3, 97
dogs, injury to livestock, 94, 100
duty to prevent straying on highway, 99
exceptions from liability, 96
keepers of, 93, 94, 97, 100
livestock
detention and sale of, 98
injured by dogs, 94, 100
liability for damage and expenses due to trespassing, 95, 99

APOLOGY
defamation, unintentional and, 40
libel actions, in mitigation of damages, 4, 5

APPEALS
detention of goods, against, 322
suspension notices, against, 305

APPRAISAL
goods accepted for, 147

ARREST
citizen's, 267
police powers regarding, 264, 265, 267, 268
summary, 267
use of force in making, 74

ARRESTABLE OFFENCES
interpretation of, 267

ARSON
criminal injuries and, 339B

ASSAULT
criminal injuries and, 339B

AUCTION
contracts made in course of, 353
sale by, 161

AUTHORISED INSURER
interpretation of, 343
membership of Motor Insurers' Bureau, 343
motor insurance to be issued by, 343

AWARDS
time limits for enforcement of, 202

B

BAILEE
hire by description, implied terms, 237
interpretation of, 247
powers of
imposing obligation to collect goods, 147
right to transfer possession, 237
sale of uncollected goods, 142, 143, 148

BAILOR
interpretation of, 247

BANKRUPTCY
creditors, rights after decease of debtor, 17
insured or secured persons, not to affect claims by third parties, 351
insurers
 duty to give necessary information to third parties, 18
 liabilities to third parties, 17-19
 rights of third parties against, 17-19
 settlement with insured persons, 19
married women, husbands, liabilities of, 24

BENEFITS
disregard of in assessment of damages, 126

BEREAVEMENT
claim for damages for, 21, 123, 204, 339D

BIRTH
interpretation of, 120C

BLACKMAIL
theft and, 198

BLASPHEMY
newspaper reports and, 10

BODY CORPORATE
documents, service of, 333
liability of, 329

BREACH OF DUTY
nuclear installations and, 330

BREACH OF THE PEACE
police powers to deal with or prevent, 264

BROADCASTING
defamation, 78-80, 356-7
 defences against, 45
 qualified privilege and, 356
interpretation, 50

BUILDING REGULATIONS
breach of and civil liability, 262
duty to build dwellings properly, 105-6
power to make, 261

BUSINESS
interpretation of, 163, 193, 247, 334
records, production of for enforcement authorities, 318

BUYER
acceptance of goods, 187B
interpretation of, 193
right of examining goods, 187A

C

CAR-SHARING AGREEMENTS
motor insurance and, 348

CARAVANS
provision of facilities and services for, 311

CARE
duty of
 acceptance of risk and, 255
 animals, to, 98
 children, towards, 56

CARE—contd
duty of—contd
 common, 56, 57, 151
 negligence and, 151
 occupiers' liability and, 151, 255
 persons using highway, to, 255
 with respect to work done on premises, 107

CARE AND SKILL
implied terms, 243

CAUSE OF ACTION
accrual of, latent damage to property, in respect of, 281

CHAMPERTY
tort of, 74
 civil rights in respect of, 76

CHATTELS
interpretation of, 222
obtaining, 198

CHILDREN
civil liability to child born disabled, 120-1
contracts made by
 guarantees, 288
 restitution, 289
disability, treated as if under, 222
duty of care towards, 56
loss of services of, abolition of actions for, 251
protection of, 268
radiation causing disabled birth, 120B, 120C
unborn, mother's duty of care to, 120A

CIVIL AVIATION
regulation of, liability of aircraft in respect of trespass, nuisance and surface damage, 229

COMMON LAW
occupiers' liability, 55

COMPANIES
authority of directors, no duty to enquire as to, 274
capacity of
 execution of documents, 276
 no duty to enquire as to, 274
contracts, 275
liability of, consumer safety, 329
liquidator, vesting of property in, 281
registration of memorandum and articles
 company's capacity not limited by, 272
 effect of, 271
winding-up of, third-party claims and, 351

COMPENSATION
children, disabled birth due to radiation, for, 120B
civil liability, for, 176
Criminal Injuries Compensation Scheme, 339A-E
earnings, for loss of, 339D

COMPENSATION—*contd*
  false or misleading prospectus, for, 285
    exemption from liability, 286
  loss of society, for, 339D
  rape, for, 339D
  reimbursement and recovery, 339E
  rights of data subjects to
    inaccuracy, for, 258
    loss or unauthorised disclosure, for, 259
  seizure and detention of goods, for, 323
  suspension notice, payable for, 304

COMPETITIVE TENDER
  sale by, 161

CONCEALMENT
  limitation periods, postponement in case of, 218
  third parties, innocent, and, 218

CONCURRENT ACTIONS
  wrongful interference with goods, for, 139

CONGENITAL DISABILITIES
  civil liability to child, 120-1

CONSERVATION
  building regulations and, 261

CONSUMER
  interpretation of, 309

CONSUMER GOODS
  interpretation of, 300

CONSUMER PROTECTION
  legislation, short title,
    commencement and transitional provision, 336
  product liability
    defective products, 292
    generally, 291
  safety regulations, 301
    forfeiture of goods, 306
      appeals against, 306
    notices
      prohibition, 303, 307, 334, 337
      suspension, 304, 305, 319, 334
      warn, to, 303, 307, 334, 338
    offences against, 302
    power to obtain information, 307
    provisions, 301
    standards, 301
    statutory powers, 301
  safety requirements, 300
    failure to comply with, 300
      defences, 300
  See also HEALTH AND SAFETY

CONTEMPT OF COURT
  contemporary reports of proceedings, 227
  innocent publication or distribution, defence of, 226
  strict liabilty rule, 226-7

CONTRACT
  actions founded on
    time limits, 200
      loans, in respect of, 201

CONTRACT—*contd*
  auction, made in course of, 353
  breach of, 153
    actions for, 188-92
      non-acceptance, 189
      non-delivery, damages for, 190
      performance, specific, 191
      price, 188
      warranty, remedy for breach of, 192
    effect of, 158
  characteristics, 164
  children, made by, 288-90
  choice of law clauses, 165
  company, 275
    pre-incorporation contracts, deeds and obligations, 277
  "consumer, dealing as", 161
  employment, of, 169
  exceptions, 166
  exclusion from, safety regulations and, 330
  exemption clause, 162
  financial services legislation and, 353
  frustrated, 26-7
  generally, 167
  hire of goods, 236-40
    defined, 236
  insurance, of. 169 *See also* MOTOR INSURANCE, 169
  international supply, 164
  interpretation of, 231
  lease, to grant, 353
  liability in
    implied term, 58
    strangers to the contract, 57
  marine, 169
  misrepresentation and, 70-2
  performance of, building work as, 335
  reasonableness test, 160
  sale of land, to be made by signed writing, 353-5
  sale, of, 180
    agreement to sell, 180, 183
    agreement to sell at valuation, 183
    breach of contract, actions for, 188
    buyer's right of examining goods, 187A
    conditions to be treated as warranty, when, 183B
    goods perishing before sale, 181
    implied terms about title, 184
    interpretation of, 193
    sale by description, 185
    sale by sample, 187
    time stipulations, 183A
  secondary, evasion by means of, 159
  transfer of property in goods, for, 231
  unfair, 151-70

CONTRIBUTION
  assessment of, 172
  entitlement to, 171
  time limit for claiming, 205

CONTRIBUTORY NEGLIGENCE See
  NEGLIGENCE
CONVERSION
  goods
    denial of title, 141
    receipt of by way of pledge, 141
    time limit for actions founded on tort, 197
CONVICTIONS
  evidence in civil proceedings, as, 81, 82
COUNCILS
  motor insurance, exceptions from requirements of, 342
COURT
  contempt of
    contemporary reports of proceedings, 227
    innocent publication or distribution, defence of, 226
    strict liabilty rule, 226-7
COURTS
  authorisation of sale of uncollected goods, 143
  county, 134, 139, 143, 322
  Crown, 322
  interpretation of, 220
  rules of, 134
COURTS-MARTIAL
  convictions as evidence, 81
  definition, 81
CREDIT
  interpretation of, 311
CREDIT-BROKER
  hire-purchase agreements and, 114
  interpretation of, 193, 247
  sale of goods and, 186
CRIMINAL INJURIES
  compensation awards, 339D
  death as result of, 339D
  interpretation of, 339B
  qualifying injuries, 339C
  reimbursement and recovery, 339E
CRIMINAL INJURIES COMPENSATION BOARD, 339A
CRIMINAL OFFENCES
  disclosure of information and, 327
CROWN
  legislation binding on
    civil liability, 175
    defective premises legislation, 109
    highway legislation, 224
    latent damage, 281
    liability for damage done by animals, 103
    occupiers' liability, 256
    product liability, 299
  liability in tort, 33
    interference with goods, 145

CUSTOMS AND EXCISE AUTHORITIES
  detention of goods, 320
  power to disclose information, 326
  seizure of goods and records, 319

D

DAMAGE
  interpretation of, 262, 295, 330
  latent, property, to, 281-2
  liability, giving rise to, 295
    prohibition on exclusions from, 297
  surface, civil aviation and, 229
DAMAGES
  assessment of
    benefits, disregard of, 126
    contributory negligence and, 127
    re-marriage prospects of widows, 125
    unmarried couples, 125
    wrongful interference with goods, 135
  bereavement, for, 123
    assessment of, 125
    sum awarded, 123
  children with congenital disabilities, for, 120
  contributory negligence affecting, 29, 127
  defamation, evidence of other damages recovered by plaintiff, 48
  defective products, actions in respect of, 207
  detention of goods, for, 133
  funeral expenses, in respect of, 125
  misrepresentation, for, 70
  personal injuries
    loss of expectation of life, abolition of claim for, 250
    loss of income, 250
    loss of services, 251
    maintenance at public expense, 252
DATA PROTECTION
  police powers regarding information on computer, 265
  rights of subjects
    compensation for inaccuracy, 258
    compensation for loss or unauthorised disclosure, 259
DEATH
  actions in respect of
    time limits, 206, 208, 213
      discretionary exclusion, 220
    wrongful act causing, 122, 123
      assessment of damages, 125
      persons entitled to bring action, 124
  bankruptcy following, 351
  defective products causing, 296
  disability and, time limit, 213
  effect of
    bereavement claims, 21, 123, 125
    on certain causes of action, 21
    on creditors of insured, 17
    criminal injuries claims, 339D
  employment, arising out of and in course of, motor insurance and, 343

DEATH—*contd*
　Fatal Accidents legislation
　　time limit, 208
　　　different dependants, 209

DEBTS
　mortgages, foreclosure of, 215
　promissory notes, 201
　time limits for actions in respect of, 201

DEEDS
　pre-incorporation, 277

DEFAMATION
　broadcasting and, 44, 356-7
　　qualified privilege, 356
　consolidation of actions, 49
　convictions as evidence, 82
　defences
　　broadcasting, 44, 356
　　elections, limitation of privileges at, 46
　　evidence of other damages recovered by plaintiff, 48
　　fair comment, 42
　　indemnity, agreements for, 47
　　justification, 41
　　newspapers, qualified privilege of, 43, 356
　　reporting privileges, 43-4, 52-3
　　unintentional defamation, 40
　interpretation, 50
　theatre, law respecting, 78-80
　unintentional, 40
　See also LIBEL; SLANDER

DEFECT
　meaning of, 293

DEFECTIVE PREMISES
　duty to build dwellings properly, 105
　　exceptions, 106

DEFECTIVE PRODUCTS
　actions in respect of, 207
　knowledge of, 294
　meaning of, 293
　safety regulations, 292

DELIVERY
　interpretation of, 193

DEPENDANTS
　criminal injuries compensation and, 339D
　Fatal Accidents legislation, action brought under, 209
　interpretation of, 122, 176, 291, 339D
　right of action for wrongful act causing death, 122, 123

DEPOSITS
　motor insurance
　　exception from requirements of, 342
　　securities, in respect of, 344

DETINUE
　abolition of, 132

DIRECTOR OF PUBLIC PROSECUTIONS
　safety regulations and, 301

DIRECTOR-GENERAL OF FAIR TRADING
　codes of practice, approval of, 314
　regulations, making of, 315

DIRECTORS, COMPANY
　authority of, no duty to enquire as to, 274
　execution of documents, 276
　liability incurred by, 272
　powers to bind company, 273

DISABILITY
　actions in respect of, time limits, 213, 214
　children treated as if under, 222
　congenital
　　liability for, 120-1, 296
　　radiation, due to, 120B
　unsound mind, treated as if, 222

DISCLOSURE
　duty of, prospectus, in, 284
　information, of
　　Customs and Excise authorities, power of, 326
　　penalties for offences, 327
　　restrictions on, 327

DISPOSITION
　interpretation of, 353

DOCUMENT OF TITLE TO GOODS
　interpretation of, 193

DOCUMENTS
　execution of, 276
　service of, 333

DRIVING LICENCE
　holding of and liability, 349

DRUG, CONTROLLED
　interpretation of, 308

DUE DILIGENCE
　defence of, 328

DUTY
　breach of, 151
　　building regulations and, 262
　　concealment as, 218
　　nuclear installations and, 296, 330

DUTY OF CARE
　acceptance of risk and, 255
　animals, to, 98
　common, 151
　negligence and, 151
　occupiers' liability and, 56, 57, 151, 255
　　persons other than his visitors, to, 255
　persons using highway, to, 255
　pregnant women and, 120A
　work done on premises, with respect to, 107

E

ELECTIONS
　defamation, limitation of privileges regarding, 46

EMPLOYER
　interpretation of, 311

EMPLOYER—*contd*
liability
compulsory insurance, 86-8
defective equipment, 84-5
personal injuries claim, 36-7
work equipment, *See under* WORK EQUIPMENT

EMPLOYMENT
contract of, 169
defence to personal injuries claim, as, 36-7
motor insurance and, 341
motor insurance, liability not covered by, 343
risks entered into incidental to, 97

ENACTMENT
interpretation of, 247

ENFORCEMENT
recovery of expenses, 324
safety provisions, of, 316

ENFORCEMENT AUTHORITIES
interpretation of, 334
obstruction of officers, 321
powers of, 316-20
purporting to be officer of, 319
See also CUSTOMS AND EXCISE; POLICE

EUROPEAN COMMUNITY
disclosure of information legislation, 327
product liability Directive, 291
work equipment requirements, 369

EVIDENCE
convictions as
in civil proceedings, 81, 82
defamation actions, 82
false statements, 302
perjury, prevention of, 1
retention of, 266

EXPECTATION
life, of, loss of, abolition of right to damages, 120C, 250
misleading price indications and, 310

EXPERT
interpretation of, 286

F

FACILITIES, PROVISION OF
consumer legislation affecting, 311

FALSE STATEMENTS
offences against safety regulations, as, 302

FAULT
interpretation of, 193

FELONY AND MISDEMEANOUR
law reform regarding, 74-5

FERTILISER
interpretation of, 308

FINANCIAL SERVICES
unlisted securities, offers of, prospectus form and content, 283

FINES
consumer safety requirements, failure to comply with, for, 300
contravening prohibition notice or notice to warn, for, 303
contravening suspension notice, for, 304
misleading indications of price, for, 315

FIRE
prevention of, 2
where accidentally begins, no action to lie against person, 2

FIREARMS, POSSESSION OF
criminal injuries and, 339B

FOOD
interpretation of, 308

FOREIGN CURRENCY
sale of, 311

FORFEITURE
goods, of, 324

FRAUD
actions not maintainable unless in writing, 3
innocent third parties, 218
limitation periods, postponement in case of, 218
prevention of, 1

FUNERAL EXPENSES
damages in respect of, 125

FUTURE GOODS
interpretation of, 193

G

GAMING
contracts by way of
promises to repay, 15
to be void, 8

GOOD FAITH
actions in, 193, 273

GOODS
appraisal, accepted for, 147
contracts for hire of
contracts concerned, 236
implied terms
about right to transfer possession, 237
hire by sample, 240
quality or fitness, about, 239
where hire is by description, 238
contracts for transfer of property in
contracts concerned, 231
implied terms
quality or fitness, 234
title, 232
transfer by description, 233
transfer by sample, 235

GOODS—*contd*
conversion and trespass to
co-ownership, 140
contributory negligence, 141
denial of title, 141
receipt by way of pledge, 141
detention of, 132
appeals against, 322
customs officers, by, 320
form of judgement, 133
interlocutory relief, 134
forfeiture of, 306, 324
appeals against, 306
future, interpretation of, 193
guarantee of, liability arising from, 155
imported, 317, 319, 320
interpretation of, 163, 193, 247, 334
perishing before sale, 181
quality or fitness, implied terms, 186
relevant, 303
repair or other treatment, accepted for, 147
sale or supply of
acceptance, 187B
buyer's right of examining, 187A
liability arising from
guarantee of consumer goods, 155
miscellaneous contracts, 157
sale and hire-purchase, 156
seizure and detention of, 319
compensation for, 323
specific, interpretation of, 193
storage and warehousing, 147
supply of, 335
testing of, 317, 319
uncollected
bailee's power of sale, 142, 143, 148
bailee's power to impose obligation to collect, 147
sale authorised by court, 143
valuation, agreement to sell at, 183
valuation, accepted for, 147
wrongful interference with, 131
allowance for improvement of, 136
competing rights, 138
concurrent actions, 139
damages for, 135
double liability, 137

GOVERNMENT BUSINESS
reporting of, 53

H

HEALTH AND SAFETY
building regulations and, 261
employment
access and place of employment, 64
amendments, 325
compulsory insurance for employers, 86–8
defective equipment, 84–5
disclosure of information and, 327
floors, passages and stairs, 63
general provisions, 60
machinery generally, 62

HEALTH AND SAFETY—*contd*
employment—*contd*
prime movers, 60, 65
safety regulations, 301
transmission machinery, 61, 65
See also under WORK EQUIPMENT
See also CONSUMER PROTECTION; WORK EQUIPMENT

HEALTH AND SAFETY COMMISSION, 301

HIGHWAY
animals straying on to, duty to prevent damage from, 99
duty of care to persons using, 255
interpretation of, 255
maintenance of, enforcement of liability for, 224-5

HIGHWAY CODE
alterations in, 340
failure to observe, 340
interpretation of, 340
printing and sale of, 340

HIRE
contract of, motor insurance and, 341

HIRE-PURCHASE AGREEMENTS
bailing or hiring by description, 113
conditional sale agreements, special provisions as to, 117
credit-brokers and, 114
definition of, 163
detention of goods and, 133
goods supplied under, 335
interpretation of, 118, 247, 334
liability for breach of obligations arising from, 156
quality or fitness, implied undertakings as to, 114, 116, 118
samples, 115
title, implied terms as to, 112

HOUSING LEGISLATION
fitness for human habitation, 278, 279
new houses, 312
See also BUILDING REGULATIONS

I

IDENTIFICATION
motor vehicles, carrying on, 346
supplying to police, 268

IMPLIED TERMS
exclusion of, 241, 246
hire-purchase agreements and, 114, 116
quality or fitness, about, 234, 239
supply of services, in
care and skill, 243
consideration, 245
performance time, 244
tenancy agreements, fitness for human habitation, 278

IMPLIED TERMS—contd
  title, about, 232
  transfer
    description, by, 233, 238
    sample, by, 235, 240

IMPRISONMENT, FALSE
  criminal injuries and, 339B

INDECENCY
  newspaper reports and, 10

INDEMNITY
  contractual right and, 177
  defamation and agreements for, 47
  unreasonable, 154

INFORMATION
  disclosure of
    Customs and Excise authorities, power of, 326
    penalties for offences, 327
    restrictions on, 327
  false, 307
    penalties for, 307
  publicised, interpretation of, 327

INJURY
  arrest in order to prevent, 268
  interpretation of, 255
  See also PERSONAL INJURIES

INSOLVENCY
  interpretation of, 193
  See also BANKRUPTCY

INSURANCE
  compulsory
    employers' liability, 86-8
      amount limited, 91
      exceptions, 87
      family members, 87
      general regulations, 89
      prohibited conditions, 90
  motor See MOTOR INSURANCE

INSURERS
  authorised, 343
  duties of, 349, 350
  third party rights against, on bankruptcy of insured, 17-19

INVALID CARRIAGES
  motor insurance and, 341

J

JUDGMENTS
  motor insurance
    duty of insurers or persons giving security to satisfy, 349
    exceptions, 350

JUSTICES OF PEACE
  seizure of goods and records, and, 319

K

KIDNAPPING
  criminal injuries and, 339B

KNOWLEDGE
  damage, of, 295
  date of, 220
    time limits and, 210
  defective product and, 294
  latent damage, time limits and, 211
  motor insurance, pertaining to, 341
  reasonable expectations of, 281

L

LAND
  access orders, 358
    effect of, 359
    waste disposal, 359
  contracts for sale of, to be made by signed writing, 353-5
  interest in, interpretation of, 353
  interpretation of, 222
  possession of, 144
  rights of action to recover, 144
  settled, interpretation of, 222
  supply of goods and, 335
  test purchases, exemption from, 317

LANDLORDS
  duty of care, repairs, 108
  See also TENANCY AGREEMENTS

LATENT DAMAGE
  actions in respect of, time limit, 211

LAW REFORM
  contributory negligence, apportionment of liability, 29
  death, effect of, 21
  felony and misdemeanour, 74-5
  frustrated contracts
    application of law, 27
    exceptions, 27
    rights and liabilities of parties to, 26
  husband and wife, actions in tort between, 67-8
  married women
    capacity, property and liability of, 23-5
    husbands, liabilities of, 23-5
  personal injuries, 36-7

LEGAL AID
  contempt of court legislation and, 228

LIABILITY
  aircraft, of, in respect of trespass, nuisance and surface damage, 229
  animals
    damage done by, 92-5, 98
    exceptions, 96
  avoidance of
    breach of contract, 153
    contract terms excluding or restricting, 152
    negligence, 152
    unreasonable indemnity clauses, 154
  business, 151
  civil
    breach of building regulations and, 262

LIABILITY—*contd*
  civil—*contd*
    child born with congenital disabilities, to, 120-1
    contribution
      assessment of, 172
      entitlement to, 171
      recovery of, 177
      same debt or damage, proceedings for, 173, 174
      savings and, 177
    company directors, incurred by, 272
    contract terms, 164
    double, definition, 137
    employers
      compulsory insurance, 86-8
      defective equipment, 84-5
    "excluded", 349
    failure to observe Highway Code, 340
    highway, maintenance of, 224-5
    joint, 292
    misrepresentation, for, 72
    motor insurance
      avoidance of certain exceptions, 346
      conditions not covered by, 343
      duty of insurers or persons giving security to satisfy judgment, 349
      passengers, avoidance of certain agreement as to liability towards, 347
    occupiers
      in contract, 57
      duty to persons other than his visitors, 255
      in tort, 55-7
        contract, effect of, 57
        generally, 55
        ordinary duty, extent of, 56
    payments in respect of, 349
      recovery of, 349
    persons other than principal offender, of, 329
    product
      defect, meaning of, 293
      defective products, 292
      defences, 294
      generally, 291
    sale or supply of goods, arising from
      guarantee of consumer goods, 155
      miscellaneous contracts, 156
      sale and hire-purchase, 156
    secondary contract and, 159
    strict, contempt of court, 226-7
    third-party, motor insurance, duty of insurers or persons giving security to satisfy judgment, 349

LIBEL
  actions for, time limits, 219
  amends, payment into court by way of, 7
  consolidation of actions, 49
  death of plaintiff, effect of, 21
  newspapers
    actions against, 5

LIBEL—*contd*
  newspapers—*contd*
    reports of proceedings in court privileged, 10
    offer of apology admissible in evidence in mitigation of damages, 4, 5
  Scottish law, 6, 11
  time limits for actions, 199
  See also DEFAMATION; SLANDER

LIMITATION
  disability, extension of period in case of, 213, 214
  fraud, concealment or mistake, postponement in case of, 218
  time limits for different classes of action, 195
    theft, 198
    tort, 196

LIVESTOCK *See* ANIMALS

LOANS
  time limits for actions in respect of, 201

LOSS OF EXPECTATION OF LIFE
  damages, abolition of right to, 250

LOSS OF SERVICES
  actions, abolition of, 251

M

MACHINERY
  See under WORK EQUIPMENT

MAGISTRATES' COURT
  goods, application for release of, 322
  Northern Ireland, 334
  suspension notices, appeals against, 305

MAINTENANCE
  tort of, 74
    civil rights in respect of, 76

MARKS
  interpretation of, 334

MARRIAGE
  husband and wife, actions in tort between, 67-8
  loss of services, abolition of actions for, 251
  married women
    capacity, property and liability of, 23-5
    husbands, liabilities of, 23-5
  re-marriage prospects and assessment of damages, 125
  unmarried partners, assessment of damages, 125

MEDICINAL PRODUCTS
  interpretation of, 308

MENTAL CONDITION
  criminal injuries causing harm to, 339B

MINORS *See* CHILDREN

MISDEMEANOUR
  law reform regarding, 74-5

MISREPRESENTATION
    damages for, 70
    innocent, rescission for, removal of certain
        bars to, 69
    liability for, avoidance of provision
        excluding, 71
    liability for, exceptions, 72
MISTAKE
    limitation periods, postponement in case of,
        218
    third parties, innocent, and, 218
MOBBING
    criminal injuries and, 339B
MORTGAGE
    excepted contract, as, 231
    foreclosure of, 215
    payments in respect of, 216, 217
MOTOR INSURANCE
    authorised insurers, 343
    car-sharing agreements, 348
    certificates
        issue and surrender of, 345
        loss or destruction of, 350
    criminal injuries and, 339C
    Highway Code, observation of, 340
    policies
        avoidance of certain agreements as to
            liability towards passengers, 347
        avoidance of certain exceptions, 346
        cancellation, 345
        coverage outside Britain, 343
        issue and surrender of certificates, 345
        requirements in respect of, 343
    requirements
        policies, 343, 345
        securities, in respect of, 344, 345
    securities
        avoidance of certain exceptions, 346
        issue and surrender of certificates, 345
        requirements in respect of, 344
    third party, exceptions from requirement,
        342
    third-party claims
        bankruptcy, etc of insured or secured
            persons, 351
        compulsory insurance or security against,
            341
        duty of insurers or persons giving security
            to satisfy judgment, 349
        exceptions, 350
        stolen vehicles and, 349
        time limits, 350
    third-party risks, 341
MOTOR INSURERS' BUREAU
    membership of, 343
MOTOR VEHICLE
    insurance *See* MOTOR INSURANCE
    interpretation of, 120C, 334
    supply of goods and, 335
MOVABLE STRUCTURE
    interpretation of, 255

N

NAME AND ADDRESS
    supplying to police, 268
NEGLIGENCE
    actions in respect of
        time limit, 211
            overriding, 212
    animals straying on to highway, failure to
        prevent, 99
    civil aviation liability and, 229
    contributory
        apportionment of liability, 29
        assessment of damages and, 29, 127
        defective products and, 296
        exceptions, 30
        interpretation, 31
        wrongful interference with goods and,
            135
    definition of, 151, 163
    goods, damage to or interest in, 131
    latent damage to property and, 281
    liability, 296
        avoidance of, 152
        motor insurance and, 347
    personal injuries claims, 36-7
    unfair contracts and, 151
NEWSPAPERS
    libel claims, qualified privilege as defence,
        43-4, 52-3, 356
NORTHERN IRELAND
    civil liability legislation, 178
    county courts, 143
    High Court of Justice, 144
    hire-purchase agreements, quality or fitness
        undertakings, 114, 118
    limitation legislation, 223
    magistrates' court, 334
    resale prices, 130
    road traffic legislation, 351
    safety regulations and, 301
    supply of goods legislation, 247, 249
NOTICES
    information, to obtain, 307
    interpretation of, 334
    prohibition, 303, 307, 334, 337
    suspension, 304, 319, 334
        appeals against, 305
        compensation for, 304
    warn, to, 303, 307, 334, 338
NOTIFICATION
    generally, 339
    interpretation of, 339
    notices to warn and, 338
    prohibition notices and, 337
NUISANCE
    civil aviation and, 229

O

OBSOLETE CRIMES
    abolition of, 74

OCCUPIERS
duty of care, 151
interpretation of, 255
liability
  in contract, 57
  contract, effect of, 57
  duty to persons other than his visitors, 255
  generally, 55
  ordinary duty, extent of, 56
  in tort, 55-7

OMISSION
acts of, liability for damage and, 296

OWNERSHIP
retention in order to establish, 266

P

PAIN AND SUFFERING
damages for, 250
See also PERSONAL INJURIES

PARENTS
children with congenital disabilities, and, 120-1

PARKING FACILITIES
provision of, 311

PEACE, BREACH OF
police powers to deal with or prevent, 264

PERFORMANCE TIME
implied terms, 244

PERJURY
prevention of, 1

PERSONAL ESTATE
interpretation of, 222

PERSONAL INJURIES
actions in respect of
  time limits, 206
    discretionary exclusion, 220
claim
  employment as defence, 36-7
  other persons, through, 222
damages, loss of expectation of life, abolition of claim for, 250
defective equipment causing, 84-5
interpretation of, 163, 222, 334

PERSONAL PROPERTY
interpretation of, 222

PERSONAL REPRESENTATIVES
interpretation of, 206, 207

PLAINTIFF
interpretation of, 193

POLICE
motor insurance, exceptions from requirements of, 342
powers of arrest
  entry for purposes of, 264
  general arrest conditions, 268

POLICE—*contd*
powers of arrest—*contd*
  without warrant for arrestable offences, 267
powers of entry, search and seizure
  arrest, for purposes of, 264
  general power of seizure, 265
  retention, 266

PREGNANCY
duty of care of women driving during, 120A
radiation affecting child during, 120B, 120C

PRICE
action for, breach of contract, 188
ascertainment of, contract of sale, 182
interpretation of, 309
misleading indication
  interpretation of, 310
  offence committed, 309
  penalties, 309, 315
  regulations, 315
prohibition of resale price maintenance, 129

PRIVILEGE
legal, items subject to, 265
qualified, newspapers, of, 43-4, 52-3, 356

PRIZES
subscriptions and contributions, recoverable at law, 8

PRODUCER
interpretation of, 291

PRODUCT
defective
  actions in respect of, 207
  knowledge of, 294
  liability for, 292
  meaning of, 293
  safety regulations, 292
interpretation of, 291
licensed medicinal, interpretation of, 308

PRODUCT LIABILITY
damage giving rise to, 295
defective products, 292
defences, 294
Directive, interpretation of, 291
power to modify, 298
prohibition on exclusions from, 297
tort, in, 296

PROHIBITION NOTICE, 303, 307, 334, 337
notification, 337
representations, 337
revoking or varying, 337

PROOF, BURDEN OF
contempt of court cases, 227

PROPERTY
fitness for human habitation, 278, 279
interpretation of, 193, 247
latent damage to, 281-2

PROSPECTUS
disclosure, general duty of, 284

PROSPECTUS—*contd*
false or misleading
compensation for, 285
exemption from liability, 286
form and content of, 283

PUBLIC EXPENSE
maintenance at, assessment of damages and, 252

PUBLIC MEETINGS
reporting of, 53

PURCHASER
interpretation of, 276

Q

QUALITY OR FITNESS
implied terms, 186, 234, 239
implied undertakings as to, hire-purchase agreements, 114, 116, 118
interpretation of, 193, 247

R

RADIATION
disabled birth due to, 120B, 120C

RAPE
compensation for, 339D
criminal injuries and, 339B

REASONABLE CARE
data inaccuracy and, 258

REASONABLE CHARGE
implied terms, 245

REASONABLENESS
breach of contract and, 158
liability, avoidance of, and, 152, 153
test of, 160
guidelines for application of, 170

RECORDS
business, production of for enforcement authorities, 318
interpretation of, 334
seizure of, 319

REDEMPTION
interpretation of, 247

REGULATIONS
power to make, 315

RELATIVES
interpretation of, 291

RELEVANT INTEREST
interpretation of, 312

RELEVANT PERSON
interpretation of, 327

RENT
interpretation of, 222

REPAIRS
goods accepted for, 147
highway, 224
state of and fitness for human habitation, 279

REPORTING
contempt of court and, 227

REPORTS
safety regulations, on, 331

REPRESENTATIONS
notices to warn and, 338
prohibition notices and, 337

RISK
acceptance of, 255
employer's responsibilities for work equipment, 366, 370
occupiers' liability and, 255
protection against specified hazards, 371

ROAD SAFETY
Highway Code, alterations in, 340

S

SAFETY
interpretation of, 308
provisions
enforcement of, 316
search, powers of, 318-19
seizure and detention of goods, compensation for, 323
seizure of goods and records, 319
statutory instruments, 319

SAFETY REGULATIONS
civil proceedings, 330
defences, due diligence, 328
documents, service of, 333
employment
defective equipment, 84-5
floors, passages and stairs, 65
floors, safe means of access and place of employment, 66
machinery generally, 64
prime movers, 62, 67
transmission machinery, 63, 67
financial provisions, 332
interpretation of, 334
liability of body corporate, 329
reports on, 331
test purchases, 317
testing of goods, 319
work equipment *See* WORK EQUIPMENT
See also CONSUMER SAFETY

SALE
interpretation of, 193

SALE AGREEMENT
conditional, 334, 335
credit-, 334, 335
See also CONTRACT

SALE, CONTRACT OF, 180
agreement to sell, 180, 183
buyer's right of examining goods, 187A
conditions to be treated as warranty, when, 183B

SALE, CONTRACT OF—*contd*
  goods perishing before sale, 181
  price, ascertainment of, 182
  quality or fitness, 186
    fitness for purpose, 186
  sale by description, 185
  sale by sample, 187
  time, stipulations about, 183A
  title, implied terms about, 184

SALVAGE
  motor insurance, exceptions from requirements of, 186

SAMPLE
  hire by, 240
  sale by, 187
  transfer of goods by, 235

SAVINGS
  civil liability, and, 177

SCOTLAND
  contempt of court legislation and, 228
  hire-purchase agreements, 112, 113, 114
  libel law, 6, 11
  limitation legislation, 223
  loss of society, compensation for, 339D
  safety regulations and, 301
  supply of goods legislation, 249
  weights and measures regulations, 316

SEA
  carriage by, 169, 330

SEAL, COMMON
  execution of documents by affixing, 276

SEARCH WARRANT
  police powers of entry without, 264

SECRETARY OF STATE
  codes of practice, approval of, 314
  Highway Code alterations, 340
  notices to warn and, 338
  power to make regulations, 315, 316
  prohibition notices and, 337
  safety regulations and, 301, 319, 331

SECURITIES
  motor insurance
    amounts secured, 344
    avoidance of certain exceptions, 346
    issue and surrender of certificates, 345
    requirements in respect of, 344
    undertakings to discharge liabilities, 344
  unlisted
    prospectus
      form and content of, 283
      general duty of disclosure in, 284

SELLER
  interpretation of, 193

SERVICES
  supply of
    contracts concerned, 242
    implied terms
      care and skill, 243

SERVICES—*contd*
  supply of—*contd*
    implied terms—*contd*
      consideration, 245
      performance time, 244

SERVICES, PROVISION OF
  consumer legislation affecting, 311

SEXUAL OFFENCES
  powers of arrest and, 267

SHIPS
  supply of goods and, 335

SLANDER
  actions for, time limits, 219
  consolidation of actions, 49
  death of plaintiff, effect of, 21
  reputation, official, professional or business, affecting, 38
  time limits for actions, 199
  title, of, 39
  women, of, 13
  See also DEFAMATION; LIBEL

SOCIETY, LOSS OF
  compensation for, 339D

SPECIALTY
  time limit for actions on, 203

SPECIALTY DEBTS
  money payable under company memorandum or articles as, 271

SPECIFIC GOODS
  interpretation of, 193

SPECIFIC PERFORMANCE
  breach of contract, remedies for, 191

STATEMENTS
  false, enforcement authorities, to, 321

STATUTE
  time limit for actions for sums recoverable by, 204
  contributions, 205

STATUTORY PROVISION
  interpretation of, 340

SUMMONS
  service of, 268

SUPPLY
  meaning of, 335

T

TENANCY AGREEMENTS
  duty of care
    repairs, 108
    with respect to work done on premises, and, 107
  implied terms, fitness for human habitation, 278
  interpretation of, 108, 110
  occupiers' liability, 57

Index

TEST PURCHASES
  safety provisions and, 317

THEATRE
  defamation law
    amendment of, 78
    exceptions for performances given in certain circumstances, 79

THEFT
  interpretation of, 198
  time limits in cases of, 198

THIRD PARTIES
  on bankruptcy of insured
    duty to give necessary information to, 18
    rights against insurers, 17
  innocent, fraud, concealment or mistake, in cases of, 218

THIRD PARTY
  motor insurance
    bankruptcy, etc of insured or secured persons not to affect claims by, 351
    compulsory against risks of, 341
    exceptions from requirement, 342
  risks
    motor insurance
      duty of insurers or persons giving security to satisfy judgment, 349
      exceptions, 350
      stolen vehicles and, 349

TIME LIMITS
  actions based in tort, for, 196
  actions founded on simple contract, for, 200
  actions to enforce certain awards, for, 202
  conversions and extinction of title, 197
  date of knowledge, definition of, 210
  death, cause of actions surviving, 206
  death, actions in respect of, discretionary exclusion, 220
  defective products, actions in respect of, 207
  disability, actions in respect of, 213
  equitable jurisdiction and remedies, 221
  extension or exclusion of, acknowledgment and part payment, 215
  latent damage, actions in respect of, 211, 212
  libel and slander actions, 199, 219
  motor insurance claims, 350
  overriding, 212
  personal injuries actions, 206
    discretionary exclusion, 220
  sums recoverable by statute, 204-5
  theft, in case of, 198

TITLE
  goods, to, interpretation of, 193
  implied terms about, 232
    contract of sale, 184

TRADE MARKS
  interpretation of, 334

TRADER
  interpretation of, 339

TRADING STAMPS
  excepted contract, as, 231
  goods provided in exchange for, 335
  interpretation of, 247
  redemption of, 157

TRANSFEREE
  interpretation of, 247

TRANSFEROR
  interpretation of, 247

TRESPASS
  access orders and, 359
  animals, by, 95, 96, 98
  civil aviation and, 229
  goods, to
    co-ownership, 140
    contributory negligence, 141

TRUST
  interpretation of, 222
  for sale, interpretation of, 222

TRUSTEE
  interpretation of, 222

U

UNSOUND MIND
  disability, treated as if, 222
  interpretation of, 222

V

VALUATION
  agreement to sell at, 183
  goods accepted for, 147

VENDING MACHINES
  safety provisions, enforcement of, 318
  seizure of goods from, 333

VISITORS
  interpretation of, 255
  occupiers' liability for, 255

W

WAGERS
  deposits not recoverable, 8

WARN, NOTICES TO
  notification, 338
  representations, 338
  revoking, 338

WARRANTY
  breach of, remedy for, 192
  conditions of sale to be treated as, 183B
  interpretation of, 193

WEIGHTS AND MEASURES
  regulations, 316

WOMEN
  driving when pregnant, liability of, 120A
  husband and wife, actions in tort between, 67-8
  married
    capacity, property and liability of, 23-5
    husbands, liabilities of, 23-5

WOMEN—*contd*
   slander of, 13
   widows, re-marriage prospects and assessment of damages, 125

WORK EQUIPMENT
   interpretation of, 362
   provision and use of
      controls changing, 373
         generally, 376
         starting, 373
         stop, 374, 375
         systems, 377
      dangerous parts of machinery, 370
      disapplication of regulations, 363
      energy sources, isolation from, 2378
      European Community regulations, conformity with, 369
      generally, 361

WORK EQUIPMENT—*contd*
   provision and use of—*contd*
      hazards, specified, protection against, 371
      information and instructions, 367
      interpretation of terms, 362
      lighting, 380
      maintenance, 365
      maintenance operations, 381
      markings, 382
      risks, specific, 366
      stability, 379
      suitability, 364
      temperature extremes and, 372
      training, 366, 368
      warnings, 383

WRITTEN REPRESENTATIONS AND ASSURANCES
   fraud cases, 3